$25.28

5672

AGGRESSIVE BEHAVIOR:
Genetic and Neural Approaches

The contributors to this volume. First row (left to right): J. P. Scott, Patricia Ebert, Kirsti Lagerspetz, Edward Simmel. Second row: Bruce Svare, Michael Sheard, James Walters, Martin Hahn, Klaus Miczek. Third row: Neal Simon, J. K. Hewitt.

AGGRESSIVE BEHAVIOR:
Genetic and Neural Approaches

Edited by

Edward C. Simmel
Miami University

Martin E. Hahn
William Paterson College

and

James K. Walters
White Haven Center

LEA LAWRENCE ERLBAUM ASSOCIATES, PUBLISHERS
1983 Hillsdale, New Jersey London

Lawrence Erlbaum Associates, Inc., Publishers
365 Broadway
Hillsdale, New Jersey 07642

Library of Congress Cataloging in Publication Data
Main entry under title:

Aggressive behavior.

Bibliography: p.
Includes index.
1. Aggressiveness (Psychology)—Genetic aspects.
2. Aggressiveness (Psychology)—Research. I. Simmel, Edward C. II. Hahn, Martin E. III. Walters, James K.
[DNLM: 1. Aggression—Physiology—Congresses. 2. Genetics, Behavioral—Congresses. WM 600 A2664]
BF575.A3A58 1983 155.2′32 83-1722
ISBN 0-89859-253-4

Printed in the United States of America
10 9 8 7 6 5 4 3 2 1

Contents

II. GENETICS, EVOLUTION, AND AGGRESSION

Preface

Since the heyday of research on aggression in the late 1960s, developments in several varied areas have enabled us to take a new look at this important though difficult topic. Recent findings and sophisticated new techniques in behavior genetic analysis have made it possible not only to enhance our understanding of the genetic mechanisms underlying aggressive behavior, but also to provide some reasonable suggestions as to the role of aggression in evolution. Current research in neurochemistry and neuropharmacology provide promising approaches toward understanding the neural correlates of aggression. Fortunately, together with these significant advances in genetic and neural research, there has developed a much more sophisticated and heuristic approach to the measurement and conceptualization of aggressive behavior.

The ten chapters of this volume provide a thorough overview of these new approaches and methodologies. There are also suggestions regarding the scope of future research on aggressive behavior, since much of what is presented describes the ongoing research activities of the contributors.

This book is divided into four sections: The first provides a systematic foundation for research on aggression, and a description of some of the newer strategies for research in this area; the second concerns quantitative genetic analyses, selection data from both wild and laboratory populations, and situational determinants of aggressive behavior; the third section details new and exciting findings in neurochemical and neuropharmacological effects; and the last section contains a chapter that provides a summary and synthesis of all that has come before.

The chapters of this book are based on original contributions presented at the Miami University Symposium on Social Behavior in September of 1981. However, this volume is not a "proceedings" of the conference, but rather can be considered an "outcome," in that the final manuscripts were prepared afterwards, so that each author could take into account the comments and contributions of the others. In organizing the symposium, our goal was to bring together those working in diverse areas (genetic, or neural, or behavioral), but all focusing on the topic of aggressive behavior. We also sought to invite individuals who are clearly recognized as major inovators and pioneers in the field as well as some highly promising younger investigators.

We owe much to a great number of persons whose support and encouragement made possible the successful symposium that made this book possible. We are most grateful to the following Miami University administrators for their support: John Dolibois, Vice President for University Relations; David Brown, Executive Vice President for Academic Affairs; C. K. Williamson, Dean of the College of Arts and Science; Spiro Peterson, Dean of the Graduate School and Research. All of these individuals have since moved on to even more exalted positions. We also thank Don Parker and Ray White, whose terms as Chair of the Department of Psychology overlapped the planning and execution of the symposium. Also, we were honored when Paul Pearson took the time during his first busy days as new President of Miami University to deliver the welcoming remarks at the symposium.

We are most appreciative of the efforts of many others at Miami University, at William Paterson College, and at LEA for their efforts in putting on the symposium and in the preparation of this volume. Space does not permit listing all of them by name, but we would be remiss if we did not extend special thanks to Kathy Wiley in the Office of University Relations, and Maria Lavooy, graduate assistant in psychology, for their outstanding efforts.

Edward C. Simmel
Martin E. Hahn
James K. Walters

AGGRESSIVE BEHAVIOR:
Genetic and Neural Approaches

I
SYSTEMS AND METHODOLOGY

1 A Systems Approach to Research on Aggressive Behavior

J. P. Scott
Bowling Green State University

In the latter part of this century we are experiencing a slow revolution in scientific thought, away from dualistic, mechanistic, and reductionistic thinking, toward theories based on the concept of systems. Research on aggression is particularly affected by this revolution, as aggressive behavior is always expressed within the context of organismic systems, and nearly always, with the possible exception of predatory behavior, within the context of social systems. In this chapter I indicate how the systems concept affects such research, where it provides new understanding, and where it shows the need for new research.

GENERAL PRINCIPLES OF SYSTEMS THEORY

1. A system may be defined as a group of interacting entities.
2. Living systems are organized as a set of nested systems and subsystems.
3. A system may act as an entity on a higher level of organization.
4. Interaction implies two-way causation—the principle of *feedback*. (This is not interaction in the statistical sense, where two independent factors act simultaneously on a third. Rather, the entities within a system act on each other.)
5. Interaction occurs between lower and higher levels as well as between entities on the same level, and in all directions simultaneously.
6. Interactions within systems on higher levels produce phenomena that do not occur on lower levels—the principle of *creativity*. As an example, genes do not "think."
7. Living systems tend to become increasingly organized—the principle of *development*.

8. Living systems tend to become increasingly stable—the principle of *stability* or homeostasis.

9. Contrary to the last principle, living systems possess organized processes of change—the principle of *evolution*.

10. Living systems tend to protect their constituent entities, that is, to prolong their own existence—the principle of *adaptivity*.

Agonistic Behavior

Using the systems concept as a reference point, I have defined agonistic behavior as behavior that is adaptive in situations involving conflict between two or more members of the same species. This definition excludes predation, which involves attacking and defending behavior between members of two different species. As well as the behavior that is ordinarily considered to be aggressive (i.e., attacking behavior directed against a conspecific), agonistic behavior includes other patterns of adaptive behavior such as defensive behavior, escape behavior, defensive and aggressive signaling, and passivity. Agonistic behavior is therefore expressed primarily on two levels: within social systems, and as a physiological–behavioral–motivational system on the organismic level. In studying agonistic behavior we must therefore always consider three levels of organization: the social, the organismic, and the physiological.

Although all systems levels include the general characteristics previously outlined, each level has its own peculiar characteristics. On the physiological level, the basic entities are organs, which interact in organ systems. It is easy to forget that all organ systems are involved in behavior, because of the obvious importance and integrating function of the neuroendocrine system, which usually receives the most attention. Organs are organized anatomically, that is, they have fixed spatial relationships to each other, and the interactions between them are physical and chemical in nature. Likewise, the organ systems comprising an organism (or organismic system) bear fixed spatial relationships to each other and also interact through physical and chemical processes.

Here there is a great divide in the systems organization of animal organisms: that of behavior. Such systems have the capacity to move from one spatial situation into another, so that organization between organisms, and also between organisms on other systems levels, are no longer based on anatomical organization. A major effect is to greatly increase the variability and speed of functional adaptation. Accompanying this transition, many animal organisms have the capacity for the process of learning, a new type of organizational process that relates behavioral interactions in the past to those in the future.

Thus, a social system has certain unique aspects that are the result of the basic creativity principle. A social system may be defined as a group of behaviorally interacting organismic systems belonging to the same species. This definition separates social organization from colonial organization, which consists of organization between organismic systems based on structure. We may, therefore, list certain unique aspects of social systems:

1. The spatial relationships between entities are not fixed. Therefore, the concept of social structure is inherently misleading.
2. In organisms that are mobile, the entire social system is potentially, though not necessarily, mobile also.
3. The interactions between the entities within social systems may be symbolic and conducted through signals, as well as through direct behavioral interaction and involving physical and chemical interactions. Social interactions thus involve a novel form of communication.
4. Depending on the capacity for learning of the constituent entities, social organization may be the product of the learning process but is not wholly the product of this process.

TECHNIQUES FOR THE STUDY OF ORGANIZATIONAL PROCESSES

Whatever the concepts used, biologists and psychologists have never been able to avoid the study of organizational processes. Consequently, some of the techniques for their study are well developed and are of long standing; others are suggested by the concept of systems and by the hypotheses that are suggested by this concept.

Agonistic Behavior is Expressed Within Social Relationships. The fact that agonistic behavior is expressed within social systems has several implications. One of the major ones is that the nature of the relationships in which the agonistic behavior is expressed is a major determinant of aggression. Further, the way in which other factors affect agonistic behavior will depend on the degree of organization of such relationships. Thus, I found in my experiments with the effect of hunger on the expression of agonistic behavior in goats, that the nature of the relationship in each pair was unchanged; dominant goats remained dominant and subordinate goats remained subordinate. On the other hand, the amount of fighting actually expressed increased chiefly because the subordinate animals were willing to take more of a beating when hungry (Scott, 1948).

The Effect of an Extrinsic Factor or Process on Agonistic Behavior Depends on the State of Development of the Social Relationship in Which It is Expressed. It follows that the major technique for the study of the nature of a social relationship is the developmental one. Behavior shown at the outset of the development of a relationship changes with time. Therefore, if one wishes to get a complete picture of the effect of an extrinsic process, it should be carried on within a developmental context and studied until the relationship has reached stability. (Of course, one of the effects of the experimental factors may be to delay the production of stability.) At the very least, studies should be made at the outset of the relationship (i.e., with naive animals), at some point midway in its development, and finally at the point when the relationship becomes stable. Depending on the species and the conditions, the development of a stable social relationship may be a matter of hours, days, weeks, or years.

From this point of view, most of the studies of agonistic behavior in mice have been done with naive animals and hence at the very outset of the development of a relationship. It would be predicted that the same factors applied after mice have developed stable dominance–subordination relationships might have very different effects, and it is only recently that experimenters have begun to work with the effects of drugs and other factors on dominant and subordinate animals at the stage of stability.

At the outset of relationship formation, whether naive or experienced animals are involved, a social system is unorganized, and previously existing systems may be disorganized. It is precisely under these conditions that the great majority of fatal and injuriously violent acts occur in animal societies (Scott, 1975), and I have stated that a major, if not *the* major cause of harmful violence is the disorganization (or unorganization) of social systems.

Hahn (this volume), Labov (1980), and others (Bertram, 1975; Hrdy, 1977) have proposed a simple evolutionary explanation of the male infanticide and cannibalism that may occur in mice and certain other species; namely that it is to the competitive advantage of the male to eliminate the offspring of others.

There is always a danger of circular reasoning in applying the concept of natural selection to an existing phenomenon, to argue that because a phenomenon exists, it must be adaptive, and to end up with an explanation that may be emotionally satisfying but little better than a "Just So" story. This danger is particularly acute in the case of behavioral phenomena whose evolution took place in the remote past, and for which confirmatory historical evidence is impossible.

From the viewpoints of genetic theory and systems theory, we must always consider the following hypotheses as alternates to that of selection for an adaptive response:

1. The null hypothesis: that the characteristic has no adaptive value, either positive or negative. Such variation is inevitable as a result of random mutations.
2. That the characteristic is maladaptive, arising from a distortion or destruction of the systems under which the characteristic evolved in an adaptive form.
3. The organizational systems of the species are themselves maladaptive, and the species is headed toward extinction. There is differential survival among species as well as among individuals within species.

It follows that each species must be considered independently, and I comment here only on male infanticide and associated cannibalism in the house mouse. The experimental conditions that induce this behavior are definitely those of unorganized social relationships; a strange male is placed in the small nest box of a lactating female, who attacks him. Further, there is no way that the male can escape the attacks of the female and so develop the normal spatial organization of a mouse society. A similar comment applies to the technique described by Svare and Mann (1981), of isolating a male and introducing a solitary strange infant.

Applying the foregoing alternate hypotheses, we can eliminate number 3; there is no evidence that house mice are becoming extinct, although this might be argued in the case of lions.

Both the other hypotheses are possible: (1) male infanticide may occur so rarely in natural populations that it has no appreciable selective effect; or (2) that evolution of mouse behavioral patterns has occurred chiefly within well-organized social systems, and that infanticide is a maladaptive distortion of normal behavior that occurs only under special conditions of unorganized or disorganized social relationships.

I suspect that the latter explanation is the most likely of the four, that under natural conditions a wandering male mouse would rarely, if ever, try to stick his nose into the nest of a lactating female without being previously attacked by a resident male and, even if he found a lone female, he would be likely to leave after getting his nose bitten. Also, as Hahn (this volume) points out, although an infanticidal male might obtain some genetic advantage at the cost of being bitten, there is a larger cost to the female with no compensating advantage. Females as well as males contribute to the evolutionary process, a fact that male investigators tend to forget.

Unfortunately, evolutionary arguments are seldom testable by experiment. In this case, the best evidence would be provided by observing what happens in a well-organized population under seminatural conditions with plenty of space, and then to disorganize the population in various ways.

I conclude that this case of harmful and destructive violence, like so many others (Scott, 1975), is the result of social disorganization, and that there should be in most species and under most conditions, strong selective pressures against such violence and toward the maintenance of social organization that prevents it.

Study of the development of a relationship can take place over a relatively short period, as when a relationship develops between two adult animals that is capable of becoming stable in a short time. Or, on the contrary, one can look at development over the lifetime of an individual. From the latter viewpoint, it can be predicted that *the relationships developed by young animals will determine the nature of the relationships they exhibit as adults*. Such relationships may be simple continuations of the immature ones, but they also form models for the formation of other relationships or sometimes interfere with the formation of new ones.

The most general problem is to determine how the organization of social relationships that affect the expression of agonistic behavior can be modified. Systems theory indicates that relevant organizational processes should exist on every level of organization and that these processes should effect processes on other levels. Thus one can study genetic, physiological, organismic, social, and ecological processes of organization. The systems concept, however, insists that these do not occur independently of each other.

The usual experimental technique is to try to hold all variable conditions constant except one or two similar ones on the same level of organization. Thus, an experimenter might try to hold conditions stable on all levels except that of the physiological. The danger of this approach is that it may lead to a disregard of all but one sort of major variable, and the history of science is full of occasions where authors have claimed that the major factor affecting behavioral variation is genetic, or physiological, or experiential, or social. Systems theory suggests that a better strategy would be to include at least two systems levels in every experiment. For example, as well as a social factor, an experiment might include the genetic level to the extent of at least sex differences and, in those species where pure strains exist, of strain differences. In the long run, the strategy would be to include all systems levels that affect a particular phenomenon, including the ecological and physiological. The program of research reported by Lagerspetz (this volume) is a notable example of the application of this broad-based technique.

Systemic Analysis Versus Mechanistic Analysis. Most experimental work of the past has been guided by mechanistic theory, which assumes one-way causation. Although this technique has often been used to great effect in analyzing certain parts of systems, it can never lead to satisfactory analysis of the system as a whole. For example, one can attach electrodes to an otic nerve and record electrical impulses in response to sound stimulation. The result is very regular, certainly, and implies one-way causation. But the results can never explain the way in which the nervous system as a whole reacts to such input.

One might ask, how else can one study a system other than by breaking it up into its constituent parts? There are actually several alternatives. The first is a basic descriptive one. In any system the first task is to describe the entities composing the system and their interactions. As a part of this descriptive process one should describe developmental changes in interaction. It is not always possible to determine the nature of the entities and their interactions in a purely descriptive fashion, but assuming that these have been identified, or at least hypothesized, there are two major ways in which they can be analyzed. One is to modify or remove the entities involved in a systematic fashion, and the other is to modify or block the interactional processes between them.

In themselves, these techniques are nothing new. In fact, they correspond closely to the traditional techniques of lesioning and stimulating the central nervous system. In this case the systems concept emphasizes and adds meaning to what is already being done and also adds the possibility that the interactive functions can be recognized, as entities or hypothesized entities appear in development. In short, development provides an ongoing natural experiment that does not involve the disturbance and perhaps irrevocable destruction of the system.

APPLICATIONS OF THE SYSTEMS CONCEPT TO CURRENT RESEARCH ON AGGRESSION

Behavior Genetics. There is a tendency among nongeneticists to "geneticize," or make armchair genetic hypotheses on the basis of inadequate information regarding the nature of genetic systems. A gene always exists within a genotype system, and its ultimate action on higher levels of organization is based on interaction with other entities within the genetic system. There can be no gene for a particular characteristic, such as altruism; rather, the genetic variation produces variation in the characteristic under study. The organization of the characteristic as a whole depends on the function and interaction of the entire genotypic system.

On the basis of our knowledge of the functioning of genetic systems we can state the following general theory: Genetic organization with respect to behavior or any other phenotypic characteristic forms a stable system that cannot be divided and indeed cannot be modified extensively without destroying the system; however, genetic variation will produce variation in the behavioral expression of the system, or in any other expression. The concept of genetic homeostasis (Lerner, 1958) is associated with this theory.

The primary task of behavioral genetics with respect to the study of aggression is therefore the description of genetic variation in agonistic behavior. Once these phenotypes are established, analysis can proceed in several directions. One is the genetic analysis of the transmission process: Are the variations in behavior produced by autosomal or sex-linked genes, by multiple or single factors, or by variations in the chromosomes? Because genes must produce their effects through physiological process, a second line of research is to determine how the genes produce variations in the underlying physiology of agonistic behavior. Such variation might involve irritability, the depth and mode of expression of emotional behavior, and the like.

On a higher level, genetic variation has an effect on the interactions between organisms and the social relationships that they establish. A major field of interest is the difference between social relationships that are established between genetically similar individuals and genetically different ones. The most pervasive example is the relationship between individuals of similar sex as contrasted with those between different sexes. In our studies of the dominance–subordination relationship in dogs (Pawlowski & Scott, 1956; Scott & Fuller, 1965), we found that, in purebred dogs whose genetic constitutions were similar, males most universally become dominant over female littermates.

We made relatively few studies of interactions between puppies of different breeds, but when we did there was the expected result that the more aggressive breeds became dominant over the less aggressive ones, fox terriers over beagles, for example (James, 1951). Then there was the fascinating case that arose out of fostering Shetland sheepdogs and beagles together. The Shelties are only moderately aggressive, but in every case they became dominant over the beagles. All dogs, once they become adults, will bark at approaching strangers. When reared in groups, our sheepdogs formed a dominance order with respect to such barking, only the dominant animal in the group being allowed to bark. In the Sheltie–beagle combinations the Shelties would not allow the beagles to bark and we ended up with barkless beagles.

In human families, this general question has great relevance to the relationships that are established between monozygotic twins as opposed to dizygotic twins. To my knowledge this question has never been studied.

By its very nature, much of the results of the genetic variation can only be predicted on the basis of the probability that a particular gene will be passed on from one generation to the next. Consequently, the results of social interaction based on genetic differences (relating two independent probabilities) are to a large extent unpredictable. However, one broad generalization is possible: The greater the degree of genetic differences between individuals the greater the degree of differentiation of behavior in the relationship that they develop. Applied to agonistic behavior, this can be stated as: The greater the degree of variation in aggressiveness, the greater the degree of unequal reciprocal influence. I have termed this inequality of reciprocal interaction *prostasia,* in order to generalize the concept further than dominance–subordination relationships. But with respect to agonistic behavior this is the concept of relative power.

Physiology. Physiologists have traditionally been mechanists. Such titles as Carlson's *The Machinery of the Body* were commonplace during the first half of this century, although such volumes often included an apology to the effect that the body is not really a machine. The physiologists of today appear to be realizing that although mechanistic theory may provide starting points for research, such items never give complete answers regarding the functioning of systems.

For example, most physiologists used to look for a center in the brain that would activate aggression, the same way that twisting the starter key will activate an automobile engine. Instead, they have found that numerous parts of the brain are involved in the production of agonistic behavior, and that none of these has a key function. As Delgado (1981) figuratively puts it, the brain acts as a democracy rather than as a dictatorship. Karli (1981) reminds us that the past history of the brain has an effect on its function. A lesion in the rat septum will increase the rate of muricide in rats from approximately 25% to almost 100% of the population. But a similar operation on rats that have peacefully cohabited with mice for a month or more has no effect on muricide; such rats do not attack their cage mates. Karli therefore recommends a developmental approach as a standard method for analyzing the organization of function. Because development is essentially the study of change in organization, it should rank as one of the major methods to be used in the study of any system.

Thus, physiologists can make use of the natural experiments produced by developmental change in physiological function. In a recent example, Hood (1981) studied changes in agonistic behavior in females in relation to the sexual cycles. Female rates fight off males—albeit in a relatively gentle fashion—except during estrus. In human females there is the case of the premenstrual syndrome—naturally occurring endocrine dysfunction resulting in recurring outbursts of violence, and which can be prevented by appropriate treatment with the hormone progesterone (Dalton, 1981).

Research on the physiology of aggression has traditionally fallen into three areas: pharmacological studies, neurological studies, and hormonal studies. Each of these attempts to modify the function of the neuroendocrine system, but different techniques are involved in each. Pharmacologists of the past, working with mechanistic theory, have usually placed their faith in measuring a single aspect of behavior, such as the bar-pressing response of rats. Such a measure is, of course, totally inadequate to measure the overall function of a complex system. At the present time pharmacologists are following the technique of measuring the effects of a given drug in as many life situations as possible (see Miczek, this volume). The theory is that a drug will be expected to modify a particular physiological state, but the organism's response to this will vary according to conditions in which it is placed and also its previous history. Of particular importance is the technique of testing the drug in animals that occupy different sorts of social relationships to each other. A simple example is the winner–loser relationship that mice develop.

Simon (this volume) argues for a composite measure of aggression based on correlational analysis of different behavior patterns. This is an obvious improvement over single measures or composite measures arbitrarily added together and implicitly suggests that there is an overall organization of such behavior, consistent with the concept of systems. But, as we have already seen, there is a distinct possibility that the weights of the components would vary in different social relationships.

Similar considerations apply to the traditional neurological techniques of brain stimulation and lesioning. A newer technique that should have unusual promise for the study of an ongoing system is that of the CAT scan, and similar methods. Here it is possible to study the structure of the brain in relation to ongoing functions, not merely in an anatomical specimen.

Still another direction in which neurological study should go is that of studying feedback relationships between different parts of the brain.

Hormonal and endocrine studies provide another example of the changeover from mechanistic to systems concepts. The discovery of testosterone was originally hailed as a mechanism; removing the testes and consequently testosterone from the organismic system caused gross changes in secondary sex characteristics, including the expression of aggression in males, implying one-way causation. But it soon became apparent that testosterone is part of a complex neuroendocrine system with intricate feedback relationships not only among different endocrine glands but also the central nervous system itself. Svare (this volume) summarizes our present knowledge of the neuroendocrine system and points out the problems of research on aggression.

So what do testosterone and other endocrine substances have to do with agonistic behavior? For years, evidence has accumulated in adult mammals to the effect that the absolute amount of testosterone has no significance; it is only the threshold level that is important. The fluctuation of the amount of testosterone in circulating blood serum turns out to be more an effect of function than a cause, reflecting disturbances in the equilibrium of the neuroendocrine system. But in perinatal mice, testosterone is the organizer of future brain function, leading to later differences between the sexes with respect to the frequency of fighting (vom Saal & Bronson, 1978).

Psychology. In the past, some psychologists have been hypnotized by mechanistic theory with respect to learning and so have attempted to measure "aggression" with some simple single variable. Although this technique has paid many dividends to the followers of Pavlov and Skinner with respect to the analysis of the organizational process of learning, a single variable is hopelessly inadequate to describe a complex system such as that within which aggression is expressed.

An example is the technique of shock-induced fighting in male rats, using the upright or boxing posture as an index, and equating electric shock with pain. Aside from the fact that electric shock is a peculiar form of noxious stimulation and one that rats are extremely unlikely to meet in nature (they being literally "grounded" at all times), the upright stance is actually the defensive posture (Blanchard, Blanchard, & Takahaski, 1977; Scott, 1966). Thus, the experimenters were measuring a defensive response to pain, only one element in the rat's repertory of agonistic behavior. Of course, rats may show a variety of other behavior patterns in response to shock, including attack biting (Morgan, 1967), but one has to measure these, also, if one wishes to understand the rat's agonistic behavior system (Blanchard & Blanchard, 1977).

Hutchinson (1972) has developed a more sophisticated approach to the single-variable technique, first demonstrating that a great variety of animal species respond to pain by biting, and then reducing the measurement of behavior to jaw clenching and changes in tension of the masseter muscle. In my opinion, this technique has extensive possibilities as an objective measure of emotional responses, especially in humans who are trained to repress overt behavior.

Thus, the single-variable technique has its use when one wishes to study a single organizational process. But one such variable is inevitably inadequate to measure the numerous processes and interactions of a complex living system.

A more fruitful technique is the obverse of the foregoing, to explore the effects of one independent variable at a time, but to measure its effects in as many situations as possible and to measure all important patterns of behavior. For example, experimenters over the years have established that the agonistic behavioral system of mice includes some 10 or so common behavior patterns that are easily recognized and counted, that these patterns appear differentially in males, females, and young, and that their expression is different in winners and losers. Thus, it is possible to measure the effect of any independent experimental variable under standard and comparable situations, as many experimenters are beginning to do.

By tradition, psychologists tend to use the individual organism as a unit for studying the organization of behavior. This is true even of social psychologists, who have studied social learning in individuals. This approach has gone about as far as it can go, and we need to study the simultaneous and mutually adaptive processes in two or more organisms, as Schuster (1981) has begun to do.

The Social Level. Here most of the problems are associated with the dominance–subordination relationship. There is a tendency for behaviorists, especially those trained in the tradition of working with individual organisms, to turn this concept upside down and postulate an organismic characteristic of "dominance." It cannot be a general characteristic; dominance has relevance only in particular relationships, as a simple example will illustrate. In a group of three hens (or dogs) showing a linear hierarchy, the alpha animal can be said to be dominant and the gamma animal subordinant. But what about the beta animal who is dominant in one relationship and subordinant in another?

It is important to keep our concepts sharp and clear, as fuzzy concepts lead to fuzzy thinking. The important concept here and for which we must maintain a clear definition is that of the dominance–subordination relationship. This is an old concept but not a universal one. Once the relationship is clearly defined it is obvious that relationships arising from agonistic actions between animals can vary considerably. In the past most authors have neglected to describe such variation. I have already referred to the kind of variation that occurs in dogs. Among goats (Scott, 1948), I found that a competitive situation gave rise to a widely varying series of relationships: (1) one goat was so afraid of the other that it never came near; (2) one goat butted the other but the other never butted back; (3) one of them butted and the other always responded with a butt but never initiated one; (4) the two goats might eat peacefully side by side. This last relationship occurred between twin kids or between mother and her kid and is one that I have never seen in dogs. It can be understood in the light of the function of agonistic behavior in goat flocks: the regulation of space. Whether standing or moving, goats maintain a distance of about 2 feet between animals. Agonistic behavior between a mother and her kid, or between twin kids attempting to feed from the same mother, would be obviously maladaptive.

This raises the question of genetic variation in the capacities of species to develop dominance–subordination relationships. Chickens, dogs, and monkeys live in groups, but reduce agonistic behavior to a symbolic level and are able to develop complex dominance hierarchies between members. On the other hand, male mice in groups are able to organize only as one winner and all the rest losers. Furthermore, there are always bite wounds in such groups. Typically what one sees is one sleek individual and all the rest rather ragged mice with various scars and bite wounds and who among themselves have no special relationships. Rats seem to be capable of a little more complexity, with one dominant and one subordinate male living together with females in a group, with a little outright fighting, but never any greater complexity. Then there are such species as woodchucks, in which agonistic behavior is never reduced to a harmful or even a moderately harmful level. One never sees woodchucks in groups, or even two woodchucks together, except briefly in the mating season and the rearing of the young.

A dominance–subordination relationship is not a necessary result of competition nor should it be equated with competition. Competition can lead to a variety of other relationships. Schuster (1981) has pointed out that the effect of competition varies a great deal with the nature of the preexisting relationship. He finds that if rats have been taught to coordinate their behavior in order to receive a certain food reward, competition will enhance this behavior. But if competition is presented at the outset of the relationship, it is highly disruptive, and coordinated behavior is difficult to achieve. This raises the whole problem of the conditions under which competition may be either adaptive or nonadaptive for a species.

Ecological Systems. Here research on aggression has in the past been woefully inadequate and deficient. However, there are now numerous documented cases where social organization of animal species varies according to the ecosystem of which it is a part. For example, in the western pine forests, which are more or less open and where each tree has a supply of pine nuts, red squirrels are territorial and defend boundaries (Smith, 1968). But in the eastern hardwood forests, where trees include only scattered sources of nuts and where visibility is poor, the same species does not defend boundaries, although mutual threats may keep individuals distributed over wide areas (Banks, 1974). Similarly in the Indian Rhesus monkey, Southwick (1972) has shown that the transition from a jungle habitat, with scattered sources of food, to a human setting with concentrated food supplies that the monkeys can obtain without effort results in measureable increases in the amount of aggression, as well as harmful scarring and wounding.

SYSTEMS-ORIENTED RESEARCH ON HUMAN AGGRESSION

Research on human behavior is enormously complicated (as well as being simplified in certain respects) by the phenomenon of language, but the same general systems principles apply. One of the most important is that *agonistic behavior is expressed in social relationships that are major determinants of behavior,* but even these are strongly influenced by language. Every human culture has a symbolic relationship system as well as the interactive behavioral relationships expressed by individuals within the culture. This brings up the problem of studying the nature and effect of symbolic systems.

Symbolic Systems. These systems are attempts to either describe or influence real behavior, but they have several important characteristics that differ from behavioral systems or social systems:

1. Symbolic systems are *nonliving*. Consequently (and especially if they are written down) they can be extraordinarily stable.
2. Symbolic systems are *logical* and so often depart from living systems or give a distorted picture of them.
3. Symbolic systems (which may also be called belief systems) tend to define what people *should do,* and hence provide guides for behavior that is seldom achieved in actuality except perhaps in very clearly defined situations.
4. *Symbolic systems are by their nature nondynamic*. They may indicate function and activity, but the systems themselves ordinarily remain fixed. They have no potentiality for change, adaptation, and adjustment, apart from the living humans who may alter them.
5. As a major hypothesis we may state that *symbolic systems are always important determinants of human agonistic* behavior and in many cases may be overwhelming ones.

Therefore, in research on agonistic behavior a first task is to find out the symbolic systems held by each individual studied. The usual questionnaire method is likely to be inadequate, as the rather simplified questions and judgments required tend to bring out conclusions from the individual's belief system rather than the system itself. We need new techniques of ascertaining belief systems. In fact, a whole new field of research could be devoted to the identification of these systems and their development by individuals. A preliminary hypothesis to guide this sort of research would be that individuals should vary with respect to the development and extent of symbolic systems that affect behavior. Such a hypothesis is well supported by the work of Kohlberg and his associates, but they have chosen (following the stage theories of Piaget) to concentrate on the "development of moral thinking," the ultimate stage being that of the philosopher, rather than concentrating on the nature of the belief systems themselves (Kohlberg & Gilligan, 1971). The latter and more objective field of research may well, in my opinion, replace the rather sterile debates on ethics that are now going on among researchers. Lagerspetz and Westman (1980) have made a beginning in this area by examining the codes regulating aggressive behavior held by Finnish adults. Such research should supplement rather than replace the basic research on the nature of social relationships that is being done in other animals.

Future Directions of Work on Human Aggresssion. In the past, most research on human aggression has been done with very little attention to either cultural differences or to the nature of the relationship in which the aggression is being expressed. For example, most of the experimental research on human aggression is done on college sophomores. Furthermore, this is done within a classroom or laboratory setting. Looked at from the point of relationship systems, such research is being done within the larger context of Western European culture and specifically the context of North American culture of English speaking peoples. If I were to do such research I would first find out what the belief systems regarding aggressive behavior are in this culture, and particularily those systems that are peculiar to the individuals involved. For example, we have a wide array of religious teachings regarding aggressive behavior within our culture that may or may not be taken seriously by the individuals chosen for an experiment. Second, we have legal and political rules regarding the expression of agonistic behavior, and again the individuals may or may not follow these. Finally and most specifically, the experiments are being done in the context of a teacher–student relationship in which college sophomores have had some 14 years of experience. The usual symbolic belief regarding such relationships is that the teacher knows best and that you should do what he or she asks. It does not follow that the same individual would do the same thing in any other relationship.

A second important relationship in which research on aggression is done is that of the peer group. This relationship is also present among the college population; students are usually asked to aggress not against their professors but against fellow students. Again this relationship system would be expected to have its own rules and regulations codified into a logical symbolic system. Such codes permit the expression of certain kinds of aggression and punishment.

Most of the studies of agonistic behavior actually expressed in school settings deal with peer groups, and with developmental changes seen within such groups

(Omark, Strayer, & Freedman, 1980). As anyone knows, such interactions involve strongly held belief systems that may vary from individual to individual and in different parts of our culture. For example, most boys in middle-class families are taught that fighting is justified only in self-defense, whereas boys in lower income classes are usually taught that fighting is a good thing, and that it is important to win. It is perhaps no coincidence that most boxers come from lower income families.

Finally, one of our major problems in American culture today is the occurrence of violence within family relationships. As we all know there are symbolic belief systems that have strong influence in the expression of violent behavior in such relationships. One is the ancient belief that a man must be master of his wife and that it is justifiable to keep her in line by physical force when needed. Another is the belief that it is not only justifiable to punish children for their misdemeanors but that punishment is good for them.

There are obviously other variables involved in expression of violence within such relationships, including genetic predispositions: sex and relative strength, outside pressures, family models for children, and the like, but no researcher can afford to neglect the symbolic framework in which such violence occurs. One of the major aspects of this phenomenon is the assumption that violence is legitimate provided it does not involve death or serious injury, and the further assumption that violence within the family is not otherwise subject to remedy.

These are of course, not the only relationships within which human aggression takes place, but a useful research project would be to make a list of all the relationships within which violence occurs in our society. Even a cursory survey of this sort indicates that there are certain relationships within which violence is common, as for example the police–suspect relationship, contrasted with certain others such as the salesman–customer relationship, in which violence is extremely rare. If such a survey were seriously done, it would do much to define the problem of undesirable violence within our culture.

This topic has more than theoretical interest, for it is virtually impossible to apply what we know about the control of violent behavior without inducing cultural change, which includes changes in belief systems. Even such a direct and relatively minor change as handgun control becomes enormously difficult in a culture whose belief systems include the justification of guns as defensive weapons.

More importantly, we have both the theoretical know-how and the practical experience to bring about the development of nonviolent social relationships (Scott, 1977). The basic theoretical principle of passive inhibition was derived from Pavlov's work. It states that an organism learns to do nothing by doing nothing; therefore, a person learns to be nonviolent by being nonviolent.

Systems theory adds that, because agonistic behavior is expressed within social relationships, this implies the development of nonviolent relationships.

The best technique for doing this is not to enforce inactivity but to reward nonviolent activity, and the easiest way to do this is to encourage self-rewarding and constructive behaviors. Nursery school teachers long ago discovered what they called the "positive method"; instead of punishing violent behavior they encouraged interesting and constructive play. Thus, they laid the developmental groundwork for nonviolent social relationship in an educational system. The end result is a nonviolent academic community such as exists on a college or university campus. Violent crime in such a setting is, in my estimation, about as low as it can be. But except for teachers and professors, people move out of the social relationships of an educational institution. One would theoretically predict that the longer the educational relationship continued, the less would be the probability of violence in future relationships, simply on the basis of learning theory.

But there is more to it than this. The more education a person has, the greater the chance of obtaining a satisfactory, well-paying, and constructive job. In this new relationship the training in nonviolence continues, often over a lifetime.

I am not saying that education per se is a panacea for crime prevention. It is what goes on in the social relationships within such an institution that counts; destructive and violent relationships can also be found within an educational institution. Further, many individuals have neither the capacity nor the motivation to continue long-range educational pursuits. Such individuals become dropouts and frequently become unemployed.

Outside educational institutions the principle of passive inhibition applies equally well to the work situation. The equivalent of the "positive method" is the offering of good pay to do an interesting, constructive, and socially valuable job.

Therefore, if we really want to lower the crime rate we must offer universal employment, being especially sure that this is available to young males as soon as they leave the educational system, and possibly before. This is not easy, and one of the reasons is that it requires a change in our belief systems with respect to work, toward the goal of universal employment (Scott, 1977).

To begin with, we should do away with unemployment insurance and substitute *employment insurance,* in effect, to guarantee everyone the opportunity for employment. This does not mean abandoning the Protestant work ethic, which says that work is a good thing. It does mean abandoning the notion that people don't work because they are lazy and don't try hard enough.

There are numerous ways by which the goal of full employment could be reached, but the benefits are obvious. The economy would prosper with everyone except the totally disabled working productively. Further, with the great reduction of crime, the costs of law enforcement and prisons would be correspondingly reduced. This would not be Utopia, as no system remains fixed forever, and it would require constant effort to maintain. All that I am saying is that we now know how to scientifically develop a nonviolent society.

REFERENCES

Banks, E. M. *Ecological and evolutionary effects on social organization.* Paper presented at the AAAS Meeting, San Francisco, 1974.

Bertram, B. C. R. Social factors influencing reproduction in wild lions *Journal of Zoology,* 1975, *177,* 463–482.

Blanchard, R. J., & Blanchard, D. C. Aggressive behavior in the rat. *Behavioral Biology,* 1977, *21,* 197–224.

Blanchard, R. J., Blanchard, D. C., & Takahaski, L. K. Reflexive fighting in the albino rat: Aggressive or defensive behavior? *Aggressive Behavior,* 1977, *3,* 231–240.

Dalton, K. *Violence in the premenstrual syndrome.* Paper presented to the International Society for Research on Aggression, Boston, 1981.

Delgado, J. M. R. *Psychophysiology of freedom.* Address to International Society of Political Psychology, Mannheim, Federal Republic of Germany, 1981.

Hood, K. E. *Aggression in female rats over the estrous cycle.* Paper presented to the ISRA, Boston regional meeting, 1981.

Hrdy, S. B. *The langurs of Abu.* Cambridge, Mass.: Harvard University Press, 1977.

Hutchinson, R. R. The environmental causes of aggression. *Nebraska Symposium on Motivation.* Lincoln: University of Nebraska Press, 1972.

James, W. T. Social organization among dogs of different temperaments, terriers and beagles reared together. *Journal of Comparative and Physiological Psychology,* 1951, *44,* 71–77.

Karli, P. *Experimental approaches to the study of aggressive interactions.* Address to the European section of the International Society for Research on Aggression, Strasbourg, France, 1981.

Kohlberg, L., & Gilligan, C. The adolescent as a philosopher: The discovery of the self in a post-conventional world. *Daedalus,* Fall 1971, 1051–1086.

Labov, J. B. Factors influencing infanticidal behavior in wild male house mice (*Mus musculus*). *Behavioral Ecology & Sociobiology,* 1980, *6,* 297–303.

Lagerspetz, K. M. J., & Westman, M. Moral approval of aggressive acts: A preliminary investigation. *Aggressive Behavior,* 1980, *6,* 119–130.

Lerner, I. M. *The genetic basis of selection.* New York: Wiley, 1958.

Morgan, D. J. *Sex differences in the shock-elicited agonistic behavior of paired rats.* Master's thesis, Bowling Green State University, 1967.

Omark, D., Strayer, F., & Freedman, D. (Eds.). *Dominance relations.* New York: Garland STPM, 1980.

Pawlowski, A. A., & Scott, J. P. Hereditary differences in the development of dominance in litters of puppies. *Journal of Comparative and Physiological Psychology,* 1956, *49,* 353–358.

Schuster, R. H. *Aversive experiences and coordinated behavior: An animal model.* Paper presented to the European section of The International Society for Research on Aggression, Strasbourg, France, 1981.

Scott, J. P. Dominance and the frustration–aggression hypothesis. *Physiological Zoology,* 1948, *21,* 31–39.

Scott, J. P. Agonistic behavior in mice and rats: A review. *American Zoologist,* 1966, *6,* 683–701.

Scott, J. P. Violence and the disaggregated society. (Presidential address, International Society for Research and Aggression). *Aggressive Behavior,* 1975, *1,* 235–260.

Scott, J. P. Agonistic behavior: Function and dysfunction in social conflict. *Journal of Social Issues,* 1977, *33,* 9–21.

Scott, J. P., & Fuller, J. L. *Genetics and the social behavior of the dog.* Chicago: University of Chicago Press, 1965.

Smith, C. C. Adaptive nature of social organization in the genus of tree squirrels, *Tamiasciurus. Ecological Monographs,* 1968, *38,* 31–63.

Southwick, C. H. *Aggression among nonhuman primates*. Reading, Mass.: Addison–Wesley Module No. 23, 1972 (Anthropology).

Svare, B., & Mann, M. Infanticide: Genetic, developmental and hormonal influences in mice. *Physiology and Behavior,* 1981, *27,* 921–927.

vom Saal, F. S., & Bronson, F. H. In utero proximity of female mouse fetuses to males: Effect on reproductive performance during later life. *Biology of Reproduction,* 1978, *19,* 842–853.

2 New Strategies for Aggression Research

Neal G. Simon*
Long Island Research Institute

A survey of the literature on the genetic and neural aspects of aggression confronts the reader with a choice if the goal is to elaborate new research concepts for the field. One could present a number of specific issues and propose experimental approaches that would presumably help provide new insights into these problems. Alternatively, a more philosophical tack can be taken by presenting conceptual themes for aggression research. I have chosen the latter approach because it affords the opportunity to illustrate what I consider as the principle factor limiting our progress toward delineating the mechanisms that regulate aggressive behavior. Specifically, I refer to the separatism that exists among the subdisciplines in the field. Given the state of aggression research at this time, there is a pressing need for *integration* and *cohesion* within the area. The importance of these themes can best be demonstrated by considering their potential impact on two major issues in aggression research. These are: (1) the neuroendocrine processes that mediate the activation of aggressive behavior in adult male mice; and (2) the need for a common evaluative system for intermale aggression.

HORMONAL REGULATION OF INTERMALE AGGRESSION IN MICE: AN EXAMPLE OF THE NEED FOR INTEGRATION

The mechanisms through which testosterone (T) activates aggressive behavior in adult male mice have been the subject of considerable speculation and controver-

*Dr. Simon is now at the Department of Psychology, University of California at Riverside.

sy in recent years. At the heart of this issue is the question of the importance of hormone metabolism within the central nervous system (CNS) in the promotion of aggression by T. More precisely, T undergoes aromatization to estradiol (E_2) (Naftolin, Ryan, Davies, Reddy, Flores, Petro, Kuhn, White, Takaoka, & Wolin, 1975) and 5α-reduction to dihydrotestosterone (DHT) (Denef, Magnus, & McEwen, 1973; Jouan & Samperez, 1980; Noma, Nakao, Sato, Seki, Hanasaki, Takeuchi, & Yamamura, 1978) in the cytoplasmic compartment of limbic tissues that are thought to be regulatory centers for male-typical behaviors. These metabolic products then complex with hormone-specific receptor proteins, undergo a temperature-dependent transformation, and translocate to the nucleus, where they bind to chromatin and/or DNA acceptor sites (the interested reader is referred to Liao, 1975; Muldoon, 1980; or O'Malley & Means, 1974, for a general discussion of the mechanism of action of steroid hormones). Because the induction of behavior is presumably a product of hormone action at the level of the nucleus, it has been plausible for investigators to suggest that either E_2, DHT, T itself, or some combination of these products is the active aggression-promoting agent. Figure 2.1 summarizes the cellular events that provide the basis for each of these proposed mechanisms.

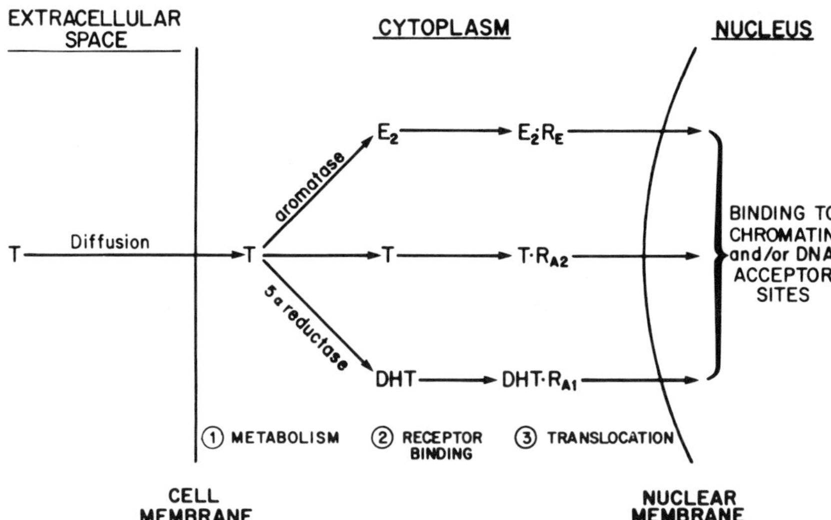

Fig. 2.1. The pathways through which testosterone or its metabolites can act to promote aggression. After entering the cell by diffusion, testosterone is enzymatically converted to estradiol by aromatase and to 5-dihydrotestosterone by 5-reductase. These products bind to cytoplasmic receptor proteins, undergo a thermolabile conformational change, and then translocate to the nucleus where they bind to acceptor sites. Behavioral effects presumably depend on the induction of protein synthesis at this level.

The aforementioned factors indicate that enzyme function and interactions between hormones and the genome are critical variables when considering the neuroendocrine regulation of aggression. It is therefore surprising that this issue has not attracted greater interest from behavior geneticists, because there is ample evidence for genetic influences on a variety of enzymatic systems in the brain (Ingram & Corfman, 1980). The few studies that have brought a genetic perspective to the question of hormonal factors in aggression have investigated strain differences in circulating T (Selmanoff, Goldman, Maxson, & Ginsburg, 1977); genetic influences on both behavioral and tissue responsiveness to exogenous T (Lagerspetz, Tirri, & Lagerspetz, 1968; Luttge, 1972; Luttge & Hall, 1973; Selmanoff, Abreu, Goldman, & Ginsburg, 1977), and the possible relationship between plasma levels of T and dominance (Raab & Haedenkamp, 1981; Selmanoff, Goldman, & Ginsburg, 1977). Although there are differences among males from different strains in the first three parameters, little evidence has thus far been obtained to suggest that dominance is correlated with endogenous T (for a more comprehensive treatment of these topics, see Selmanoff & Ginsburg, 1981). However, these observations provide little insight into the question of neuroendocrine regulatory mechanisms for aggressive behavior.

Concern with the hormonal processes that regulate aggression, not surprisingly, has been the province of behavioral endocrinologists. In this field, castration-replacement paradigms and pharmacological manipulations with hormone antagonists or enzyme inhibitors are used to examine the endocrine control of aggression.

Many of these investigations, conducted over the past 10 years, have led researchers to conclude that the behavioral action of T is mediated by estradiol (the aromatization hypothesis) (Beatty, 1979; Bowden & Brain, 1978; Brain & Bowden, 1979; Clark & Nowell, 1979, 1980). Several lines of evidence support this view. First, estradiol benzoate is as effective as testosterone proprionate as an aggression-restoring agent in gonadectomized Swiss–Webster (CFW) and Rockland–Swiss (R–S) male mice (Edwards & Burge, 1971; Simon & Gandelman, 1978a). Further, DHT, an androgen that is not aromatized to estrogen, is less effective than T in promoting aggression in CD-1 and CFW males (Luttge, 1972; Luttge & Hall, 1973). Also, the administration of an antiestrogen (CI-628) or an inhibitor of aromatase activity (4-androstene-3,6,17-trione) in conjunction with T reportedly blocks the ability of T to restore the aggressive behavior of castrated adult CF-1, CD-1, and TO males (Bowden & Brain, 1978; Clark & Nowell, 1979; Luttge, 1978). Antiandrogen administration in conjunction with T, on the other hand, presumably does not block the activation of aggression by T (Clark & Nowell, 1980; Edwards, 1970; Heilman, Brugmans, Greenslade, & DaVanzo, 1976).

These data provide strong support for the aromatization hypothesis. However, there are a number of studies that indicate that a direct androgenic effect of T can support aggressive behavior. Two reports have shown that EB is less effective than TP in restoring the aggressive behavior of CD-1 mice (Finney & Erpino,

1976; Luttge, 1972). Further, in contrast to other reports, cyproterone acetate, an antiandrogen, did reduce the ability of T to restore aggression in SPF male mice (Kurischko & Oettel, 1977). And MER-25, an antiestrogen that blocked the induction of aggression by EB, did not attenuate the activation of aggression by T (Simon, Gandelman, & Howard, 1980).

More compelling evidence regarding the role of androgen in the induction of aggression can be found in studies that used adult female mice as subjects. It is well known that chronic T administration to ovariectomized females will induce malelike aggressive behavior (Barkley & Goldman, 1977; Svare, Davis, & Gandelman, 1974). However, estrogen, unlike testosterone, appears incapable of activating aggression when administered to adult ovariectomized females in a similar fashion. Simon and Gandelman (1978b) treated R–S female mice with doses of EB that ranged from .5 μg to 40 μg per day. Of the 119 females exposed to EB, only one fought (after 32 days of 40 μg/day of EB). As can be seen in Table 2.1, 80% of females given 500 μg/day of TP attacked the stimulus animal. Additional support for the hypothesis that an androgen per se can be active also is found in a study that showed that chronic DHT treatment could induce fighting in ovariectomized females, although not as effectively as T (Schechter, Howard, & Gandelman, 1981). Obviously, these results support the concept of direct androgenic mediation of aggression and argue against the necessity for aromatization for the activation of fighting by T.

The third possible mechanism through which T might activate fighting is through a combined effect of E_2 and DHT, its major metabolites. Finney and Erpino (1976) suggested this possibility after treating orchiectomized CD-1 male mice with either T, EB, DHT, or EB + DHT. They found that only the combined regimen was as effective as T in promoting aggression.

There are clearly major differences among these proposed neuroendocrine

TABLE 2.1
The Proportion of Ovariectomized Rockland–Swiss Female Mice That Fought Following Exposure to Daily Injections of Either .5, 10, 20, or 40 μg EB or 500 μg TP Solely During Adulthood (Data are from Simon & Gandelman, 1978b)

Group	*Proportion Fighting (%)*[a]
EB–.5 μg	0/15 (0)
EB–10 μg	0/15 (0)
EB–20 μg	0/15 (0)
EB–40 μg	1/15 (7)
TP–500 μg	12/15 (80)

[a]Significant differences among groups ($p < .05$).

regulatory mechanisms for aggressive behavior in mice. Because evidence that both supports and contradicts each of these mechanisms is available, it seems reasonable to suggest that there may not be a unitary process through which T activates aggression. Rather, there are probably different mechanisms that vary as a function of genotype. Therefore, it appears that both behavior-genetic and behavioral endocrinologic techniques will be required to assess the hormonal processes involved in the regulation of aggression. Further, the inclusion of molecular endocrinological investigations would enhance these studies by providing a direct assessment of a possible biochemical basis for the sensitivity and insensitivity of various strains to the aggression-promoting property of certain hormones (for example, such studies have established that the insensitivity of Tfm mice to testosterone is due to an androgen receptor deficiency (Attardi & Ohno, 1978; Bardin & Wright, 1980)). Thus, the adoption of an experimental strategy that integrates behavior genetic, behavioral endocrinological, and molecular biological methods should permit a systematic examination of the genotype–hormone interactions involved in the regulation of androgen-dependent aggressive behavior in male mice.

The foregoing strategy was used in a recently completed study (Simon & Whalen, submitted for publication). Adult male CF-1, CFW, and CD-1 mice, which represent strains commonly used in studies of hormones and aggression, were gonadectomized and then treated daily with various doses of either T, DHT, E_2, diethylstilboestrol (DES, a synthetic estrogen), or methyltrienolone (R1881, a synthetic androgen[1]). The synthetic hormones were included as treatments because they bind to the appropriate receptors. More specifically, DES, in contrast to E_2, complexes with estrogen receptor (R_E) but has no affinity for androgen receptor (R_A), whereas R1881 binds avidly to R_A but does not interact with R_E (Chamness, King, & Sheridan, 1979; Raynaud, Bouton, Moguilewsky, Ojasoo, Philibert, Beck, Labrie, & Mornon, 1980). These properties of the synthetic ligands allow a direct assessment of whether androgenic or estrogenic stimulation alone is sufficient to promote aggression, thereby avoiding the complexities that arise when antagonists or enzymatic inhibitors are given in conjunction with T (Landau, 1980; Sutherland & Murphy, 1982). Bulbectomized males of the same strain were used as stimulus animals and tests were given daily for 10 days.

In the androgen series, the most striking finding was seen with methyltrienolone (Table 2.2). CF-1 males readily responded to the aggression-promoting property of this androgen as compared to CD-1 and CFW males. The response to the behavior-activating effect of DHT was moderate in all three strains. The seeming inconsistency in CF-1 males (i.e., a differential response to R1881 versus DHT) is due probably to differences in the potency of the two hormones. Finally, genetic influences on responsiveness to T, as reflected in the proportion

[1]Methyltrienolone was a generous gift from Dr. J. P. Raynaud of Roussel-Uclaf, Romanville, France.

TABLE 2.2
The Proportion of Gonadectomized Males From Three Different Strains That Fought in Response to Treatment With Either Testosterone, Dihydrotestosterone, or Methyltrienolone

Treatment	*CFW*	*Genotype* *CD-1*	*CF-1*
Dihydrotestosterone			
100 μg	4/10	4/8	4/10
500 μg	4/10	6/9	4/9
Methyltrienolone			
100 μg	3/10	3/6	9/10
500 μg	NA[a]	2/6	NA[a]
Testosterone			
100 μg	5/6	1/7	5/6
500 μg	NA[a]	6/10	NA[a]
Oil	2/6	0/6	2/8

[a]NA = Not administered.

fighting at a given dose level, were also found. CD-1 males required a higher dose of T to activate aggression in comparison to CF-1 and CFW males.

Pronounced differences among the strains were also observed following exposure to the estrogenic treatments (Table 2.3). CFW and CF-1 males were highly sensitive to the aggression-activating property of DES and E_2. In contrast, CD-1 males did not fight in response to DES or the low dose of E_2. The failure of these treatments to induce aggression suggests that the activation of fighting by the high dose of E_2 may be due to more than a specific estrogenic effect.

These data, in addition to demonstrating strain differences in responsiveness to androgens and estrogens, strongly argue against the notion that there is a unitary mechanism through which T promotes aggression. The findings suggest

TABLE 2.3
The Proportion of Gonadectomized Males From Three Different Strains That Fought in Response to Treatment With Either E_2, DES, or Oil

Treatment	*CFW*	*Genotype* *CD-1*	*CF-1*
Estradiol			
1 μg	8/9	1/9	9/9
5 μg	8/9	5/8	7/9
Diethylstilbestrol			
1 μg	7/9	1/9	8/90
5 μg	7/9	1/9	8/9
Oil	2/6	1/6	1/6

that there are independent androgen- and estrogen-sensitive aggression-activating systems. CF-1 males appear to have both systems. CFW males also seem to have both, but it appears that the estrogen-based system predominates. CD-1 males, in contrast to the other strains, appear to lack (or have a very limited) capacity to respond to the aggression-inducing property of estrogens. Direct androgenic stimulation, however, was moderately effective in activating aggression in this strain. A pilot study (Simon, unpublished data) also showed that a high percentage of CD-1 males will fight when exposed to a combined DES–DHT regimen. These observations suggest that the regulation of aggression in CD-1 males is mediated primarily by an androgenic effect of T that can be facilitated by estrogen action. Alternatively, there may be a synergistic system for aggression activation that depends on a combined effect of the major metabolites of T. This latter possibility is in accord with the view advanced by Finney and Erpino (1976).

Our next step was to investigate a possible biochemical correlate of the observed strain differences in sensitivity. This was accomplished by assessing the relationship between genotype and the level of androgen and estrogen receptors in the hypothalamic–septal–preoptic region. Six-point saturation analyses, depicted in Fig. 2.2, were analyzed by Scatchard analysis (Scatchard, 1949). Table 2.4 summarizes the differences found among the strains in the number of binding sites (B_{max}) and/or in the avidity of the binding between the ligand to the receptor (K_d). In the estrogen receptor assays, CFW males had the highest B_{max} (12.81 fmol/mg protein), followed by CD-1 (9.22 fmol) and CF-1 (6.8 fmol) males. The apparent K_d in CF-1 males ($.14 \times 10^{-10}$ M) was lower than that observed in the other two strains (both $.32 \times 10^{-10}$ M). Androgen receptor levels were also greatest in CFW males (B_{max} = 10.36 fmol) followed by CF-1 (9.68 fmol) and CD-1 males (8.13 fmol). The apparent K_d values for DHT binding to AR were 1.04×10^{-10} M (CFW), 2.36×10^{-10} M (CD–1), and 2.89×10^{-10} M (CF-1).

By combining the behavioral and biochemical data, a picture emerges as to how genotype might influence biochemical systems that affect sensitivity to the aggression-promoting property of T and its metabolites. Enhanced responsiveness to estrogens seems to be a product of either a higher concentration of binding sites (CFW) or higher affinity binding between estrogen and its receptor (CF-1). The androgen receptor data are not as easily interpreted. There are no clear relationships between behavioral responsiveness and the two aspects of receptor biology that were measured. Rather, it seems that other biochemical factors, such as binding kinetics or nuclear processing (Horowitz & McGuire, 1978; Olsen & Whalen, 1980; Whalen & Massicci, 1975), modulate sensitivity to the agression-promoting property of androgen.

Thus, the use of an integrative research strategy provided a wealth of data concerning the neuroendocrine mechanisms that regulate aggression. This same strategy can be applied, for example, to the study of the pharmacological control

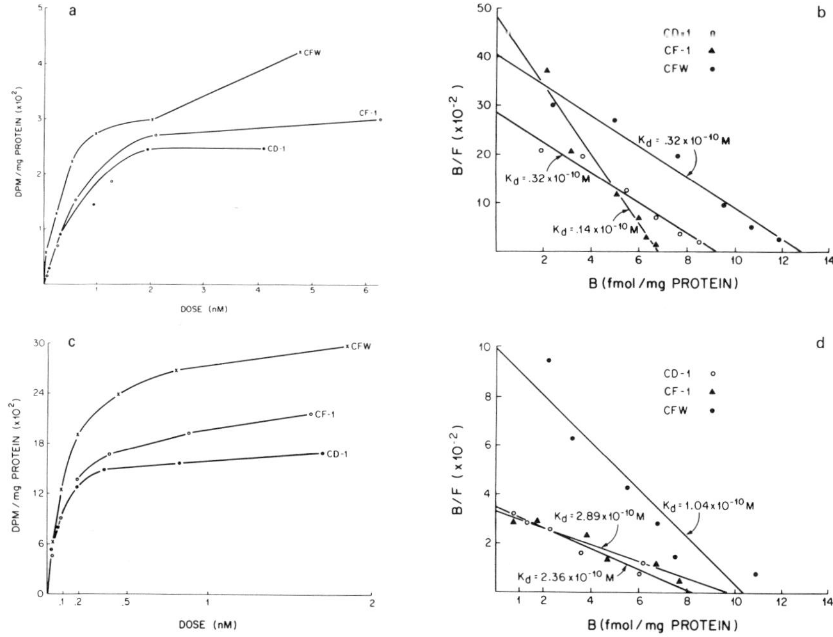

FIG. 2.2. Saturation and Scatchard analyses of [^{3}H]-DES and [^{3}H]-DHT binding to hypothalamic–preoptic–septal cytosols from CF-1, CD-1, and CFW male mice. A modification of the Chamness et al. (1979) hydroxylapatite assay was used. Cytosols were incubated for 3 or 4 hr with varying concentrations of [^{3}H]-DES (.04–1.84 nM) or [^{3}H]-DHT (.078–6.28 nM) at 0–4°C with or without a 100-fold excess of the appropriate unlabeled hormone. Specific binding was calculated by subtracting nonspecific from total binding. (a) Specific binding of [^{3}H]-DES; (b) Scatchard analysis of DES binding; (c) Specific binding of [^{3}H]-DHT; (d) Scatchard analysis of DHT binding.

TABLE 2.4
A Summary of the B_{max} and K_d Values Obtained by Scatchard Analysis From the Androgen ([^{3}H]-DHT) and Estrogen ([^{3}H]-DES) Binding Studies in CD-1, CFW, and CF-1 Male Mice

	Estrogen		*Androgen*	
Genotype	B_{max} *(fmol/mg protein)*	K_d $(\times 10^{-10} M)$	B_{max} *(fmol/mg protein)*	K_d $(\times 10^{-10} M)$
CD-1	9.22	.32	8.13	2.36
CF-1	6.8	.14	9.68	2.89
CFW	12.81	.32	10.36	1.04

of aggression. Such an integrated approach will serve to enhance our understanding of the processes involved in the control of intermale aggression.

THE EVALUATION OF INTERMALE AGGRESSION IN MICE: AN EXAMPLE OF THE NEED FOR COHESION

A variety of evaluative systems have been employed in studies of intermale aggression. Basically, these systems can be classified as either discrete or composite. In discrete scoring systems, a number of parameters are measured and each is analyzed separately. Composite indices, on the other hand, generate a single "aggression score" by combining the behavioral measurements in some fashion.

Discrete scoring systems vary in the number and kind of behaviors that are sampled. They may include assessments of the presence or absence of fighting (Edwards & Burge, 1971; Eleftheriou, Bailey, & Denenberg, 1974); the frequency and incidence of wounding (Collins, 1970); the frequency and duration of attack behavior (Simon & Gandelman, 1978a); the latency to attack and fight frequency (Luttge, 1972); latency to attack, total attack duration, and frequency of attacks or bites (Brain & Poole, 1974; Clark & Nowell, 1980; Finney & Erpino, 1976); or frequency of chases, attacks, fights, and grooming (Vale, Vale & Harley, 1971). More ambitious discrete systems have included all these plus either tail rattling, sniffing, and anogenital investigation (Kessler, Elliott, Orenberg, & Barchas, 1977); nosing, grooming, and squeaking (Hahn, Haber, & Fuller, 1973); or anogenital investigation, autogrooming, allogrooming, and head sniffing (Erpino, 1975).

Composite scoring systems for aggressive behavior, although less frequently utilized, also differ substantially. One such index simply sums the frequency of chases, attacks, and fights (Southwick, 1968). Another composite system divides the test session into 20-sec intervals and assigns one or two points for each interval that contains either bites, chases, tail rattling, or attacks (Selmanoff, Maxson, & Ginsburg, 1976). A third type of composite index is the scaled score system. This is based on either the latency for the appearance of certain agonistic behaviors (Elias, Elias, & Schlager, 1975) or on the intensity of fighting as assessed by the frequency of nosing, allogrooming, threats, tail rattling, wrestling, or fighting (Brain & Bowden, 1979; Ebert & Hyde, 1976; Lagerspetz, 1981).

The scoring systems just described obviously differ in some of the behaviors selected for measurement and, in certain cases, in the weightings assigned to the behaviors that comprise the aggression ethogram. This lack of methodological congruence has no doubt contributed to the disparate results obtained in different laboratories even when, for example, the same inbred strains have been studied (see a review by Simon, 1979). More importantly, this type of methodological variation has probably hindered progress in our understanding of aggressive behavior because it makes comparisons among studies difficult.

The differences among available evaluative systems, when coupled with the interpretive problems engendered by these differences, indicate that there is a need for a common, statistically derived system that can be used in the analysis of intermale aggression. We have developed two such systems for the evaluation of offensive aggressive behavior in mice (Simon, Gray, & Gandelman, in press). One is a short-form discrete index and the other a composite system for use when more detailed measurements are required.

Male mice from four different strains (Rockland–Swiss, (R–S), CF-1, CD-1, and CFW) were used in an effort to minimize biasing the systems. They were given a single test for aggression toward an olfactory bulbectomized stimulus male of the same genotype 20 days after they were individually housed. The test consisted of leaving the olfactory bulbectomized stimulus male in the home cage of the experimental animal and recording the test male's behavior prior to the onset of attack and then for 5 minutes after the initiation of fighting. Throughout this period, the frequency, duration, and sequential display of anogenital investigation, rough grooming, tail rattling, threat postures (often accompanied by side-to-side movements of the head toward the flanks of the stimulus male), and biting attacks were recorded. Detailed descriptions of these behaviors can be found in Banks (1962), and Grant and MacKintosh (1963).

Because of the differences in interval length, all data were normalized by converting to per minute scores prior to analysis. Preliminary analyses were performed to determine whether the frequency or duration measure of the various behaviours should be used in the formal analyses of the data. These tests indicated that the duration of anogenital investigation (AGD), duration of rough grooming (RGD), tail-rattling frequency (TRF), frequency of threat postures (THF), and frequency of attacks (ATF) were the appropriate parameters for the actual analyses.

Behavioral Transitions in Aggression

The first set of analyses was designed to determine whether sequential behavior patterns on the part of the experimental male could be detected. To examine this possibility, the test period was partitioned into four intervals, two preattack and two following the onset of fighting. The relationship of each behavior to the behaviors in the adjacent interval was then assessed by correlational analyses. The results are depicted in Fig. 2.3. A careful examination of this figure makes it evident that the behaviors separate into two paths after Interval 1. Anogenital investigation during the second preattack interval is the beginning of a path that is significantly associated with aggression during Intervals 3 and 4. Animals that exhibit high levels of rough grooming during Interval 2, on the other hand, continue to exhibit this behavior during Intervals 3 and 4.

TRANSITION PATHS IN AGGRESSIVE BEHAVIOR

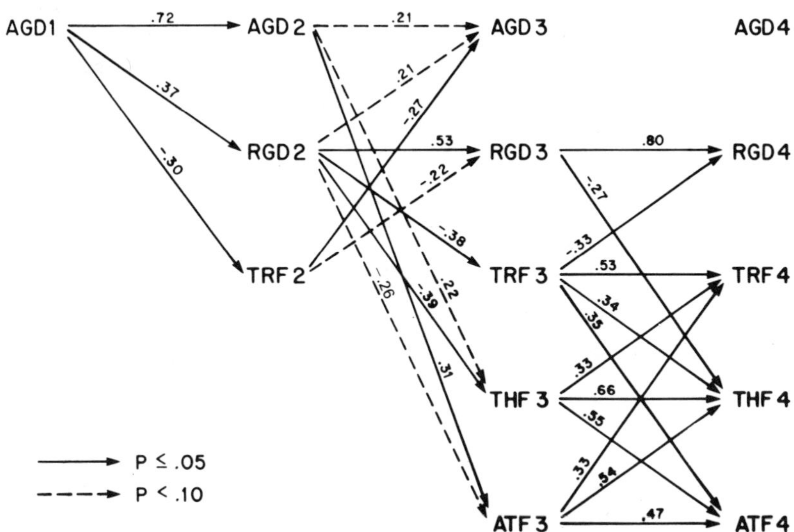

FIG. 2.3. The results of a series of correlational analyses designed to detect the relationship among the behaviors from adjacent intervals. Significant (—) and marginal (---) relationships are included.

These observations, when combined with the results of several stepwise regressions, indicated that two distinct behavioral sequences were exhibited by the experimental males. One of these behavioral profiles was characteristic of highly aggressive males, whereas the other was displayed by males that engaged in little attack behavior (see Fig. 2.4). In highly aggressive males, anogenital investigation during Interval 2 predicts attack behavior during the third interval. Engaging in high levels of attack behavior indicates that this and related behaviors (tail rattling, threats) will continue to be exhibited. Males that are not highly aggressive show extended amounts of rough grooming prior to the initiation of fighting. They continue to exhibit high levels of rough grooming over the course of testing and are less likely to display either biting attacks or behaviors associated with attacks.

Structure of Aggressive Behavior

The variables extracted from the series of intercorrelations were subjected to factor analysis to determine the underlying structural relationship. The behaviors included in this analysis were anogenital investigation during Intervals 1, 2, 3; rough grooming and tail rattling during Intervals 2, 3, 4; and threat frequency and attack frequency during Intervals 3 and 4.

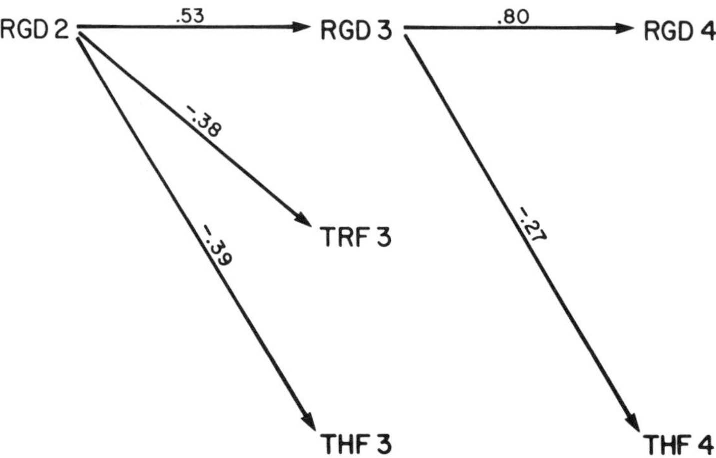

FIG. 2.4. The extracted pathways that characterize males that were high or low in aggressiveness toward a bulbectomized stimulus male during a home-cage test. (A) Behavioral transitions of a low aggression male; (B) Behavioral pathway typical of a highly aggressive male.

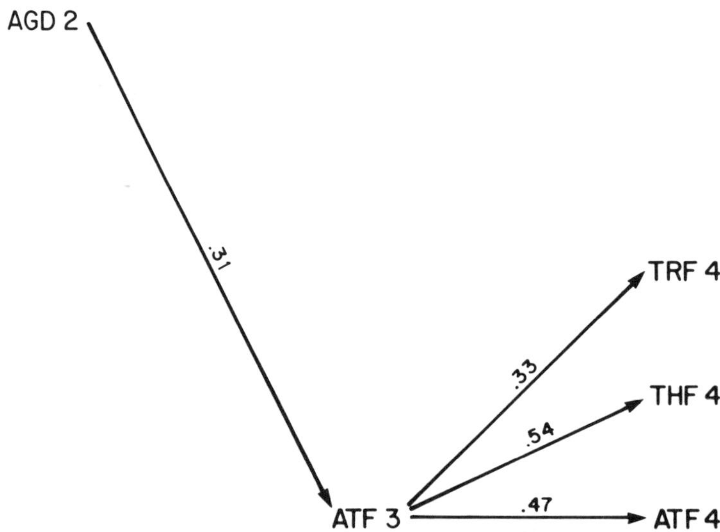

The least overlap among the factors, which indicates the best means for analyzing aggressive interactions, was found when two factors were initially extracted and a quartimax rotation was performed. The results are summarized in Table 2.5 and Fig. 2.5. In this analysis, Factor 1 can be termed *aggression*. Attacks, threats, and tail rattling have positive loadings whereas rough grooming is negatively weighed. The second factor was termed *investigation* because rough grooming and anogenital investigation had high positive loadings.

The results indicate that two general features of an attacking male's behavior should be designed into an evaluative system for offensive aggression. One such feature is the shift in the behaviors that comprise offensive aggression over the course of an interaction. This was detected in the series of intercorrelations. The other salient feature is that the component behaviors within each interval should be differentially weighted. The need for this is apparent from an examination of the loadings in the factor analysis.

These considerations are incorporated into a composite aggression index that is presented in Table 2.6. The index is based on the aggression factor (Factor 1) in the 2 factor structure (see Table 2.5). Coefficients were derived for all behaviors with factor loadings above .25. The weightings for each variable have also been adjusted so that they can be applied to raw scores (i.e., per minute scores) to produce the equivalent of a factor score. It should also be noted that the components of the composite index can be analyzed individually if a detailed discrete scoring system is deemed appropriate.

TABLE 2.5
A Summary of the Results of a Factor Analysis When Two Factors Were Extracted and Subjected to a Quartimax Rotation. Only Loadings With an Absolute Value Greater Than .25 Are Presented. These Values Were Used To Construct the Composite Aggression Index Shown in Table 2.6.

Variable	*Factor 1* *Aggression*	*Factor 2* *Investigation*
Anogenital investigation 1		.78
Anogenital investigation 2	.26	.72
Rough grooming 2	−.51	.53
Tail rattling 2		−.68
Anogenital investigation 3		.47
Rough grooming 3	−.61	.39
Tail rattling 3	.71	
Threat 3	.86	
Attack 3	.81	.27
Rough grooming 4	−.48	.29
Tail rattling 4	.62	
Threat 4	.82	
Attack 4	.75	

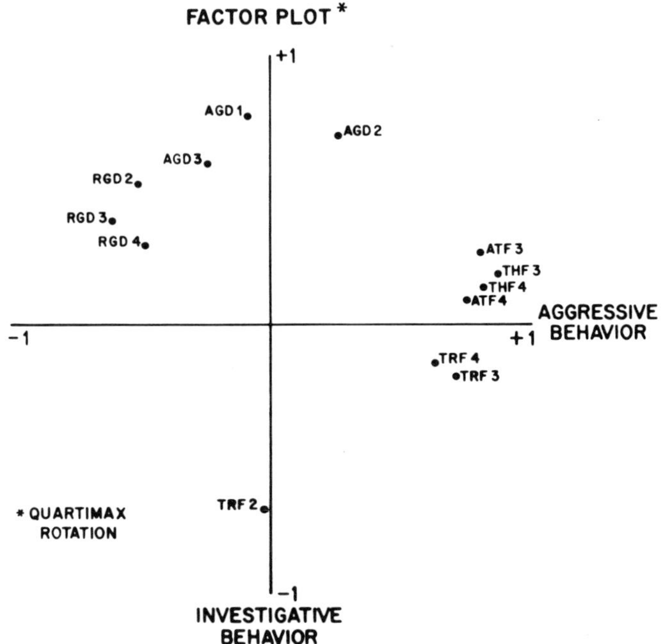

FIG. 2.5. A graphical representation of the two factors that represent the underlying structure of offensive aggressive behavior. The horizontal axis, which reflects aggression, loads attacks, threats, and tail rattling with positive signs. Rough grooming is negatively related to aggressiveness. The second factor, shown on the vertical axis, reflects investigative behaviors and loads anogenital investigation and rough grooming with positive signs.

In addition to the aforementioned features, there is one other noteworthy aspect of the new scoring index. This is the negative weighting given to rough grooming. Those systems that have included this behavior have generally classified it as an aggressive act (Elias et al., 1975; Vale et al., 1971). In fact, previous studies have not clearly established whether this is an aggressive or nonaggressive behavior. Some investigators considered grooming to be an extension of

TABLE 2.6
The Formulas for the Statistically Derived Composite and Short-Form Indices for Offensive Intermale Aggression

I. Composite index aggression score	=	.03 (AGD2) − .04 (RGD2) − .07 (RGD3) + .1 (TRF3) + .37 (THF3) −.41 (RGD4) + .51 (TRF4) + .39 (THF4) + .38 (ATF4)
II. Short-form aggression score	=	$\frac{\Sigma \text{ (THF3 + ATTF3 + THF4 + ATTF4)}}{\text{\# Minutes}}$

attack (Kahn, 1954; Warne, 1947), whereas others have not observed such a clear relationship (Clark & Schein, 1966). The obtained negative loadings for this behavior suggest that it is a nonaggressive act. Further, animals exhibiting high amounts of rough grooming engaged in less attack behavior. Additional support for this classification of rough grooming is also evidenced by the observation that females, which are nonaggressive, readily engage in rough grooming during an interaction with a bulbectomized male (Gandelman, Simon, & Gray, unpublished data).

The results also provide an empirical basis for a short-form index of fighting behavior. Presented in Table 2.6, this index is calculated by summing threats and attacks and then converting this value to a per minute rate. These behaviors were the obvious choices for the short-form system because they have the highest loadings on factors that are best interpreted as aggressive (see Table 2.5 and Fig. 2.5).

The short-form index is generally consistent with other basic discrete indices that have appeared in the literature (Luttge, 1972). It is distinguished by two features: the inclusion of threats and the absence of attack duration as a measure of aggression. The inclusion of the former was based on its loading in the factor analyses. The decision to exclude attack duration was based on the finding that this parameter was subject to greater measurement error than attack frequency and also was not as well predicted by the other components of the model.

The two new scoring systems herein described contrast with other indices in that they are statistically derived. Their adoption would increase methodological consistency in aggression research, a step that will enhance the ability of investigators to make comparisons among studies from different laboratories.

Conclusion

The field of aggression research has reached a crossroads. The choice confronting those who study various aspects of intermale aggressive behavior is either to continue the parallelism in lines of inquiry that is a product of specialization or to adopt new research strategies that can bring fresh perspectives to aggression research. I believe that it is time for the latter and that an emphasis on integrated, interdisciplinary approaches, along with cohesive methodology, will significantly enhance future endeavors designed to increase our understanding of the regulation of aggressive behavior.

ACKNOWLEDGMENT

The preparation of this chapter and parts of the research presented were supported by NICHD Grant HD–15647 to the author.

REFERENCES

Attardi, B., & Ohno, S. Physical properties of androgen receptors in brain cytosol from normal and testicular feminized mice. *Endocrinology,* 1978, *103,* 760–770.

Banks, E. M. A time and motion study of prefighting behavior in mice. *Journal of Genetic Psychology,* 1962, *101,* 165–183.

Bardin, C. W., & Wright, W. Androgen receptor deficiency: Testicular feminization, its variants, and differential diagnosis. *Annals of Clinical Research,* 1980, *12,* 236–242.

Barkley, M. S., & Goldman, B. D. Testosterone-induced aggression in adult female mice. *Hormones and Behavior,* 1977, *9,* 76–84.

Beatty, W. W. Gonadal hormones and nonreproductive behaviors in rodents: Organizational and activational influences. *Hormones and Behavior,* 1979, *12,* 112–163.

Bowden, N. J., & Brain, P. F. Blockade of testosterone-maintained intermale fighting in albino laboratory mice by an aromatization inhibitor. *Physiology and Behavior,* 1978, *20,* 543–546.

Brain, P. F., & Bowden, N. J. Sex steroid control of intermale fighting in mice. *Current Developments in Psychopharmacology,* 1979, *5,* 403–465.

Brain, P. F., & Poole, A. E. Some studies on the use of "standard opponents" in intermale aggression testing in TT albino mice. *Behavior,* 1974, *50,* 100–110.

Chamness, G. C., King, T. W., & Sheridan, P. J. Androgen receptor in the rat brain–assays and properties. *Brain Research,* 1979, *161,* 267–276.

Clark, L. H., & Schein, M. W. Activities associated with conflict behavior in mice. *Animal Behaviour,* 1966, *14,* 44–49.

Clark, C. R., & Nowell, N. W. The effect of the antiestrogen CI-628 on androgen-induced aggressive behavior in castrated male mice. *Hormones and Behavior,* 1979, *12,* 205–210.

Clark, C. R., & Nowell, N. W. The effect of the non-steroidal antiandrogen flutamide on neural receptor binding of testosterone and intermale aggressive behavior in mice. *Psychoneuroendocrinology,* 1980, *5,* 39–45.

Collins, R. A. Aggression in mice selectively bred for brain weight. *Behavior Genetics,* 1970, *1,* 169–171.

Denef, C., Magnus, C., & McEwen, B. S. Sex differences and hormonal control of testosterone metabolism in rat pituitary and brain. *Journal of Endocrinology,* 1973, *59,* 605–621.

Ebert, P. D., & Hyde, J. S. Selection for agonistic behavior in wild female *Mus musculus. Behavior Genetics,* 1976, *6,* 291–304.

Edwards, D. A. Effects of cyproterone acetate on aggressive behaviour and the seminal vesicles of male mice. *Journal of Endocrinology,* 1970, *46,* 477–481.

Edwards, D. A., & Burge, K. G. Estrogenic arousal of aggressive behavior and masculine sexual behavior in male and female mice. *Hormones and Behavior,* 1971, *2,* 239–245.

Eleftheriou, B. E., Bailey, D. W., & Denenberg, V. H. Genetic analysis of fighting behavior in mice. *Physiology and Behavior,* 1974, *13,* 773–777.

Elias, J. W., Elias, M. F., & Schlager, G. Aggressive social interaction in mice genetically selected for blood pressure extremes. *Behavioral Biology,* 1975, *13,* 155–166.

Erpino, M. J. Androgen-induced aggression in neonatally androgenized female mice: Inhibition by progesterone. *Hormones and Behavior,* 1975, *6,* 149–157.

Finney, H. C., & Erpino, M. J. Synergistic effect of estradiol benzoate and dihydrotestosterone on aggression in mice. *Hormones and Behavior,* 1976, *7,* 391–400.

Grant, E. C., & MacKintosh, J. H. A comparison of the social postures of some common laboratory rodents. *Behaviour* 1963, *21,* 246–259.

Hahn, M. E., Haber, S. B., & Fuller, J. L. Differential agonistic behavior in mice selected for brain weight. *Physiology and Behavior,* 1973, *10,* 759–762.

Heilman, R. D., Brugmans, M., Greenslade, E. C., & DaVanzo, J. P. Resistance of androgen-mediated aggressive behavior in mice to flutamide, an antiandrogen. *Psychopharmacology,* 1976, *47,* 75–80.

Horowitz, K. B., & McGuire, W. L. Nuclear mechanisms of estrogen action. *Journal of Biological Chemistry,* 1978, *253,* 8185–8189.

Ingram, D. K., & Corfman, T. P. An overview of neurobiological comparisons in mouse strains. *Neuroscience and Biobehavioral Reviews,* 1980, *4,* 421–435.

Jouan, P., & Samperez, S. Metabolism of steroid hormones in the brain. In M. Motta (Ed.), *The endocrine functions of the brain.* New York: Raven Press, 1980.

Kahn, M. W. Infantile experience and mature aggressive behavior in mice: Some maternal influences. *Journal of Genetic Psychology,* 1954, *84,* 65–75.

Kessler, S., Elliott, G. R., Orenberg, E. K., & Barchas, J. D. A genetic analysis of aggressive behavior in two strains of mice. *Behavior Genetics,* 1977, *7,* 313–321.

Kurischko, A., & Oettel, M. Androgen-dependent fighting behaviour in male mice. *Endokrinologie,* 1977, *70,* 1–5.

Lagerspetz, K. M. J. Genetic and social causes of aggressive behaviour in mice. *Scandinavian Journal of Psychology,* 1981, *2,* 167–173.

Lagerspetz, K. Y. H., Tirri, R., & Lagerspetz, K. M. J. Neurochemical and endocrinological studies of mice selectively bred for aggressiveness. *Scandinavian Journal of Psychology,* 1968, *9,* 157–160.

Landau, I. T. Facilitation of male sexual behavior in adult male rats by the aromatization inhibitor, 1,4,6,-androstatriene-3,17-dione (ATD). *Physiology and Behavior,* 1980, *25,* 173–177.

Liao, S. Cellular receptors and mechanisms of action of steroid hormones. *International Review of Cytology,* 1975, *41,* 87–172.

Luttge, W. G. Activation and inhibition of isolation-induced intermale fighting behavior in castrate male CD-1 mice treated with steroidal hormones. *Hormones and Behavior,* 1972, *3,* 71–81.

Luttge, W. G. Anti-estrogen inhibition of testosterone-stimulated aggression in mice. *Experientia,* 1978, *35,* 273–274.

Luttge, W. G., & Hall, N. R. Androgen-induced agonistic behavior in castrate male Swiss–Webster mice: Comparison of four naturally occurring androgens. *Behavioral Biology,* 1973, *8,* 725–732.

Muldoon, T. G. Regulation of steroid hormone receptor activity. *Endocrine Reviews,* 1980, *1,* 339–364.

Naftolin, F., Ryan, K., Davies, I., Reddy, V., Flores, F., Petro, Z., Kuhn, M., White, R. J., Takaoka, Y., & Wolin, L. The formation of estrogens by central neuroendocrine tissues. *Recent Progress in Hormone Research,* 1975, *31,* 295–315.

Noma, K., Nakao, K., Sato, B., Seki, T., Hanasaki, N., Takeuchi, N., & Yamamura, Y. Testosterone metabolites associated with cytosol receptors and nuclei of anterior pituitary and various brain regions. *Journal of Steroid Biochemistry,* 1978, *9,* 257–264.

Olsen, K. L., & Whalen, R. E. Sexual differentiation of the brain: Effects on mating behavior and (^{3}H)-estradiol binding by hypothalamic chromatin in rats. *Biology of Reproduction,* 1980, *22,* 1068–1072.

O'Malley, B. W., & Means, A. R. Female steroid hormones and target cell nuclei. *Science,* 1974, *183,* 610–620.

Raab, A., & Haedenkamp, G. Impact of social conflict between mice on testosterone binding in the central nervous system. *Neuroendocrinology,* 1981, *32,* 273–277.

Raynaud, J. P., Bouton, M. M., Moguilewsky, M., Ojasoo, T., Philibert, D., Beck, G., Labrie, F., & Mornon, J. P. Steroid hormone receptors and pharmacology. *Journal of Steroid Biochemistry,* 1980, *12,* 143–157.

Scatchard, G. The attractions of proteins for small molecules and ions. *Annals of the New York Academy of Science,* 1949, *51,* 660–672.

Schechter, D., Howard, S. M., & Gandelman, R. Dihydrotestosterone promotes fighting behavior of female mice. *Hormones and Behavior,* 1981, *15,* 233–237.

Selmanoff, M. K., Abreu, E., Goldman, B. D., & Ginsburg, B. E. Manipulation of aggressive behavior in adult DBA/2/Bg and C57BL/10/Bg male mice implanted with testosterone in silastic tubing. *Hormones and Behavior,* 1977, *8,* 377–390.

Selmanoff, M. K., & Ginsburg, B. E. Genetic variability in aggression and endocrine function in inbred strains of mice. In P. F. Brain & D. Benton (Eds.), *Multidisciplinary approaches to aggression research*. New York: Elsevier/North-Holland Biomedical Press, 1981.

Selmanoff, M. K., Goldman, B. D., & Ginsburg, B. E. Serum testosterone, agonistic behavior, and dominance in inbred strains of mice. *Hormones and Behavior*, 1977, *8*, 107–119.

Selmanoff, M. K., Goldman, B. D., Maxson, S. C., & Ginsburg, B. E. Correlated effects of the Y chromosome of mice on developmental changes in testosterone levels and intermale aggression. *Life Sciences*, 1977, *20*, 359–366.

Selmanoff, M. K., Maxson, S. C., & Ginsburg, B. E. Chromosomal determinants of intermale aggressive behavior in inbred mice. *Behaviour Genetics*, 1976, *6*(1), 53–69.

Simon, N. G. The genetics of intermale aggression in mice: Recent research and alternative strategies. *Neuroscience and Biobehavioral Reviews*, 1979, *3*, 97–106.

Simon, N. G., & Gandelman, R. Aggression-promoting and aggression-eliciting properties of estrogen in male mice. *Physiology and Behavior*, 1978, *21*, 161–164. (a)

Simon, N. G., & Gandelman, R. The estrogenic arousal of aggressive behavior in female mice. *Hormones and Behavior*, 1978, *10*, 118–127. (b)

Simon, N. G., Gandelman, R., & Howard, S. M. MER-25 does not inhibit the activation of aggression by testosterone in adult Rockland–Swiss mice. *Psychoneuroendocrinology*, 1980, *6*, 131–137.

Simon, N. G., Gray, J., & Gandelman, R. An empirically derived scoring system for intermale aggression in mice. *Aggressive Behavior*, in press.

Simon, N. G., & Whalen, R. E. Hormonal regulation of aggression: Evidence for a relationship among genotype, receptor binding, and sensitivity to androgen and estrogen. Submitted to *Endocrinology*.

Southwick, C. H. Effect of maternal environment on aggressive behavior of inbred mice. *Communications in Behavioral Biology*, 1968, *1*, 129–132.

Sutherland, R. L., & Murphy, L. C. Mechanisms of oestrogen antagonism by nonsteroidal antiestrogens. *Molecular and Cellular Endocrinology*, 1982, *25*, 5–23.

Svare, B., Davis, P. G., & Gandelman, R. Fighting behavior in female mice following chronic androgen treatment during adulthood. *Physiology and Behavior*, 1974, *12*, 399–403.

Vale, J. R., Vale, C. A., & Harley, J. P. Interaction of genotype and population number with regard to aggressive behavior, social grooming, and adrenal and gonadal weight in male mice. *Communications in Behavioral Biology*, 1971, *6*, 209–221.

Warne, M. C. A time analysis of certain aspects of the behavior of small groups of caged mice. *Journal of Comparative and Physiological Psychology*, 1947, *40*, 371–387.

Whalen, R. E., & Massicci, J. Subcellular analysis of the accumulation of estrogen by the brain of male and female rats. *Brain Research*, 1975, *89*, 255–164.

II GENETICS, EVOLUTION, AND AGGRESSION

3 Genetic Architecture and the Evolution of Aggressive Behavior

J. K. Hewitt
P. L. Broadhurst
University of Birmingham
England

In this chapter we consider aggressive behavior from the viewpoint of that particular approach to behavior genetics that attempts to relate the pattern of gene action and interaction manifested in intraspecific behavioral variation to the possible evolutionary pressures on the behavior and, hence, its adaptive significance. An overview of the fruitfulness of this approach for a wide range of behaviors has been provided by Broadhurst (1979), whereas the general thesis and methodology have been outlined by Broadhurst and Jinks (1974) and Jinks and Broadhurst (1974), and a summary of the approach to a particular behavior, escape–avoidance conditioning in the rat, has been presented by Hewitt, Fulker, and Broadhurst (1981). Following the format of these earlier papers, we first outline the arguments relating the consequences of different evolutionary pressures to patterns of genetic architecture, then discuss the biometrical specification and methods of analysis of the genetic variation, and lastly consider some of the relevant data available in the literature. Our detailed discussion focuses on same-sex aggression in mice because it is for this phenomenon that the kinds of data we require are available in some scope and variety. Furthermore, as a contribution to a symposium subtitled "Synthesis and New Directions," we would be satisfied if this chapter were in part a prospective view as well as a retrospective review; for this reason we indicate some methods of analysis that we hope might find their way into the research armamentarium of students of the genetics of aggression even though there are as yet no clear examples of their application. Before embarking on this proposed program there are some remarks we would like to make about the phenotype that is the object of our analysis and that may help to set the scene for some of our later comments and conclusions.

From the outset we are not faced with a single phenotype but with a collection of phenotypes or perhaps, if we understood better the relationships among these phenotypes, what we would probably hope to describe as a system of phenotypes. Thus, even when restricting discussion to one sex of one species, Simon (1979) defines intermale aggression in mice as referring to "interactions between adult males that include the elements of threat (postural adjustments and/or facial expressions), attack (outright biting directed to the flank areas), avoidance (behaviors which minimize attack duration), escape, or some combination of these [p. 97]." Naturally, much broader definitions are often adopted, perhaps the broadest coming from sociobiologists like Wilson (1975) who, when obliged to offer a short characterization of the concept, defines aggression as, "a physical act or threat of action by one individual that reduces the freedom or genetic fitness of another [p. 577]." Wilson does, of course, offer considerable guidance to the intended interpretation of the definition when he suggests an eightfold categorization of the forms that aggression may take: territorial (that directed towards achieving dominance over subordinates); sexual; parental disciplinary (that directed towards one's own weanlings); moralistic (aimed at enforcing reciprocation of altruism); and predatory and antipredatory aggression. As Wilson (1975) says, he is concerned that his categories of aggression should conform to adaptive categories; that is, to the different mechanisms of enhancement of individual genetic fitness. Simon's (1979) definition was more closely concerned with specification of the precise behaviors that were to be seen as aggressive, irrespective of their ultimate adaptive functions. Our view is that the two approaches exemplified by Simon and Wilson are both necessary for a full understanding of aggressive behavior; we need clear operational definitions of the behaviors under investigation on the one hand, while we seek, on the other, to discover the significance or nonsignificance of these behaviors for individual animals seen as participants in the process of evolution. However, the very complexity of the phenotypes involved makes us wary of following Wilson too readily in asserting the adaptive function of this or that behavior, without at least some alternative form of evidence to support our assertions.

Apart from its complexity, perhaps one of the most obvious features of aggressive behavior is that it is by definition a social phenomenon (Scott, 1977); that is to say that the occasion for aggressive behavior is always the interaction of at least two individuals. The consequences of this have been explored by Fuller and Hahn (1976), who remind us that aggressive or, more generally, agonistic behavior shares this property of being social with sexual and cooperative behaviors such as parental care giving, but differs in this respect from the individual behaviors, like learning performance or activity in a standard test situation, that are more commonly the subject of behavior-genetic analysis. One reason for the relative neglect of social behaviors is surely that the additional dimensions of complexity of analysis have proved too daunting to prospective investigators. However, because those behaviors that are central to the direction of the evolutionary process, namely sexual behavior, the control of the mating system, and competitive interactions to determine the allocation of resources, are precisely those that are social in character, if we want to understand the interplay of behavior and evolution we must develop methods of analysis appropriate to social behavior. Fuller and Hahn (1976) discussed three experimental designs that might be employed, but did not pursue in detail the genetic models that could be specified or the kinds of conclusions that might be reached about the genetic architecture of social behaviors from their experimental designs. For our part, we would not claim any special insights into this problem, especially as the methods of analysis we prefer, those of biometrical genetics (Mather & Jinks, 1971), have often been developed initially within the context of plant breeding, where the problems of interaction between individuals, although not altogether absent (Breese & Hill, 1973), are not generally paramount. However, we do feel that this problem represents one of the more fertile areas for development in the study of behavior genetics, and we would point to a start that has already been made from within the biometrical genetical school on the analysis of genotypic competition (Mather, 1973) and of competition and cooperation within human families (Eaves, 1976; Eaves, Last, Young, & Martin, 1978). These provide examples of the potential for an analysis of social behaviors using biometrical genetical methods similar to that we have seen in the analysis of the genetical architecture of individual behaviors (Broadhurst, 1979; Broadhurst & Jinks, 1974).

But as we progress from the characterization of individual operationally defined components of aggressive behavior in terms of their genetic architectures to the analysis of the social encounters that these behaviors regulate, we find that the current state of knowledge permits less and less precise statement while, at the same time, the opportunities for new research aimed at understanding the evolution of aggression may become greater. Thus we want to ask: What is known, what should we be looking for, and how might we best discover it? With this in mind we turn now to a discussion of the general theory that motivates our approach to behavior genetics.

GENETIC ARCHITECTURE AND EVOLUTION

Our basic premise is that the genetic architecture controlling a trait will reflect the evolutionary pressures that have acted upon it. This situation may be brought about by a genuine evolution of the genetic system (Darlington, 1939), two examples of which are the gradual construction of "supergenes" by recombination and tight linkage to give balanced or coadapted sets of alleles (Mather, 1973), and the modification of dominance properties at one genetic locus by the accumulation of appropriate modifiers at other loci (Fisher, 1928). On the other hand, the situation might result from the selective survival of newly arising mutations that, in interaction with alternative alleles or effects at other loci, display de novo the appropriately adaptive effects. As an illustration let us consider the case of dominance at an individual locus while bearing in mind that the discussion will apply in all its essentials to other kinds of effects.

As we have noted elsewhere (Hewitt et al., 1981) the connection between dominance and evolution was made by Fisher (1928, 1958) who, taking as his starting point the observation that phenotypes of most mutant alleles are recessive to their wild type counterparts, argued that, although initially a newly arising mutation may in the heterozygous condition result in an intermediate phenotype, any modification of this expression toward the fitter heterozygote will be favored. If a mutation is recurrent, then eventually modifying genes that result in dominance in the direction of the favored homozygote will become fixed. Thus Fisher argued that dominance is a consequence of continued directional selection for a favored phenotype. As early as 1929, Sewall Wright took issue with Fisher and argued that when the mutant allele is initially very rare the selective advantage of modifying genes would be so low as to have virtually no effect on their frequencies. Wright's own view of wild type dominance was that it was a property of certain alleles ab initio and that those alleles would be selected that produced sufficient gene product for the full expression of the favored phenotype even when in the heterozygous state. But in either of these views evolutionary pressures result in dominance in the favored direction. Furthermore, both Wright and Fisher and others were agreed that where there is considerable polymorphism the conditions for the evolution of dominance are optimized (Sheppard, 1967). In the case of polygenic systems, Mather and his associates have demonstrated that polymorphism is the rule rather than the exception (Mather, 1941; Mather & Harrison, 1949) and showed experimentally that characters associated with high fitness, for example viability, exhibit dominance in the high direction (Breese & Mather, 1960). A similar demonstration for mating speed, a behavioral fitness character, was provided by Fulker (1966), and Angus (1974) has demonstrated in experimental population cages the increased selective value of a measure of spontaneous activity previously shown to be under the control of directional dominance.

Extending the argument, Mather (1960, 1973) shows how, with characters for which intermediate expression is optimal, either little or no dominance variation will be expressed, or dominance will act at some loci in one direction and at others in the opposite direction. This form of ambidirectional dominance was found by Breese and Mather (1960) for bristle number in *Drosophila* and subsequently demonstrated to coincide with maximum fitness for intermediate scores using cage populations (Kearsey & Barnes, 1970).

The emerging picture (Broadhurst, 1979) is one in which the discovery of directional dominance for a polygenically controlled trait indicates a history of evolutionary pressure toward extreme expression of the trait, whereas the absence of dominance or the presence of ambidirectional dominance indicates neutrality or stabilizing selection for intermediate scores. Thus by discovering the nature of the genetic effects controlling particular behaviors we can begin to understand their adaptive significance.

Aside from the nature of any dominance variation present, the other major aspects of what we are calling the genetic architecture of a trait are the relative importance of additive genetic variation and the extent and nature of any nonallelic interactions (Jinks, 1979). The additive genetic variance or its ratio to the total phenotypic variance, usually referred to as the narrow heritability, are of considerable theoretical and practical importance, so that estimates of their magnitudes will generally be a step in the analysis. The primary reason for the importance of this source of variation is that the level of available additive genetic variability will determine the speed of advance under selection, both artificial and natural. Thus, in one sense at least, the relative magnitude of the additive genetic variance can be considered an estimate of the evolutionary lability of a population. Applied to reproductive fitness as a phenotype, this concept leads to Fisher's (1958) *Fundamental Theorem of Natural Selection:* "The rate of increase in fitness of any organism at any time is equal to its genetic variance in fitness at that time [p. 57]."

Inasmuch as we want to generalize this concept to characters other than fitness, then, as far as natural selection is concerned, the rate of change in the character will be a joint function of its own additive genetic variability, that of fitness and the correlation between them (Falconer, 1965; Mather, 1973). As far as artificial selection is concerned, the response to selection is, to a first approximation, both predicted by and serves as an estimate of the narrow heritability as a direct linear function (Falconer, 1970). Thus the success of Tryon's (1940) original selection for maze-learning ability in rats, or Broadhurst's (1960) production of the Maudsley Reactive and Nonreactive strains depended on the presence of additive genetic variance in the foundation populations.

In addition to determining in part the consequences of selection, we have previously argued that the level of additive genetic variance may indicate the importance of, or at least the tolerance of diversity in natural populations (Hewitt et al., 1981). If there were a single unequivocally optimum expression for the phenotype, then changes in gene frequencies, the development of nonadditive variation, and the establishment of tightly linked groups of balanced genes would push the population toward phenotypic uniformity and reduce the proportion of additive genetic variability that is expressed (Mather, 1973). Thus the discovery of large amounts of additive genetic variance must suggest that there has not been strong selection pressure toward uniformity of expression.

After a consideration of the additive differences and the dominance deviations of the heterozygotes at individual loci, a survey of the types of genic variation manifest in the observable phenotype would be incomplete without some account being taken of the consequences of interactions between different loci within the genome. Such nonallelic interactions, or epistatic effects as they are often called, are in principle subject to the same kinds of analysis. In particular, the effects tend to be either complementary or duplicate (giving rise respectively to 9 : 7 and 15 : 1 segregation ratios in a classical Mendelian major locus experiment). Moreover, inasmuch as we are dealing with polygenic systems, such effects tend to be either balancing, thereby pushing the population toward some uniform optimum, or directional in that—like the directional dominance discussed previously—their net effect is to push the population toward one extreme or the other. For characters that have been selected over a long period toward one extreme of expression we might predict that the nonallelic interactions will be of the predominantly directional and duplicate kind, tending to reinforce the action of any directional dominance at individual loci (Mather, 1973). In experiments with *Drosophila,* for instance, such a prediction has been confirmed for viability (Breese & Mather, 1960) and egg hatchability (Kearsey & Kojima, 1967), both characters being prima facie fitness characters subject to directional selection. The alternative prediction of balancing or ambidirectional interactions is apparently borne out in the case of abdominal chaetae number (Breese & Mather, 1960; Mather, 1960) and sternopleural chaetae number, which has been shown to be under stabilizing selection (Kearsey & Barnes, 1970).

Let us turn lastly to the question of the number of genes or, more accurately, effective factors (Mather & Jinks, 1971). Although those researchers most concerned with isolating biochemical pathways may find those behavioral differences mediated by single major genes most congenial to work with, it seems unlikely, from the point of view of the genetic architecture and its implications, that normal variation of importance for understanding the relationship between behavior and evolution will typically be mediated by one or only a few major genes. There are at least two a priori reasons for expecting the genetic control of characters affecting the adaptation of the animal to its environment to be polygenic rather than major gene in nature. The first comes from Fisher's (1958) abstract but none the less compelling analogy of any complex adaptation to the situation that obtains when a point in space is displayed from its optimal position; if the space is one-dimensional, then a random movement has a fifty–fifty chance of being toward the optimal point, but even here only small changes are likely to leave the point closer to its optimal position because large movements will overshoot. However, as the space in which we are operating becomes two-, three-, or more dimensional, so large random changes have a rapidly decreasing probability of resulting in an improved position in relation to the optimum, and in the limit only infinitesimally small random changes have a fifty–fifty chance of resulting in an improvement, no matter how large the initial displacement (Fisher, 1958). For this reason alone we would expect the fine adjustments associated with complex adaptations, which correspond to the multidimensional space in the analogy, to have been the result of an accumulation of many small changes rather than the highly improbable single large adjustment.

The second general argument follows Mather's demonstration that the proportion of genetic variation that can be carried by a population without its being expressed phenotypically, but none the less available for selection to act upon should environmental circumstances require it, increases as a monotonic function of the number of effective factors (Mather, 1973). That is to say, those populations that have arrived at polygenic control of a given character will be at an advantage over those that use major gene control in that, for the same level of phenotypic variation about a given optimum expression, the former populations have a much greater potential for adaptation should environmental circumstances change. Taking this argument one stage further, Mather (1973) also shows that this potential for carrying genetic variability is maximized, other things being equal, when the genes involved are of equal effect.

Together these two arguments give us good reasons for expecting the assumptions of what we may call the polygenic hypothesis to be approximated wherever we are faced with the control of relatively complex adaptations in circumstances that are unlikely to be completely stable over large numbers of generations. At the very least we must be prepared with methods of analysis that can cope equally well with major gene or polygenic variation.

THE ANALYSIS OF GENETIC ARCHITECTURE

Our aim is to progress from a demonstration of inherited differences in behavior to a partitioning of the sources of environmental and heritable variation into their subcomponents (Jinks, 1979). At the first level of investigation, which, given the data available for aggressive behavior we can hardly go beyond, we would like some indication of the relative balance of dominance to additive genetic variation, and the general direction or ambidirectionality of any dominance present. Further information concerning the nature of any nonallelic interactions, the number of effective factors, the effects of linkage, and the detailed specification of genotype × environment interactions generally requires more sophisticated studies, but ones that involve no other principles than those that characterize biometrical genetics generally. These principles have been presented in detail by Mather and Jinks (1971, 1978) and have been discussed in their application to behavioral phenotypes in a number of papers (Broadhurst & Jinks, 1961; Jinks & Broadhurst, 1974).

In outline, we first specify a model for the quantitative effects of genotypic differences at individual loci (or effective factors) in terms of the additive effects of homozygotes for increasing and decreasing alleles ($+d$ and $-d$) and the dominance deviation of the heterozygote ($+h$) from the mid-value (m) of these two homozygotes. Generalizing to many loci we may define $[d]$ and $[h]$ as the corresponding net effects on the mean phenotypic expression in two inbred strains and the F_1 cross between them. Furthermore we can define additional parameters $D = \Sigma\, d^2$, $H = \Sigma\, h^2$ and $F = \Sigma\, dh$ to allow us to model the consequences of additive and dominance effects for generation variances as well as for generation means, and in so doing we will need to allow for environmental variation E.

By way of illustration, Table 3.1 gives the genetic model for the generation means and variances of a classical Mendelian cross involving two inbred strains (P_1 and P_2), their F_1 cross, and the F_2 and backcrosses (B_1 and B_2) from these generations. Given an appropriate data set, the parameters of the model may be estimated and the goodness of fit of the model to the generation means may be tested by a joint scaling test (Gale, Mather, & Jinks, 1977; Mather & Jinks, 1971), whereas additional generations would be required for a proper test of the model for variances. Going beyond this simple situation, the specification of models for nonallelic interactions will require consideration of sets of genes and the definition of additional parameters, as will allowance for unequal gene frequencies in random mating populations, and so on.

However, our simple case permits us to make two observations. In the first place our model for the generation variances assumes that the environmental variation is the same for each of the nonsegregating generations (P_1, P_2, F_1). If these variances are heterogeneous then we have a form of genotype × environment interaction that must complicate the interpretation of the other parameters of the model, and if heterogeneity is severe then the parameters of the model estimated from the generation variances will be all but meaningless. Very often, though, such heterogeneity can be removed by a scalar transformation of the raw data, and this is recommended as a preliminary to quantitative analysis wherever there is no overriding reason for retaining the original scale.

Secondly, the parameters $[d]$ and $[h]$ are the net effects in the two inbred strains and their F_1 cross of d's and h's at individual loci. There is no reason why all the increasing alleles should be carried by one inbred strain and all the decreasing alleles by the other and hence, if genes are dispersed between the parental strains, $[d]$ will underestimate the potential for additive difference; in the most extreme case of dispersion P_1 and P_2 could be phenotypically identical for a character with 100% heritability and yet differ at every genetic locus. The important consequence of this is that the F_1 cross may lie outside the range of its inbred progenitors (heterosis), even though there may be no more than partial dominance at only a few loci. But conversely, when considering $[h]$, if dominance is ambidirectional, that is at some loci in one direction and at some in the opposite direction, the value taken by $[h]$ may be small even though there is considerable dominance variation. Again in the extreme case the F_1 could lie midway between the parental strains and yet we may have complete dominance at every locus. Thus the potence ratio $[h]/[d]$ does not in general indicate the average level of dominance even though the sign of $[h]$ will indicate the prevailing direction of dominance. These comments about the canceling of effects on generation means do not, however, apply to generation variances, and thus the dominance ratio $\sqrt{H/D}$ does estimate the average level of dominance at individual loci irrespective of their directions. We have gone into this at some length partly because

TABLE 3.1
The Simple Additive-Dominance Model for the Generation Means and Variances of a Classical Mendelian Cross

Generation	*Mean*				*Variances*		
	m	[d]	[h]	E	D	H	F
P_1	1	1		1			
P_2	1	-1		1			
F_1	1		1	1			
F_2	1		½	1	½	¼	
B_1	1	½	½	1	¼	¼	-½
B_2	1	-½	½	1	¼	¼	½

Derived statistics:

potence ratio = [h] / [d]
dominance ratio = $\sqrt{H/D}$
narrow heritability = ½D / (½D + ¼H + E)
broad heritability = (½D + ¼H) / (½D + ¼H + E)
direction of dominance given by sign of [h]

there is still considerable confusion about the difference between heterosis (the F_1 lying outside the parental range) and overdominance, and chiefly because it is from the comparison of such estimates from first- and second-degree statistics that often the most interesting conclusions about the level and directionality of dominance effects may be drawn. It is therefore unfortunate that in the data for aggression in mice that we consider in the following section there has as yet been little attention paid to this source of information.

Apart from the classical Mendelian cross and its extensions, which can provide detailed information about the genetical control exerted at those loci for which the inbred progenitors differ, there is a wide range of methods at our disposal. These include selection studies (Broadhurst, 1960), the diallel cross (Broadhurst, 1960; Broadhurst & Jinks, 1966) and a range of test cross methodologies (Chahal & Jinks, 1978; Jinks, Perkins, & Breese, 1969; Jinks & Virk, 1977; Kearsey & Jinks, 1968) that are now beginning to be applied to behavioral phenotypes (Fulker, 1972; Henderson, 1978; Hewitt & Fulker, 1981, in press, submitted for publication, Hewitt et al., 1981). The more widely used strain survey on its own provides little information about genetic architecture however, although it may be an important initial step in an investigation and may be of considerable use in studying trait covariation. The various approaches we have noted in addition on the Mendelian cross provide different kinds of information and are more or less useful depending on the population we are working with and the questions we wish to answer.

The selection study can provide estimates of the narrow heritability in the early generations, although as the genetic variation is depleted with the progress of selection such estimates will become more approximate. Additionally, an asymmetrical response to selection for high and low expression of a character may indicate directional dominance, interactions, or gene frequencies (Falconer, 1970) of a kind that would maintain a level of phenotypic expression in the base population opposite to the direction of greatest selection response. Finally, bidirectional selection may be useful in providing extreme strains that, after inbreeding, may be employed in test cross studies (Hewitt & Fulker, 1981) and that provide an estimate of the maximum additive separation, $[d]$, obtainable. (If there are k effective factors of equal magnitude of effect and the genes are in complete association then $[d] = kd$, and with $D = kd^2$ an estimate of k is provided by $[d]^2 / D$). But as a source of information about the components of the genetic architecture the selection study is relatively weak (Jinks, 1979).

The diallel cross, on the other hand, which surveys a population of inbred strains together with all their reciprocal F_1 crosses, can provide in one generation tests for, and estimates of reciprocal effects (maternal, paternal, or sex-linked), levels of additive and dominance variation, and the direction of dominance. There are many different approaches to the analysis of the diallel table both through the analysis of variance and through the study of variance–covariance graphs (see for example Mather & Jinks, 1971, 1978; Walters & Gale, 1977; Wearden, 1964). A particularly clear example of the application of the designs and its interpretation is given in Fulker's (1966) study of mating speed in *Drosophila melanogaster*.

Lastly, the various test cross designs, which have yet to find wide application in behavior genetics, share the common characteristic of surveying the genetic architecture in either a random mating population or population of inbred lines by backcrossing samples from these populations to inbred tester lines or F_1 crosses between them. Analyses of variance of scores from the offspring of the various crossing schemes can provide tests for, and estimates of nonallelic interactions, level and direction of dominance variation, and level of additive variation. Importantly, although these designs require inbred tester lines, which in the case of the triple test crosses (Jinks et al., 1969; Kearsey & Jinks, 1968) have to be extreme lines for optimal efficiency, the surveyed population can be a random mating population (Hewitt & Fulker, 1981; Kearsey & Jinks, 1968). For this reason, together with the relative power of the designs (Jinks, 1979), we expect that greater use may be made of them in the future.

We should end this brief survey of some analytical methods by emphasizing that from the point of view of biometrical genetics all the methods make use of the application of the principles of Mendelian genetics to quantitative characters in a way that need not imply any prior commitment to the number of effective factors contributing to the control of a behavioral phenotype.

THE GENETIC ARCHITECTURE OF AGGRESSIVE BEHAVIOR IN MICE

As we shall discover from our discussion of some of the data available on same-sex aggression in mice, to attempt to build generalizations on the basis of one or two or even several studies may be quite misleading. For this reason we have restricted our consideration to the species and behaviors most commonly used in breeding studies of the kind that might yield some information about the genetic architecture of aggressive behavior. This is not to say that we think this restriction is desirable, for, as we have argued elsewhere (Hewitt et al., 1981), we would hope that no one species would come to dominate mammalian behavior genetics, and that cross-species comparisons of the genetic architecture of representative behavioral phenotypes might become an important theoretical tool for understanding the wider implications of the genetic analysis of behavior. But when arguing this point previously we were arguing from a position of relative strength in that we had a good enough description of the genetic architecture of escape–avoidance conditioning in the Norway rat to stand the theoretical strain of interspecific comparison. For aggressive behavior the outlook cannot be so positive and we content ourselves with a morc detailed assessment of a more restricted domain.

We consider here the three selection studies of Lagerspetz (1964), Ebert and Hyde (1976), and van Oortmerssen and Bakker (1981), and the crossbreeding programs of Southwick (1970), Eleftheriou, Bailey, and Denenberg (1974), Selmanoff, Maxson, and Ginsburg (1976), Kulikov (1980), and Kessler, Elliott, Orenberg, and Barchas (1977), together with the more recent diallel and test cross studies of Watson (1978) and Singleton (1981). In addition to these studies the classical Mendelian cross carried out by Lagerspetz and the diallel cross of Hahn are presented in detail in their chapters in this volume.

SELECTION STUDIES

In the study of male aggressiveness reported by Lagerspetz (1964, 1969) and Lagerspetz and Lagerspetz (1971), the phenotype subjected to bidirectional selection was an observer's rating, on a 7-point scale, of aggression toward another male during a 7-minute encounter in a novel test cage on each of 7 test days. The foundation population was of Swiss albino mice obtained in Sweden. The original report gave the results up to the seventh generation (S_7), after which there was apparently no further separation of the lines in response to continued selection (Lagerspetz & Lagerspetz, 1971). Selection was successful in both directions and, although Lagerspetz (1964) does not give the realized heritabilities, approximate estimates from the cumulative selection differential and response, treating the study as single-sex selection, give values of the order of .34 and .22 for high and low aggressiveness respectively. The asymmetry is consistent with the observation of Lagerspetz and Lagerspetz (1971) that some highly aggressive animals persisted in the low line even at S_{19}. The results might also be consistent with directional dominance for low aggression in this situation, the high-aggression animals in the low line resulting from heterozygote segregation. However, the relatively high narrow heritabilities are also suggestive of an absence of a close association with fitness of a single optimum phenotype. In support of this view, the most recent results reported by Lagerspetz (this volume), and in particular the Mendelian cross between the high and low lines point to an absence of nonadditive genetic effects.

A similar early response asymmetry has been reported by Hyde and Sawyer (1980) and Ebert (this volume), who give the results up to S_{11} of the replicated bidirectional selection for agonistic behavior in wild female mice first described in Ebert and Hyde (1976). Here the phenotype was an index of agonistic behavior, based on a shortened version of the Lagerspetz (1964) scale, scored over two 7-minute testing sessions with a standard opponent (a C57BL/6 female) in the subject's individual home cage. Again selection was successful in both directions and realized heritabilities were .12 and .14 for the replicated high lines and .34 and .46 for the low lines. This response asymmetry reverses that reported up to S_4 and would be consistent with a biological ceiling on the agonistic behavior of female mice maintained, one might speculate, by duplicate gene interactions nullifying the otherwise expected additive increments from the accumulation of loci homozygous for increasing alleles. That the explanation is simply an artifactual scalar effect is thought improbable by Hyde and Sawyer (1980), because the majority of the animals do not score at the upper limit of their scale. An uncomplicated appeal to directional dominance is rendered less plausible, although should not be ruled out, by the initially rapid upward progress during the first four generations. However, the notion of a biological ceiling on the ferocity of the aggressive behavior is given some support by other data reported by Hyde and Sawyer (1980) showing that, although their total index score did not increase in the high lines after S_4, the percentage of animals showing at least one attack over the two testing sessions continued to respond to selection in a symmetrical manner.

Because this is the only study of female aggression we consider in this chapter, we should note that although there has been a correlated response to selection in maternal aggressiveness (Hyde & Sawyer, 1979), there was no evidence of a correlated response in male aggressiveness (Hyde & Ebert, 1976; Hyde & Sawyer, 1980), and thus there is no reason to suppose that male and female aggressiveness are controlled by the same genetic system.

The most recent selection study to be reported is that of van Oortmerssen and Bakker (1981), who have attempted to select for short and long attack latency in a population descended from four male and three female wild mice. The phenotype was the average latency to attack a standard opponent (MAS-Gro male mouse) over three tests in a familiar cage (not the long-term home cage). Selection for short attack latency was successful with a realized heritability of .30 ± .19 over 11 generations whereas a maintained control line showed no change. However, selection for long latency failed on four occasions because in each case the line died out within two generations for unexplained reasons. Thus although one might wish to argue that the rapid downward response indicated directional dominance for long latency to attack, the unusual circumstances of the failure of upward selection detract somewhat from the strength of this conclusion.

Before leaving these selection studies we may note that if we attempt to estimate the numbers of effective factors from the additive separation of the lines and the narrow heritability we arrive at estimates varying between 1 and 12, depending on exactly what assumptions we make about the data. The general imprecision of our inferences from these selection studies underlines our earlier comments about the desirability of crossbreeding experiments to separate out the components of variation.

CROSSBREEDING STUDIES

Whereas, as we have already indicated, data from surveys of inbred strains are in themselves unlikely to throw light on the genetic architecture of behavioral traits, a variant of the inbred strain survey has considerable promise for such studies. If two inbred strains are crossed to produce an F_1 that is subsequently used to produce an F_2, genetic segregation and recombination occur. Inbreeding may then be practiced to produce a set of recombinant inbred (RI) strains (Bailey, 1971). One powerful use to which such strains may be put in the future is to provide the basis for a simplified triple test crossbreeding experiment (Fulker, 1972) that allows tests of epistasis and estimates of additive and dominance variation together with an estimate of the direction of dominance. The particular attraction of RI strains for this purpose is that extreme tester lines may be chosen from the RI set that are differentiated at the same loci for which there is variation among the testee strains. Furthermore, a provisional assumption of equality of gene frequencies may be justifiably adopted, and the genotypes may be replicated as desired. These properties, with the exception of the gene frequency assumption but with the property shared with RI strains, that they all descend from the same coadapted gene pool, may be obtained by deriving strains from a single natural population. Such strains are routinely used in *Drosophila* genetics and in our own laboratory we are using the single test cross design of Chahal and Jinks (1978) with such strains to investigate the genetics of courtship modification in *Drosophila melanogaster,* a trait that shares many of the problems of the analysis of aggression (Collins, 1980; Collins & Hewitt, 1981).

Needless to say, such studies with rodents are large and costly and as yet have not been undertaken for aggressive behavior. However, the study of Eleftheriou et al. (1974) has surveyed the between-strain variation for Bailey RI strains derived from an initial cross between the BALB/cBy and C57BL/6By mouse strains (Bailey, 1971). In addition, they report the results of a series of F_1 crosses, cross-fostering studies, ovarian transplants, and a backcross in an attempt to understand the genetic and maternal influences on aggression. We should devote some time to this study because given its complexities and those of the phenotype, the data turn out to conform reasonably well to a fairly straightforward model.

The procedure for testing was to place male mice, which had been isolated for 40+ days postweaning, in a neutral box with a standard opponent for 5 minutes on each of 5 consecutive days. The score was the total number of occasions on which the experimental animal initiated a fight (maximum score = 5). On the basis of a preliminary experiment, the standard opponent was chosen at the low aggression RI strain CXBH. A series of four experiments using various of the available genotypes was carried out over a period of 2 years using the same standard rearing and testing procedures. The data summary that we present is based on simple averaging of genotype mean scores from between one and four of these experiments with various sample sizes of the order of 20; the published account allows us to be no more specific than this and, further, does not provide details of within-genotype variation although we are told that nonparametric tests revealed significant differences among the genotypes (Eleftheriou et al., 1974).

The data summary given in Table 3.2 is thus adapted from Eleftheriou et al. (1974, p. 776). Concentrating on the top half of the table, we can see that the heterosis revealed in the F_1 crosses between the C and B6 inbred progenitors is the result not of overdominance but of the genes for high and low aggression being dispersed between these lines. After reassortment, the CXBG and CXBH recombinant inbreds provide extremes that are not outscored by an F_1 cross. However, unless variation at loci at which there is dominance has been lost by chance during the inbreeding process, we would expect the F_1 cross between the extreme RI strains to give the same phenotype as that between the original inbred progenitors. This is not the case and in particular the CXBH♀ × CXBG♂ cross has a very low mean score. But, recalling that the standard opponent is from the CXBH strain, the following hypothesis suggests itself: In addition to additive, $[d]$, and dominance, $[h]$, effects acting through the test animal's own genotype, a special maternal effect, s in Table 3.3, lowers the aggression toward the standard CXBH opponent of subjects reared by a CXBH mother. This effect does not further lower the already reduced aggression for CXBH test animals but would do so for any other genotypes. The model is specified and fitted in Table 3.3, the only further ad hoc specification being that we have allowed the special CXBH maternal effect to operate from the maternal grandmother in the (CXBH♀ × CXBG♂)♀ × XCBH♂ cross. This simple model, with just three parameters in addition to the mean, accounts for 88% of the observed variation across 14 diverse genotypes and conditions, and much of the residual variation must be due to vagaries of sampling and unreliability of measurement.

TABLE 3.2
A Summary of the Data of Eleftheriou et al. (1974) for Mean Number of Fights Initiated by Male Mice Out of 5 Encounters Against a Standard CXBH Opponent

Strain	*Mean*	*II*	*III*	*IV*	*V*	*Remarks*
		*Experiments from which the means are derived**				
BALB/cBJ (C)	1.8	√	√			Progenitors of RI
C57BL/6By (B6)	2.7	√	√			strains
$B6CF_1$	3.7	√	√	√	√	Reciprocal F_1 crosses
$CD6F_1$	3.9	√	√	√	√	
CXBD	2.5	√	√			
CXBE	3.4	√	√			Recombinant
CXBG	4.7	√	√	√	√	
CXBH	0.8	√	√	√	√	
CXBI	2.4	√	√			inbred strains
CXBJ	1.6	√	√			
CXBK	1.8	√	√			
CXBH♀ X CXBG♂	1.2			√	√	Reciprocal F_1
CXGB♀ X CXBH♂	2.9			√	√	crosses
$B6CF_1$ (CXBG)	3.2			√		Ovaries of parenthe-sized strain transplant-ed to F_1 then mated to parenthesized strain
$B6CF_1$ (CXBH)	0.6			√		
CXBH (CXBG)	0.8			√		Crossfostered to paren-thesized strain
CXBG (CXBH)	3.4			√		
(CXBG♀ X CXBH♂) ♀ X CXBH♂	2.1				√	Backcrossed to recip-rocal F_1's
(CXBH♀ X CXBG♂) ♀ X CXBH♂	1.1				√	

* Numbers refer to experimental identifiers in the original report. Sample sizes per strain were 8 (Exp. II), 10 (Exp. III), 9 - 20 (Exp. IV) and 14 - 35 (Exp. V).

Our conclusion accords with that of Eleftheriou et al. (1974) but avoids the need to specify any particular number of genes and emphasizes the overall consistency of the data. The coefficient, r, in Table 3.3 was calculated after the model had been fitted to the rest of the data and would be the coefficient of gene distribution in the progenitor inbred strains (BALB/cBy and C5 7BL/6By) if the genes controlling the trait were now in complete association in the CXBG and CXBH lines (Mather & Jinks, 1971). The clear outcome of this study is partial directional dominance for high aggression in this test situation.

A somewhat different conclusion resulted from the study reported by Kessler et al. (1977), using the A/J and BALB/cJ inbred mouse strains as progenitors of a partial Mendelian cross design (P_1, P_2, F_1, F_2, and B_1 but omitting B_2) to investigate the genetic control of intermale aggressive behavior. Rather than use a freely interacting opponent they employed the dangler paradigm (Scott &

TABLE 3.3
A Simple Model Fitted to the Data of Eleftheriou et al. (1974)

Genotype	m	Model [d]	[h]	s	Observed Mean	Expected Mean
C	1	-r			1.8	
B6	1	r			2.7	
B6CF$_1$	1		1		3.7	3.3
CB6F$_1$	1		1		3.9	3.3
CXBG	1	1			4.7	4.2
CXBH	1	-1			0.8	0.8
CXBH♀ X CXBG♂	1		1	1	1.2	2.0
CXBG♀ X CXBH♂	1		1		2.9	3.3
B6CF$_1$ (CXBG)	1	1			3.2	4.2
B6CF$_1$ (CXBH)	1	-1			0.6	0.8
CXBH (CXBG)	1	-1			0.8	0.8
CXBG (CXBH)	1	1		1	3.4	2.9
(CXBG♀ X CXBH♂) ♀ X CXBH♂	1	-½	½		2.1	2.1
(CXBH♀ X CXBG♂) ♀ CXBH♂	1	-½	½	1	1.1	0.8

m = 2.5
[d] = 1.7
[h] = 0.8 by unweighted least squares
s = 1.3
r = .26

Fredericson, 1951), wherein another mouse (in this case a CBA/J group-housed male) is dangled by its tail into the experimental subject's cage. The test session was of 5 minutes duration during which a number of behaviors were recorded including latency to first attack, number of attacks, and accumulated attack time (AAT). As previously reported by Southwick (1970; Southwick & Clark, 1966, 1968), using a homogeneous group measure of aggression, the A/J mice were nonaggressive, whereas the BALB/cJ males were moderately aggressive. The differentiation was so great that a classification into fighters (latency $\leq$ 240 seconds, number of attacks $\geq$ 2, and AAT $\geq$ 3 seconds) and nonfighters unambiguously identified the two strains. On the basis of this classification the data conformed closely to the expectations of a single-locus model with complete dominance for nonfighting, although of the 13 F_1 subjects tested, two were fighters (see Table 3.4). However, an arbitrary classification criterion can often be found that, when applied to a continuous character showing high potence and relatively little environmental variation, will mimic the operation of a single locus, and so the authors point out that their analysis does not exclude a polygenic model. We would thus like to be able to analyze the generation means and variances for latency to attack, number of attacks, and accumulated attack time but there are a number of problems arising chiefly from the short (5 minutes), one-trial observation period.

TABLE 3.4
The Data of Kessler et al. (1977) Showing the Outcome of Classification into Fighters and Non-Fighters

Genotype	Observed number of Fighters	Observed number of Non-Fighters	Expected number of Fighters	Expected number of Non-Fighters
P_1 BALB/cJ	7	0		
P_2 A/J	0	14		
F_1	2	11	0	13
F_2	30	73	25.6	77.3
B_1	31	24	27.5	27.5

During the 5-minute observation period, 64% of the experimental animals made no attacks and thus all these subjects would have to be assigned an arbitrary 300 seconds latency score even though Southwick (1970) has reported mean attack latencies for A/J males reared by A/J mothers of between 33 and 35 minutes when observed in groups of four. Thus such an arbitrarily low ceiling for the latency scores of the majority of the experimental animals precludes any meaningful analysis. Although this limitation must compromise the attack data, we have presented the approximate generation means and variances in Table 3.5, which is reconstructed from the information given in Kessler et al. (1977). Clearly the heterogeneity of the P_1, P_2, and F_1 variances, indicating a form of genotype × environment interaction to be expected with ceiling (or floor) scalar effects, would require a rescaling of the raw scores before any simple model could be fitted with any real justification. But no reasonable change of scale will alter the overwhelming evidence of strong potence toward low number of fights and low AAT during a 5-minute exposure to a dangling CBA/J intruder and, for completeness, the unweighted least squares estimates for the parameters for the m, $[d]$, and $[h]$ model gave, for number of fights, $\hat{m} = 4.8$, $[\hat{d}] = 4.9$, $[\hat{h}] = -3.5$, and for AAT, $\hat{m} = 9.1$, $[\hat{d}] = 9.4$ and $[\hat{h}] = -9.6$.

The findings of dominance for low aggression in this situation contrasts with both that of Eleftheriou et al. (1974), discussed previously, and that of Southwick (1970), who reports the performance of various F_1 crosses in a series of

TABLE 3.5
The Quantitative Data of Kessler et al. (1977)

Generation	N	Number of Attacks Mean	Number of Attacks Variance	Accumulated Attack Time Mean	Accumulated Attack Time Variance
P_1	7	8.7	28.0	18.9	90.7
P_2	14	0.0	0.0	0.0	0.0
F_1	13	0.4	1.2	0.2	17.3
F_2	103	2.6	18.6	3.1	34.1
B_1	55	7.6	67.2	8.7	104.4

studies measuring the frequency of aggressive behavior (chase–attack–fight frequency / hour) in groups of four males of the same genotype. A summary of the data, which taken together give a partial diallel cross, is shown in Table 3.6. If we pool the results of reciprocal F_1 crosses we have four out of four showing dominance for high aggression (p = .06, sign test), whereas without pooling reciprocal F_1 crosses we have six out of six showing this directional dominance (p = .02, sign test). In any case the data, such as they are, overwhelmingly point to dominance for high aggression scores in this paradigm.

We turn now to the work of Selmanoff, Jumonville, Maxson, and Ginsburg (1975), Selmanoff, Maxson, and Ginsburg (1976), and Maxson, Ginsburg, and Trattner (1979), who have pursued the possibility that the Y chromosome may carry genes controlling male aggression in mice, a possibility that was suggested by reliable reciprocal differences between crosses of the DBA/1Bg and C57BL/1OBg strains. The evidence in favor of the hypothesis has been recently reviewed by Maxson (1981), and we shall not deal with it in this chapter except to note that the available data indicate that whatever is the cause of the effect (see Hay, 1975, for a discussion of alternatives to the Y-chromosome hypothesis), it is specific to the DBA/1 × C57BL/1O cross and is not found in crosses between closely related strains (Selmanoff et al., 1976).

The data given in detail by Selmanoff et al. (1976) are from a series of experiments using two pairs of closely related strains, DBA/1Bg, DBA/2Bg, C57BL/6Bg, and C57BL/1OBg, and crosses between them. The procedure for testing aggressiveness used same-strain dyadic encounters in a neutral cage during a 10-minute period on each of 3 consecutive days, the subjects (males) having been isolated for 3 weeks prior to the encounters. A number of measures were taken, including latency to first attack (maximum 1800 seconds) and a composite 'any aggression' score. From the experiments reported it is possible to reconstitute 15 of the 16 cells of a 4 × 4 diallel cross between the strains. The data thus organized are given in Tables 3.7 and 3.8.

TABLE 3.6
The Mean Chase-Attack-Fight Frequencies for Groups of Four Male Mice of the Same Strain (Southwick, 1970)

		Strain of male parent				
		C57Br	CFW	C57BL/6	A/J	CBA
	C57Br	82.2				84.2
	CFW		67.0	249.7	107.8	
Female parent	C57BL/6			49.7		
	A/J		41.3		14.2	
	CBA	98.6			44.0	12.1

The cell sizes vary up to 40 mice and the standard errors range between 2.0 for the CBA strain to 23.1 for the CFW X C57BL/6 cross.

TABLE 3.7
Reorganized 'Latency to First Attack' Data from Selmanoff et al. (1976), Genotype Means ± SE (Cell Size in Parenthesis)

		Strain of male parent			
		DBA/1	DBA/2	C57BL/6	C57BL/10
Female parent	DBA/1	670 ± 109 (2)	873 ± 133 (22)	1693 ± 49 (26)	1315 ± 81 (42)
	DBA/2	573 ± 120 (19)	513 ± 188 (20)	1800 ± 0 (16)	1658 ± 88 (22)
	C57BL/6	1551 ± 98 (21)	1748 ± 51 (20)	1600 ± 93 (22)	–
	C57BL/10	1022*± 102 (43)	1776 ± 24 (24)	1514 ± 121 (16)	1447 ± 116 (22)

*C57BL/10 X DBA/1 cross giving significant reciprocal difference.

However rather than analyze these tables directly as 4 × 4 diallel tables, we should recognize that, because of the close relationships of DBA/1 to DBA/2 and of C57BL/6 to C57BL/1O (Festing, 1979), we have, to a close approximation, 2 × 2 blocks of genotypes represented in these experiments. The analyses of variance on this basis are given in Table 3.9, where it is apparent that although there is variation within the blocks of genotypes, this variation, apart from the special case of the C57BL/1O × DAB/1 cross already mentioned, is no more than we might expect to observe between sets of data collected over a period of time for closely related but not identical genotypes. The main effects between the DBA and C57BL genotypes are unequivocally those of a large additive dif-

TABLE 3.8
Reorganized "Any Aggression Score" Data from Selmanoff et al. (1976), Genotype Means ± SE (Cell Size in Parenthesis)

		Strain of male parent			
		DBA/1	DBA/2	C57BL/6	C57BL/10
Female parent	DBA/1	35.4 ± 4.6 (20)	27.0 ± 4.0 (22)	2.5 ± 1.0 (26)	10.7 ± 2.2 (42)
	DBA/2	37.2 ± 4.7 (19)	44.2 ± 5.1 (20)	0.0 ± 0.0 (16)	3.6 ± 1.9 (22)
	C57BL/6	5.2 ± 2.2 (21)	2.0 ± 1.1 (20)	7.4 ± 3.1 (22)	–
	C57BL/10	19.8* ±3.0 (43)	0.2 ± 0.2 (24)	7.1 ± 2.3 (16)	7.3 ± 2.3 (22)

*C57BL/10 X DBA/1 cross giving significant reciprocal difference.

TABLE 3.9
Analyses of Variance of the Data in Tables 3.7 and 3.8
Treated as 2 x 2 Blocks of Genotypes

Source of variation	*df*		*Latency to first attack* *MS* $(x10^{-5})$	*F+*	*Any aggression score* *MS* $(x10^{-2})$	*F+*
Genotype blocks	3		147.3		169.2	
[d]		1	253.3	38.4**	278.6	51.9**
[h]		1	180.1	27.3**	221.5	41.3**
Reciprocal effects		1	8.4	1.3	7.4	1.4
Within blocks	11		16.6		12.0	
DBA/1 x C57BL/10 deviation		1	117.1	17.7**	78.6	14.6**
Residual		10	6.6	2.9*	5.4	2.6*
Within cells	340		2.3		2.1	

+ All items tested against Residual within blocks (10df), except this residual which was tested against Within cells MS.
* $P < .01$
** $P < .005$

ference and strong directional dominance for low overall aggression and long latency to first attack with no reciprocal F_1 differences.

Another diallel cross, albeit a partial diallel, shows an absence of directional dominance supporting high levels of aggression in paired encounters. Kulikov (1980) formed a series of intercross combinations from the C57BL/6J, BALB/c, DD, C3H/He, and CC57Br inbred strains of mice. Subjects were male mice, between 2 and 4 months of age, that had been housed in groups of 10 until 2–3 days before testing, when they were transferred to individual cages. They were tested once by introducing an intruder male random-bred albino mouse into the cage and scoring the number of attacks made by the resident on the intruder. Table 3.10 shows the numbers of attacks (mean ± standard error) made by the different genotypes, with cell sizes given in parenthesis. The analyses of variance reported by Kulikov, taking account of the unbalanced cell sizes, indicate an absence of significant reciprocal effects or nonadditive genetic effects with reliably detected general combining ability variance. We can conclude that, with Kulikov's test procedure, the genotypic influences primarily act additively, with an absence of overall nonadditive directional effects.

The most recent diallel cross study of intermale aggression in mice is reported in detail by Hahn in this volume. Here the male offspring from a full diallel crossing of the C57BL/10, DBA, BALB/cJ, and SJL/J mouse strains were tested in same-genotype dyadic encounters in a neutral but partially familiar cage at 70+ days of age after 40+ days of individual housing. Here again, the conclusions from the Hayman analyses of variance of several measures of aggressiveness indicate a preponderance of additive genetic variation and an absence of directional dominance effects.

TABLE 3.10
Reorganized Summary of "Number of Fights" Data from Kulikov (1980), Genotype Means ± SE (Cell Size in Parenthesis)

		Strain of male parent				
		C57BL/6J	*BALB/c*	*DD*	*C3H/HC*	*CC57Br*
	C57BL/6J	7.9 ± 1.0 (24)	7.4 ± 1.0 (14)	6.8 ± 0.8 (19)		
	BALB/c	6.6 ± 0.9 (17)	4.1 ± 0.9 (10)	3.7 ± 0.8 (6)	6.5 ± 1.9 (4)	2.7 ± 0.4 (3)
Strain	DD	3.3 ± 0.6 (13)	4.5 ± 2.5 (2)	7.3 ± 1.7 (9)		
of Female	C3H/He		4.8 ± 0.8 (11)		6.3 ± 0.9 (20)	9.6 ± 1.7 (7)
Parent	CC57Br		4.3 ± 1.0 (8)		7.0 ± 0.9 (9)	5.0 ± 0.9 (9)

Unweighted mean of inbred parents = 6.1
Unweighted mean of hybrid crosses = 5.6

Thus far, the crossbreeding studies as distinct from the selection studies, have not utilized subjects from natural populations. However, two recent experiments carried out by Watson (1978) and Singleton (1981; Singleton & Hay, 1982) have made use of the wild mouse gene pool. Watson used the strains developed by Connor (1975, 1978), which were derived by continued sib mating from a population of live trapped *Mus musculus,* to carry out a 5 × 5 diallel cross study of predation and aggression in male mice. She employed Hayman analyses and estimation of variance components (Hayman, 1954a, 1954b) to describe the genetic architecture of the behaviors observed when a nonaggressive A/J strain male mouse was dropped into the subject's home cage. Subjects were isolated for 3 weeks before being tested at 90+ days of age when they were observed for 4- to 7-minute periods over consecutive days. (As the study has not yet been published in final form we do not consider the data in detail but simply quote from the conclusion to the discussion in Watson's (1978) thesis:

> The results of the present study neither confirm nor contradict the expected relationship between fitness and aggression. . . . The proportion of time spent jumping or running from the intruder showed directional dominance, in the direction of decrease, along with considerable additive variation. This indicates that selection has favored mice which run away less. . . . The proportion of time spent in the apparently defensive boxing posture (Hoffmeister & Wuttke, 1969) was inherited additively. . . . Most of the non-aggressive behavior of the mice in the intermale test was divided into cage exploration and non-aggressive contact with the intruder. Most of the genetic variation influencing these variables was dominance variation of the directional sort, in the direction of less non-aggressive contact and more cage exploration. This indicates that selection has favored mice which spend less time in non-aggressive contact with strange male mice [pp. 32–33].

Thus, as with the selection studies from wild populations (Ebert & Hyde, 1976; van Oortmerssen & Bakker, 1981), the results of this diallel study give an ambiguous picture of the genetic architecture, not least because for a number of Watson's measures there was little detectable genetic variation at all.

Turning finally to the studies of Singleton (1981; Singleton & Hay, 1982) and Hay (1980), we find an attempt to use a form of the test cross methodology (Kearsey & Jinks, 1968), which we have advocated and successfully employed for testing the assumption that the genetic architecture discovered in laboratory populations is representative of that obtaining in contemporary natural populations (Hewitt & Fulker, 1981, in press, submitted for publication; Hewitt et al., 1979, 1981). As we have indicated previously, test cross designs, in their various forms, will for this purpose usually involve crossing wild males to one or more inbred tester lines or F_1 crosses between them. Analyses of the variance of the progeny scores permit, with a number of simplifying assumptions that may or may not be testable depending on the design, partitioning of the between-sires genetic variation into additive and dominance components, together with providing a test of the direction of dominance. However, the nonadditive effects will be detected as such only for loci at which the tester lines differ, whereas loci segregating only in the wild population will contribute their effects to an inflation of the putative additive variation (Hewitt & Fulker, 1981; Mather & Jinks, 1971). The most direct way to ensure that we have adequate tester lines is to use inbred descendants of extreme bidirectional selection lines derived from the natural population. In the absence of these, other extreme lines or lines known to be genetically if not phenotypically differentiated may be used and the architecture for the wild × laboratory animal test cross compared with a laboratory × laboratory animal test cross (Hewitt & Fulker, 1981, in press, submitted for publication; Hewitt et al., 1981).

Singleton and Hay (1982) crossed wild male mice to BALB/c and C57BL/6J females, as well as to wild females. The offspring were individually housed from weaning to 60+ days of age when they were observed in successive 5-minute encounters in a neutral arena, first with a BALB/c male and then 2 days later with a C57BL/6 male opponent. Several measures were taken, including number of attacks, accumulated attack time, number of bites, and number of jumps. Now we know from our analysis of the Eleftheriou et al. (1974) data that, although BALB/c and C57BL/6J were not phenotypically extreme, the reason was largely because the genes controlling aggression in that study were dispersed between these strains and that on reassortment considerable genetic variation was revealed; thus these two strains are a reasonable choice of testers. However, a major outcome of Singleton's study was the detection of large and highly significant amounts of putatively additive variation between the wild sires. The dominance effects were either small or nonsignificant and, if present, their direction depended both on the measure and on the strain of opponent; however, against the more passive opponent (BALB/c), the direction of dominance was consistently toward low aggression, a result that contrasts with that of Eleftheriou et al. (1974), who found dominance for high aggression toward a nonaggressive opponent. It seems likely to us that this study is demonstrating both that there is much variation in the wild population sampled by Singleton and Hay (1982), which is not available in the crosses between BALB/c and C57BL/6, hence the high estimates of 'additive variation', and also that the representativeness assumption for aggressive behaviors in mice is far from confirmed, in contrast to the situation for the behaviors we have studied in rats (Hewitt et al., 1979, 1981).

DISCUSSION AND CONCLUSIONS

Although our coverage has not been exhaustive, it is sufficient for us to determine that for aggressive behaviors, even when we restrict consideration to same-sex encounters in one species, the genetic architecture depends on the particular genotypes, the test procedure, type of opponent, and so on. Thus, as far as the

TABLE 3.11
A Summary of Eleven Studies of the Genetic Architecture of Same-Sex Aggression in Mice

Study	*Genetic Design*	*Population/Strains*	*Sex*	*Behaviors*	*Outcome*
Lagerspetz (1964-1969) Lagerspetz and Lagerspetz (1971) Lagerspetz (this volume	Selection	Swiss albino stock	Male	Aggression during 7 dyadic encounters in a novel test cage with same and opposite strain opponents.	Possibly dominance for low aggression, but mainly additive genetic variation.
Ebert and Hyde (1976) Hyde and Sawyer (1980) Ebert (this volume)	Selection	Wild	Female	Aggression towards C57BL/6 opponent over 2 trials in home cage.	Possibly dominance or duplicate gene interactions for moderate/high with ceiling on ferocity.
vanOortmerssen and Bakker (1981)	Selection	Wild	Male	Latency to attack standard (MAS-Giro) opponent over 3 trials in familiar cage.	Possibly dominance for slow latency (low aggression)
Eleftheriou et al. (1974)	Inbred strains, RI strains, F_1 crosses, backcrosses, various cross parent manipulations	BALB/c, C57BL/6, and RI strains	Male	Initiation of fights against standard non-aggressive opponent (CXBH) during 5 trials in a neutral arena.	Dominance for high aggression with special maternal effect.

Kessler et al. (1977)	P_1, P_2, F_1, F_2, B_1	A/S, BALB/cJ	Male	Aggresive behaviors towards CBA/J male dangled into home cage on one trial.	Dominance for low aggression.
Southwick and Clark (1968) Southwick (1970)	Inbred strains F_1 crosses	C57Br, CFW, C57B6/6, A/J, CBA	Male	Frequency of aggressive behavior in groups of 4 same strain subjects. Continuous recordings	Dominance for high aggression.
Selmanoff et al. (1976)	Diallel cross	DBA/1, DBA/2 C57BL/6, C57BL/10	Male	Aggressive behaviors during 3 same genotype encounters in neutral arena.	Dominance for low aggression.
Kulikov (1980)	Incomplete diallel cross	C57BL/6J, BALB/c DD, C3H/H3, CC57Br	Male	Number of attacks on standard intruder.	Little non-additive variation.
Hahn (this volume)	Diallel cross	C57BL/10, DBA, BALB/cJ, SJL/J	Male	Various measures of aggression against same genotype.	No directional non-additive variation
Watson (1978)	Diallel cross	Inbred strains derived from wild population	Male	Aggressive behaviors when non-aggressive (A/J) male dropped into home cage. 4 trials.	Low heritabilities, little non-additive variation detected.
Singleton (1981) Singleton and Hay (1982)	Test cross	Wild males crossed to BALB/c and C57BL/6 males	Male	Aggressive behaviors towards BALB/c and then C57BL/6 male in neutral arena. One trial for each opponent.	High heritabilities, little dominance detected usually for low aggression (against BALB/c)

evidence from genetic architecture is concerned, the data so far preclude any firm generalizations about the adaptiveness of high or low levels of aggression. However in an attempt to discern the trends, we have summarized the studies we have been considering in Table 3.11.

Taking the study of interfemale aggression first (Ebert, this volume; Ebert & Hyde, 1976; Hyde & Sawyer, 1980), inasmuch as the ultimate asymmetry of response was consistent with a genetic architecture supporting moderate levels of aggression it may be related to the suggestion of Hyde and Sawyer (1979) that the adaptive value of this behavior comes about through its correlation with maternal aggression, or possibly through sexual selection. It is interesting to note in this connection that, in contradistinction to the observations on the wild mice used in this study, interfemale aggression has been all but lost in laboratory populations (Ebert & Hyde, 1976).

In male laboratory mice, on the other hand, the genetic architecture would indicate that in an unfamiliar situation (Lagerspetz, 1964; Selmanoff et al., 1976) or with an unusual form of intrusion (Kessler et al., 1977) during a short dyadic encounter, lower levels of aggressive behavior are adaptive, or at least there is no adaptive advantage in high levels of aggression (Hahn, this volume; Kulikov, 1980; Lagerspetz, this volume): an exception occurred when the opponent was nonaggressive but otherwise normal (Eleftheriou et al., 1974). With larger groups over longer periods, higher levels of aggression are supported (Southwick, 1970). This trend would accord with the results of DeFries and McClearn (1970), Horn (1974), and Kuse and DeFries (1976), which suggested a correlation between fitness and social dominance among laboratory mice as measured by the results of aggressive encounters in group conditions, even though the correlation may not be causal in the most obvious way (Horn, 1974). The hypothesis would be that intraspecific aggression is adaptive when it is potentially contributing to the establishment of social dominance relationships within the group, and not when it is expressed in a brief dyadic encounter in a strange situation.

With wild populations the results of Singleton's study (Singleton, 1981; Singleton & Hay, 1982) suggest that the genes segregating in the wild population are not represented by those differentiating the BALC/c and C57BL/6 inbred strains, the strains that, we may note, were the progenitors of the only crosses to show directional dominance for high aggression in a brief dyadic encounter in a novel environment. Where we have evidence of the genetic architecture for the wild population it would seem generally to favor moderate to low aggression in these situations (Singleton & Hay, 1982; van Oortmerssen & Bakker, 1981; Watson, 1978).

It has already been suggested that the aggression measured during 'bouts' has little to do with social dominance and hence, by implication, fitness (McClearn & DeFries, 1973). Our reading of the data suggests that this may well be so, but already there is a further complication, as it is likely that for these behaviors in mice the genetic architecture found in laboratory strains may not reflect that operating in wild populations. One way forward is to make further use of the test cross designs to survey the wild populations. Optimally, these designs need the extreme tester lines derived initially from the population to be surveyed, a consideration that might provide some impetus for further bidirectional selection studies from wild foundation populations.

We would like to conclude with two more general observations. Firstly, Scott (1977) has pointed to the need for new methods of analysis for social behaviors and we have already agreed that the problems of analyzing social interaction, competition, and cooperation are of central importance and have argued that progress in this direction can be made within the scope of biometrical genetical analysis (Eaves, 1976; Eaves et al., 1978). At the same time, we feel that such developments must be matched by the collection of hard data, already scarce enough for the more readily defined behaviors. The promise of future developments should not deter us from trying to understand the genetic control of the kinds of behavior we have been discussing.

Secondly, there are those who will argue that these behaviors, measured as they are under controlled laboratory conditions, are 'unnatural' and whatever we learn about them can have little to do with what happens in a natural habitat. But what is a natural habitat? One definition we might offer is that natural habitats are those that share the characteristics of that to which the genetic architecture of the breeding population is adapted; natural behaviors are those that are maintained by this genetic architecture. It is difficult to see how it is possible to know in advance which aspects of which behaviors and situations will be 'natural' and which will not. One approach is through the application of biometrical genetics to elucidate the genetic architecture of these behaviors.

REFERENCES

Angus, J. Changes in the behaviour of individual members of a *Drosophila* population maintained by random mating. *Heredity,* 1974, *33,* 89–93.

Bailey, D. W. Recombinant-inbred strains. *Transplantation,* 1971, *11,* 325–327.

Breese, E. L., & Hill, J. Regression analysis of interactions between competing species. *Heredity,* 1973, *31,* 181–200.

Breese, E. L., & Mather, K. The organization of polygenic activity within a chromosome in *Drosophila:* II. Viability. *Heredity,* 1960, *14,* 375–399.

Broadhurst, P. L. Experiments in psychogenetics. Applications of biometrical genetics to the inheritance of behaviour. In H. J. Eysenck (Ed.), *Experiments in personality* (Vol. 1). London: Routledge & Kegan Paul, 1960.

Broadhurst, P. L. The experimental approach to behavioral evolution. In. J. R. Royce & L. P. Mos (Eds.), *Theoretical advances in behavior genetics*. Germantown, Md.: Sijthoff & Noordhoff, 1979.

Broadhurst, P. L., & Jinks, J. L. Biometrical genetics and behavior: Re-analysis of published data. *Psychological Bulletin,* 1961, *58,* 337–362.

Broadhurst, P. L., & Jinks, J. L. Stability and change in the inheritance of behaviour. A further analysis of statistics from a diallel cross. *Proceedings of the Royal Society, Series B*, 1966, *165*, 450–472.

Broadhurst, P. L., & Jinks, J. L. What genetical architecture can tell us about the natural selection of behavioural traits. In J. H. F. van Abeelen (Ed.), *The genetics of behaviour*. Amsterdam: North Holland, 1974.

Chahal, G. S., & Jinks, J. L. A general method of detecting the additive, dominance and epistatic variation that inbred lines can generate using a single tester. *Heredity*, 1978, *40*, 117–125.

Collins, M. F. *An investigation and genetic analysis of a reported conditioned response in the courtship behaviour of Drosophila melangaster*. Unpublished master's dissertation, University of Birmingham, 1980.

Collins, M. F., & Hewitt, J. K. A biometrical genetical analysis of a reported conditioned response in the courtship behavior of male *Drosophila melanogaster*. *Behavior Genetics*, 1981, 11, 595. (Abstract).

Connor, J. L. Genetic mechanisms controlling the domestication of a wild house mouse population (*Mus musculus*, L.). *Journal of Comparative and Physiological Psychology*, 1975, *89*, 118–130.

Connor, J. L. Development of inbred and random stocks of wild mice. *Mouse News Letter*, 1978, *58*, 61–62.

Darlington, C. D. *The evolution of genetic systems*. Cambridge, Eng.: Cambridge University Press, 1939.

DeFries, J. C., & McClearn, G. E. Social dominance and Darwinian fitness in the laboratory mouse. *The American Naturalist*, 1970, *104*, 408–411.

Eaves, L. J. A model for sibling effects in man. *Heredity*, 1976, *36*, 205–215.

Eaves, L. J., Last, K. A., Young, P. A., & Martin, N. G. Model-fitting approaches to the analysis of human behaviour. *Heredity*, 1978, *41*, 249–320.

Ebert, P. D., & Hyde, J. S. Selection for agonistic behavior in wild female *Mus musculus*. *Behavior Genetics*, 1976, *6*, 291–304.

Eleftheriou, B. E., Bailey, D. W., & Denenberg, V. H. Genetic analysis of fighting behavior in mice. *Physiology and Behavior*, 1974, *13*, 773–777.

Falconer, D. S. Genetic consequences of selection pressures. In J. E. Meade & A. S. Parkes (Eds.), *Genetic and environmental factors in human ability*. Edinburgh: Oliver & Boyd, 1965.

Falconer, D. S. *Introduction to quantitative genetics*. Edinburgh: Oliver & Boyd, 1970.

Fisher, R. A. The possible modification of the response of the wild type to recurrent mutations. *American Naturalist*, 1928, *62*, 115–126.

Fisher, R. A. *The genetical theory of natural selection* (2nd ed.). New York: Dover Publications, 1958.

Fulker, D. W. Mating speed in male *Drosophila melanogaster:* A psychogenetic analysis. *Science*, 1966, *153*, 203–205.

Fulker, D. W. Applications of a simplified triple test-cross. *Behavior Genetics*, 1972, *2*, 185–198.

Fuller, J. L., & Hahn, M. E. Problems in the genetics of social behavior. *Behavior Genetics*, 1976, *6*, 391–406.

Gale, J. S., Mather, K., & Jinks, J. L. Joint scaling tests. *Heredity*, 1977, *38*, 47–51.

Hay, D. A. Y chromosome and aggression in mice. *Nature*, 1975, *255*, 658.

Hay, D. A. Genetics in the analysis of behavior. *Neuroscience and Biobehavioral Reviews*, 1980, *4*, 489–508.

Hayman, B. I. The analysis of variance of diallel tables. *Biometrics*, 1954, *10*, 235–244. (a)

Hayman, B. I. The theory and analysis of diallel crosses. *Genetics*, 1954, *10*, 789–809. (b)

Henderson, N. D. Genetic dominance for low activity in infant mice. *Journal of Comparative and Physiological Psychology*, 1978, *92*, 118–125.

Hewitt, J. K., & Fulker, D. W. Using the triple test cross to investigate the genetics of behavior in wild populations. I. Methodological considerations. *Behavior Genetics*, 1981, *11*, 23–36.

Hewitt, J. K., & Fulker, D. W. Using the triple test cross to investigate the genetics of behavior in wild populations. II. Escape–avoidance conditioning in Norway rats. *Behavior Genetics,* in press.

Hewitt, J. K., & Fulker, D. W. *Using the triple test cross to investigate the genetics of behavior in wild populations. III. Activity and Reactivity in Norway rats.* Manuscript submitted for publication.

Hewitt, J. K., Fulker, D. W., & Broadhurst, P. L. Genetic architecture in a laboratory and a wild rat population. *Behavior Genetics,* 1979, *9,* 460. (Abstract).

Hewitt, J. K., Fulker, D. W., & Broadhurst, P. L. Genetic architecture of escape–avoidance conditioning in laboratory and wild populations of rats: A biometrical approach. *Behavior Genetics,* 1981, *11,* 533–544.

Hoffmeister, F., & Wuttke, W. On the actions of psychotropic drugs on the attack and aggressive–defensive behaviour of mice and cats. In S. Gurattni & E. B. Siggs (Eds.), *Biology of aggressive behaviour.* Amsterdam: Excerpta Medica Foundation, 1969.

Horn, J. M. Aggression as a component of relative fitness in four inbred strains of mice. *Behavior Genetics,* 1974, *4,* 373–381.

Hyde, J. S., & Ebert, P. D. Correlated response in selection for aggressiveness in female mice. I. Male aggression. *Behaviour Genetics,* 1976, *6,* 421–428.

Hyde, J. S., & Sawyer, T. F. Correlated response in selection for aggressiveness in female mice. II. Maternal aggression. *Behavior Genetics,* 1979, *9,* 571–577.

Hyde, J. S., & Sawyer, T. F. Selection for agonistic behavior in wild female mice. *Behavior Genetics,* 1980, *10,* 349–359.

Jinks, J. L. The biometrical approach to quantitative variation. In J. N. Thompson, Jr., & J. M. Thoday (Eds.), *Quantitiative genetic variation.* New York: Academic Press, 1979.

Jinks, J. L., & Broadhurst, P. L. How to analyse the inheritance of behaviour in animals—the biometrical approach. In J. H. F. van Abeelen (Ed.), *The genetics of behaviour.* Amsterdam: North Holland, 1974.

Jinks, J. L., Perkins, J. M., & Breese, E. L. A general method of detecting additive, dominance and epistatic variation for metrical traits. II. Applications to inbred lines. *Heredity,* 1969, *24,* 45–57.

Jinks, J. L., & Virk, D. S. A modified triple test-cross analysis to test and allow for inadequate testers. *Heredity,* 1977, *39,* 165–170.

Kearsey, M. J., & Barnes, B. W. Variation for metrical characters in *Drosophila* populations. II. Natural selection. *Heredity,* 1970, *25,* 11–21.

Kearsey, M. J., & Jinks, J. L. A general method for detecting additive, dominance and epistatic variation for metrical traits. I. Theory. *Heredity,* 1968, *11,* 23–35.

Kearsey, M. J., & Kojima, K. The genetic architecture of body weight and egg hatchability in *Drosophila melanogaster. Genetics,* 1967, *56,* 23–37.

Kessler, S., Elliot, G. R., Orenberg, E. K., & Barchas, J. D. A genetic analysis of aggressive behavior in two strains of mice. *Behavior Genetics,* 1977, *7,* 313–321.

Kulikov, A. V. Izuchene zakonomernostei nasledovaniya intensivnosti "spontannoi" agressii m'ishei. [A study of the heredity of the intensity of "spontaneous" aggressiveness in mice.] *USSR Academy of Science, Siberian Section, Biological Science Series,* 1980, *3,* 69–74.

Kuse, A. R., & DeFries, J. C. Social dominance and Darwinian fitness in laboratory mice: An alternative test. *Behavioral Biology,* 1976, *16,* 113–116.

Lagerspetz, K. M. J. *Studies on the aggressive behaviour of mice.* Helsinki: Snomalainen Tiedeakatemia, 1964.

Lagerspetz, K. M. J. Aggression and aggressiveness in laboratory mice. In S. Garattini & E. B. Sigg (Eds.), *Aggressive behaviour.* Amsterdam: Excerpta Medica, 1969.

Lagerspetz, K. M. J., & Lagerspetz, K. Y. H. Changes in the aggressiveness of mice resulting from selective breeding, learning and social isolation. *Scandinavian Journal of Psychology,* 1971, *12,* 241–248.

Mather, K. Variation and selection of polygenic characters. *Journal of Genetics*, 1941, *41*, 159–193.

Mather, K. Evolution in polygenic systems. *Accademia Nazionale dei lincei*, 1960, *47*, 131–152.

Mather, K. *Genetical structure of populations*. London: Chapman & Hall, 1973.

Mather, K., & Harrison, B. J. The manifold effect of selection. *Heredity*, 1949, *3*, 1–52.

Mather, K., & Jinks, J. L. *Biometrical genetics: The study of continuous variation* (2nd ed.). London: Chapman & Hall, 1971.

Mather, K., & Jinks, J. L. *Introduction to biometrical genetics*. London: Chapman & Hall, 1978.

Maxson, S. C. The genetics of aggression in vertebrates. In P. F. Brain & D. Benton (Eds.), *The biology of aggression*. Leiden: Sijthoff, 1981.

Maxson, S. C., Ginsburg, B. E., & Trattner, A. Interaction of Y-chromosomal and autosomal gene(s) in the development of intermale aggression in mice. *Behavior Genetics*, 1979, *9*, 219–226.

McClearn, G. E., & DeFries, J. C. *Introduction to behavioral genetics*. San Francisco: W. H. Freeman, 1973.

Scott, J. P. Social genetics. *Behavior Genetics*, 1977,*7*, 327–346.

Scott, J. P., & Fredericson, E. The causes of fighting in mice and rats. *Physiological Zoology*, 1951, *24*, 273–309.

Selmanoff, M. K., Jumonville, J. E., Maxson, S. C., & Ginsburg, B. E. Evidence for a Y-chromosomal contribution to an aggressive phenotype in inbred mice. *Nature*, 1975, *253*, 529–530.

Selmanoff, M. K., Maxson, S. C., & Ginsburg, B. E. Chromosomal determinants of intermale aggressive behavior in inbred mice. *Behavior Genetics*, 1976, *6*, 53–71.

Sheppard, P. M. *Natural selection and heredity*. London: Hutchinson University Library, 1967.

Simon, N. G. The genetics of intermale aggressive behavior in mice: Recent research and alternative strategies. *Neuroscience and Biobehavioral Reviews*, 1979, *3*, 97–106.

Singleton, G. R. *A behavioral and population study of wild house mice, Mus musculus*. Unpublished doctoral dissertation, La Trobe University, 1981.

Singleton, G. R., & Hay, D. A. *A genetic study of male social aggression in wild and laboratory mice*. *Behavior Genetics*, 1982, *12*, 435–448.

Southwick, C. H. Genetic and environmental variables influencing aggression. In *Animal aggression: Selected readings*. New York: Van Nostrand Reinhold, 1970.

Southwick, C. H., & Clark, L. H. Aggressive behavior and exploratory activity in fourteen mouse strains. *American Zoologist*, 1966, *6*, 559. (Abstract)

Southwick, C. H., & Clark, L. H. Interstrain differences in aggressive behavior and exploratory activity in inbred mice. *Communications in Behavioral Biology*, 1968, *1A*, 49–59.

Tryon, R. C. Genetic differences in maze-learning ability in rats. *39th Yearbook, National Society for the Study of Education (Part 1)*, Bloomington, Ill.:Public School Publishing Co., 1940.

van Oortmerssen, G. A., & Bakker, T. C. M. Artificial selection for short and long attack latencies in wild *Mus musculus domesticus*. *Behavior Genetics*, 1981, *11*, 115–126.

Walters, D. E., & Gale, J. S. A note on the Hayman analysis of variance for a full diallel table. *Heredity*, 1977, *38*, 401–407.

Watson, P. A. *The genetic basis of aggression in wild house mice: A diallel analysis*. Unpublished doctoral dissertation, University of Nebraska, 1978.

Wearden, S. Alternative analyses of the diallel cross. *Heredity*, 1964, *19*, 669–680.

Wilson, E. O. *Sociobiology. The new synthesis*. Cambridge, Mass.: Belknap Press, 1975.

Wright, S. Fisher's theory of dominance. *American Naturalist*, 1929, *63*, 274–279.

4 Genetic "Artifacts" and Aggressive Behavior

Martin E. Hahn
William Paterson College

INTRODUCTION

Early Studies

Aggressive behavior in mice has been intensively studied over the last 40 years. Among the questions examined over that period have been: (1) what are the contributions of genetic and environmental variation to individual differences in aggressive behavior; and (2) what is the function of aggression in social interactions and social organization in mice.

Early work on mouse aggression concentrated on those questions. For example, Scott (1942), in a pioneering study, examined inbred strains of mice and found quantitative differences among mice of different strains in several types of behavior including: fighting, investigative behavior, eating, and sexual behavior. In another pioneering study, Allee and Ginsburg (1941) were able to show that a mouse's social position was a result of its prior experience with other mice. If a mouse had been defeated in the past, it was likely that it was conditioned to be a subordinate and would be defeated again. Allee and Ginsburg also demonstrated that proper experience would raise a mouse's social position. Another early paper by Scott (1944) proposed a role for aggression in social organization. Scott argued that social behavior, specifically agression, determined social organization, specifically dominance. Grouped mice that exhibited aggression should develop a dominance order, whereas those that did not engage in aggression, should not. In a test of his theory, Scott (1943) took two strains of mice and divided the males of each strain into groups, one of which was trained to fight while the other was trained to inhibit fighting. When animals were trained to fight, their groups developed dominance, and those trained to inhibit aggression did not.

Aggression and Fitness

Research that has followed over the years has broadened and extended the conclusions of that early work but those early studies laid important foundations by demonstrating genetic and environmental influences on aggression and showing that aggression led to social organization. A view held in common by the early investigators was that aggression was positively related to Darwinian fitness. The reasoning was that aggression, though involving risks, led to the establishment of individual dominance relationships between male mice and ultimately to social orders in which aggression was severely curtailed and replaced by, in the words of Wynne-Edwards (1962), "conventional competition." That is, fighting was replaced by threat and social status signals.

Although a positive relationship between aggression and fitness had been assumed, the question of the nature of the relationship between aggression and fitness had not been examined empirically until recently. Four studies have looked at the relationship between fighting-induced dominance orders and the reproductive success of males in those orders. DeFries and McClearn (1970) found that when mice established a social order, assessed by the number of wounds on each male, the dominant male sired approximately 90% of the litters when in competition with other males for mates. Although the relationship between fitness and dominance appeared clear in the DeFries and McClearn study, the results of other studies have not yielded such a clear-cut relationship. Horn (1974) employed a situation similar to that of DeFries and McClearn but found that the relationship between aggression-induced dominance and fitness was partially dependent on the inbred strains employed. Horn suggested that observed differential fecundity between males was due in part to dominance status, but also to fertility differences among males and pregnancy blocks that occurred in the females. Experiments by Levine and colleagues (Levine, 1958; Levine, Barsal, & Diakow, 1965) also found a relationship between fitness and aggression, but the results seemed to be more a function of the specific method used than the aggressiveness of the males employed. No clear picture of the relationship between intermale aggression and fitness emerged from those studies.

Biometrical Genetic Approach

Given that the nature of the relationship between aggression and fitness is an important question and that prior research had not satisfactorily analyzed the relationship in groups of males or in other situations, I decided to approach the problem employing methods of genetic analysis long used in agriculture and recently applied to behavioral phenotypes. These methods allow an investigator to study the evolution of behavior in much the same way that an anthropologist studies the evolution of stone tool use—by examining artifacts. The artifacts of interest here are not the arrowheads or stone hatchets of previous civilizations, but artifacts in the genetic structure of a population, referred to by Broadhurst and Jinks (1974) and Hewitt and Broadhurst (this volume) as genetic architecture.

The methods for studying genetic architecture fall under the title of "biometrical genetics" and have been discussed and employed by Bruell (1967) and Broadhurst (1979) among others, but the most detailed account of their use and interpretation is available in Mather and Jinks (1971). I briefly outline the approach here, but a more detailed account of the methods and their applications to the study of aggression are found in the chapter of Hewitt and Broadhurst in this volume.

1. Most behavioral traits are influenced and controlled by genetic systems composed of many genes at several loci—so-called *polygenes*. Each locus has an effect on the behavior of interest but a gene substitution at any locus will have only a minor effect. If you make a Mendelian type cross of two inbred lines of mice and measure a behavioral phenotype in the P_1, P_2 and F_1 generation, the results will be like those depicted in Fig. 4.1. What is observed is that the mean of the F_1 does not coincide with the mean of either P_1 or P_2 but lies in an intermediate position, a result of the multiple loci involved in the inheritance of the trait.

2. In order to properly analyze the results of such crossbreeding experiments, biometrical geneticists propose models that partition the phenotypic variance into several component parts, the genetic components of which may be called the genetic architecture. The results of the early studies of aggression, described

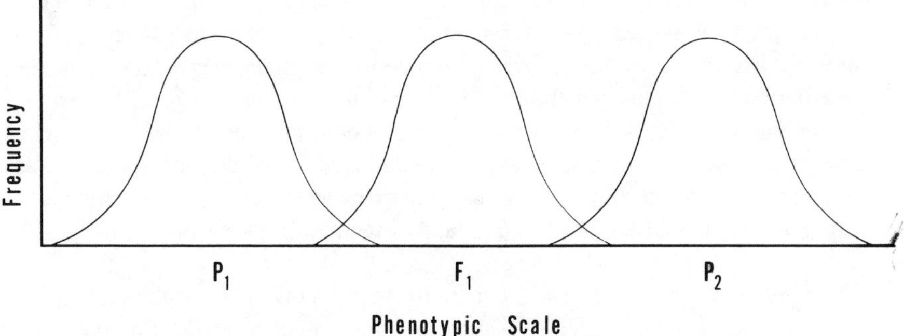

FIG. 4.1. Illustration of phenotypic values obtained from a Mendelian type cross of two inbred lines.

previously, fit an elementary model, namely that genes and environments both contribute to variation in aggression. That model is:

$$V_p = V_g + V_e$$

where the phenotypic variation (V_p) is divided into two components, genetic variation (V_g) and environmental variation (V_e).

The biometrical geneticists have proposed a number of such models, the appropriateness of any one for a particular situation being based on the conditions existing in that situation. One such model (the one I use later) is that outlined by Hayman (1954) and is a fixed sample, maternal effects model. The model is:

$$V_p = V_a + V_b\ (V_{b_1} + V_{b_2} + V_{b_3}) + V_c + V_d$$

where the phenotypic variation is divided into variance associated with: additive genetic effects or breeding values (V_a), dominance variation associated with dominance deviations (V_b), variation attributable to maternal effects such as early nutrition (V_c), and variation due to other reciprocal effects (V_d). Dominance variation is further divided into directional dominance (V_{b_1}), asymmetrical dominance (V_{b_2}), and specific combining effects (V_{b_3}).

3. The final step in the biometrical genetic system is to relate the genetic architecture to evolutionary processes. Broadhurst and Jinks (1974), for example, argue that over time, selection has operated on populations and several results are possible. The first polygon in Fig. 4.2 illustrates a population prior to any selection. Notice that the curve is normal in shape and symmetrical. If directional selection was applied to such a population over several generations (e.g., individuals low in aggressiveness were at a selective disadvantage), then the values of the population would become distributed as in the second polygon of Fig. 4.2. That population would be characterized as being lower in variability, with poor response to selection, and inheritance in the population would be primarily directionally dominant for high values of aggression. If some intermediate value of aggressiveness was favored by selection, and extreme values were at a disadvantage for several generations, stabilizing selection would be operating and the values of the population would become distributed as in the third polygon of Fig. 4.2. Such a population would be characterized by a symmetrical and roughly normal shape, have reduced variability compared to an unselected population, but remain highly responsive to selection. Inheritance in the population would be additive and ambidirectionally dominant.

The position of the biometrical geneticist, then, is that in a population where a particular phenotype has been subjected to strong directional selection pressure, variation in that population will be composed primarily of directional dominance variation (b_1) with a low proportion of additive variation (a). On the other hand,

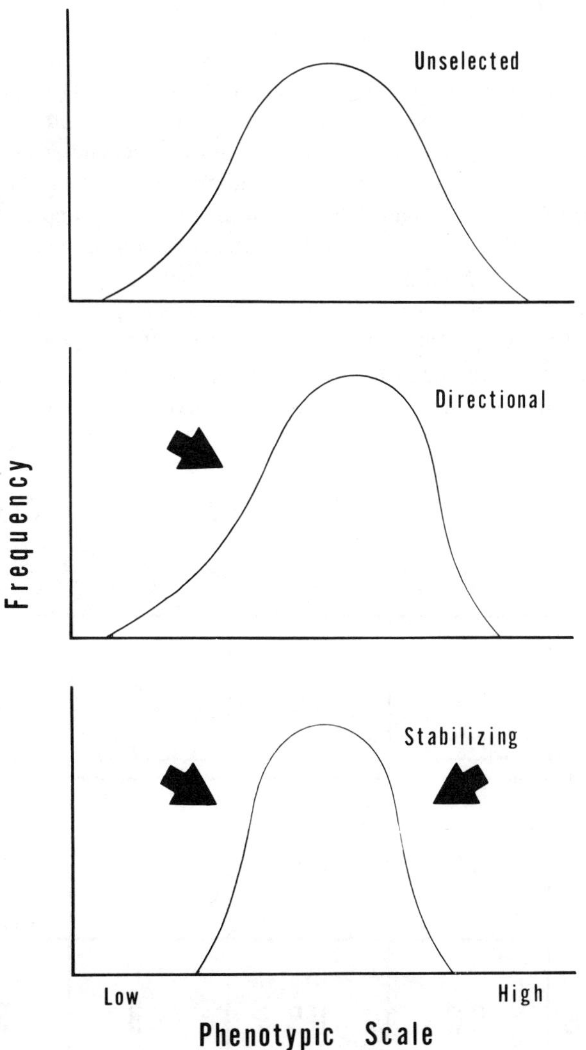

FIG. 4.2. Illustration of the results of directional and stabilizing selection on a population.

a trait subjected to stabilizing selection will have an architecture of mostly additive variation (a) and little directional dominance variation (b_1). These sources of genetic variation in a phenotype, present in a population, are the artifacts to be examined in this study of the relationship between aggression and fitness.

Diallel Cross Method

Several genetic methods allow biometrical genetic analysis, including artificial selection, the triple test cross, and the diallel cross. Perhaps the most important among these methods is the diallel cross or method of complete crossings. By using the diallel cross, one can estimate a number of genetic and environmental contributions to phenotypic variation including those in the Hayman (1954) model: a, b, b_1, b_2, b_3, c, and d. A typical diallel cross is depicted in Fig. 4.3 and involves completely crossing males and females of a number of inbred lines, in this case, four. The resulting F_1 generation is composed of 16 different genetic groups: four inbred lines, CC, DD, BB, and SS; six hybrid groups, CD, CB, DB, etc.; and six reciprocals of those hybrids, DC, BC, BD, etc. After completing measurements of all the behavioral phenotypes of interest, the data are placed in a 4 × 4 matrix and analyzed to reveal the sources of variation present.

Strain of Male Parent	Strain of Female Parent: C	D	B	S
C	CC	DC	BC	SC
D	CD	DD	BD	SD
B	CB	DB	BB	SB
S	CS	DS	BS	SS

FIG. 4.3. The breeding design for a diallel cross. All strains of females are crossed with all strains of males.

Diallel Studies of Aggressive Behavior

I am reporting here on the results of diallel crosses in three situations where aggression is a likely behavior. These situations were chosen to include the already discussed intermale pairing and also to extend into situations in which a greater range of behaviors was possible. They are:

1. *Male–male pairs (intermale aggression).* Male mice were housed individually for 30 days, until 70 days of age. At that age, pairs of males of the same genetic group—a homogeneous set (Fuller & Hahn, 1976) were placed together in a standard laboratory cage.
2. *Food competition.* Male mice were treated as in the intermale situation described previously except that at 55 days of age, they were food deprived for 24 hours. They were then placed in a standard size cage with a .5 gm piece of mouse lab chow. Pairs of mice consisted of a male from one of the various genetic groups and a standard tester (Fuller & Hahn, 1976), in this case a standard hybrid male of the C57BL/10J and SJL/J strains.
3. *Nest defense.* Pairs of sexually mature male and female mice from each genetic group were established and remained together until a litter was born. At the birth of a litter the male was removed and 72 hours later, a strange male intruder (standard tester, a hybrid of the A/J and C57BL/6J strains) was placed in the cage that contained the test female and her 3-day-old litter.

In all three social situations, the F_1 generation of a 4×4 diallel cross of the C57BL/10J (C), DBA/2J (D), BALB/cJ (B), and SJL/J (S) inbred strains, was tested.

Intermale Aggression. At 70 days of age, two male litermates, isolated since 31 days of age, were placed in a standard colony cage and observed for 30 minutes. The behaviors of the animals were recorded using one time measure; latency to aggression and nine behavioral categories: chasing, fighting, (Fig. 4.4b), social grooming, genital sniffing, tail lashing, defense posture (Fig. 4.4d), nosing (Fig. 4.4a) and squeaking (Fig. 4.4c). In order to obtain information about the intensity of fighting, a 4-point (0–3) rating scale, similar to that employed by Lagerspetz (1961), was used. After an observation was completed, the observer assigned a value of 0 (no fighting), 1 (nonvigorous, low-speed biting and wrestling), 2 (moderately vigorous biting and wrestling), or 3 (vigorous biting and wrestling with visible biting and wounding) to the observation. In all, 336 mice (164 pairs, about 10 pairs from each of the 16 genetic groups) were observed. Further details of the methods employed can be found in Hahn and Haber (1982).

Data analysis was done on the time measures, behavioral categories (scores were converted to seconds of behavior/minute), and measure of fighting inten-

FIG. 4.4. Intermale mouse behaviors: a. nosing, b. fighting, c. squeaking, d. defense posture.

sity. The method of analysis was the Hayman (1954) procedure, with modifications to include a within-cell term (Hahn & Haber, 1978, 1982). The results for a typical measure, latency to aggression, are depicted in Fig. 4.5.

Inspection of the inbred values: C, D, B, and S reveal large differences in the length of time before fighting began with the C57 strain averaging over 1400 seconds, whereas the SJL strain animals averaged under 10 seconds. Inspection

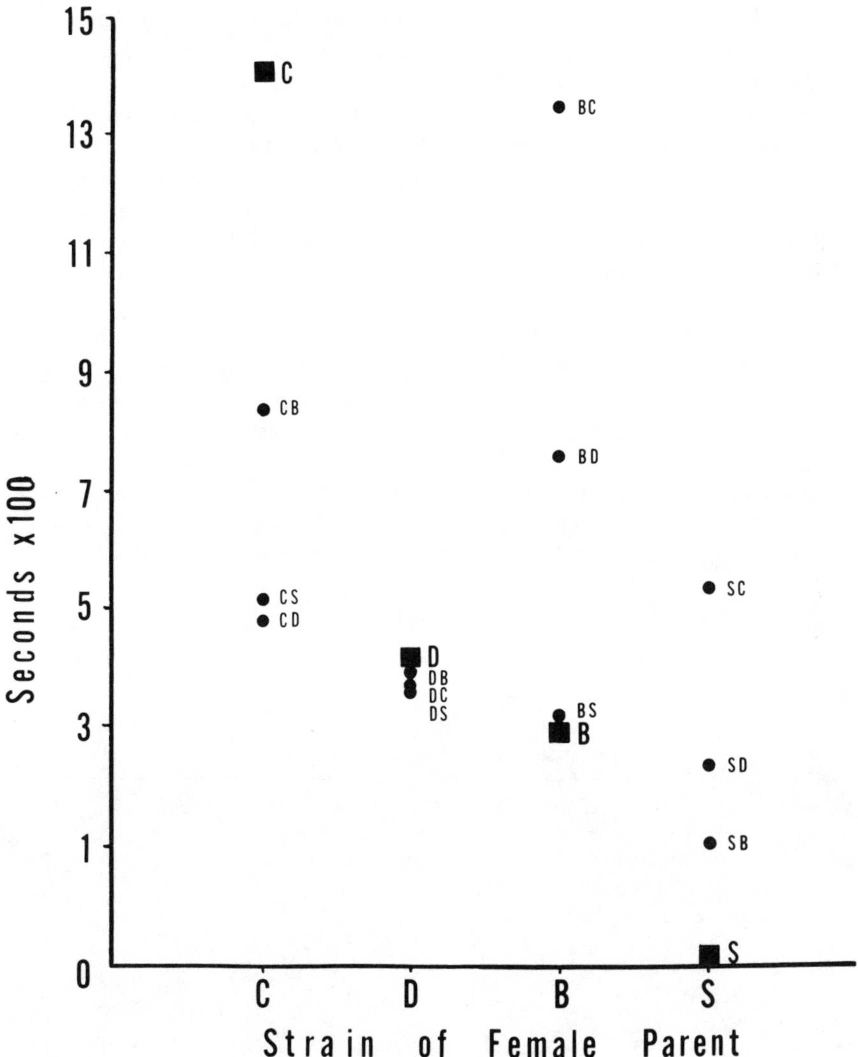

FIG. 4.5. Mean latencies to aggression in the intermale situation. Hybrid group scores are arrayed above the strain of their female parent.

of the hybrid values indicates that some hybrid means fell about halfway between their parent strain values whereas other hybrids resemble one parent strain more than the other.

The genetic analysis of these data is presented in Table 4.1. In this table, general dominance (b), asymmetrical dominance (b_2), specific combining effects (b_3), and maternal effects are significant, whereas the additive component approaches significance. In accordance with the cogent points of Henderson (1979), I have included a measure of the magnitude of effects of the various components in the model (η^2 = percentage of the total sums of squares associated with a particular component). From this statistic, it is clear that the additive component accounts for almost 30% of the total phenotypic variability, whereas the directional dominant component accounts for essentially none.

Table 4.2 illustrates the patterns of inheritance for all behaviors measured in the intermale social situation. A pattern of results emerges when the significance levels and proportions of total sums of squares associated with each component of the model are examined. It is evident that the inheritance of each trait is strongly influenced by additive genetic effects, influenced moderately by dominance deviations, and minimally by directional dominance effects. This pattern is consistent with the theoretical statements of Broadhurst and Jinks (1974) and indicates that the traits measured have undergone stabilizing selection in which a moderate value of a trait is favored over an extreme value. Such a trait would retain genetic malleability and respond well to artificial selection. The successful bidirectional selection for aggressiveness (based on a rating scale similar to the one employed here) in male mice by Lagerspetz (1961, this volume) support such an interpretation.

Food Competition. It could be argued that intermale aggression as just discussed—involving males of identical genotypes, in which escape from a small

TABLE 4.1
Genetic Analysis of Latency to Aggression

Source	*MS*	*df*	*F Ratio*	*p Value*	η^2
a	514110.0	3	7.77[a]	<.10	.296
b	90489.0	6	4.65	<.01	.104
b_1	227.5	1	.01	N.S.	.000
b_2	82917.0	3	4.23	<.01	.048
b_3	148057.0	2	7.61	<.01	.057
c	66208.4	3	3.41	<.05	.038
d	12914.2	3	.66	N.S.	.007
Within	19443.7	149			.555

[a]In this model, additive effects are tested against maternal effects (*c*) while all other effects are tested against pooled (*d*) and within, when *d*/within is not significant.

TABLE 4.2
Summary of Genetic Analyses for All Measures—Intermale Situation

	p Values of Sources of Variance						η^2 (SS_{effect}/SS_{total})					
Behavioral Measure	*a*	*b*	b_1	b_2	b_3	*c*	*a*	*b*	b_1	b_2	b_3	*c*
Latency to aggression	.10	.01	—	.01	.01	.05	.296	.104	.000	.048	.057	.038
Fighting intensity	—	.01	—	.05	.01	.01	.327	.080	.003	.040	.037	.072
Fighting	—	—	—	—	—	—	.129	.056	.003	.048	.006	.016
Social grooming	.10	.05	—	.01	—	—	.127	.072	.000	.065	.007	.015
Genital sniffing	.05	.10	—	.01	—	—	.152	.065	.000	.052	.013	.006
Tail lashing	.05	.01	—	.01	.01	—	.197	.159	.002	.056	.100	.019
Defensive posture	.01	.01	—	.05	.01	—	.214	.126	.000	.046	.080	.002
Nosing	—	—	—	—	.05	—	.086	.047	.000	.001	.044	.025
Squeaking	.05	—	—	—	—	—	.054	.012	.004	.008	.006	.012

area is not possible, is unlikely to occur in nature and artifically restricts the behavioral repertoire of the animals involved. The genetic architecture and its interpretation for behaviors measured in that situation might not be representative of mouse aggression in general. Accordingly, I chose to investigate a situation that presented a more complex set of stimuli, allowed greater possibility for responding, and involved mice of different genotypes interacting. Competition for food has been reported in wild mice living in a laboratory setting (Brown, 1953), as Brown observed dominant male mice taking food away from subordinate ones. Fredericson (1950) studied the effects of food deprivation on fighting in mice and discovered that first, latency to fighting was decreased when hunger was increased and second, that "spontaneous" aggression and aggression in food-deprived animals seemed to be controlled by distinct genetic systems. Thus, a food competition situation is more complex and perhaps more natural than an intermale aggression situation.

More recently, Manosevitz (1972) attempted to relate food competition and Darwinian fitness. In this study, he employed females of two inbred strains and of the hybrid groups between those strains. After certain training procedures and food deprivation procedure, he placed two females together and measured the time each was able to eat. His results indicated that in direct competiton, hybrids consistently ate for more seconds than their inbred competitor. Such a result, called heterosis, can be interpreted as demonstrating the effects of prior directional selection on a mouse population.

I felt that further study on food competition was desirable, using the analytical techniques of biometrical genetics. The study that was completed involved male and female mice, using the standard-tester and homogeneous set designs. In this chapter, I report only on a portion of that study, males in the standard-tester situation.

Subjects in the study were placed in individual cages at 31 days of age, where they remained until testing at 55 days of age. On day 55, each animal was weighed and placed in a clean cage that contained a water bottle but no food. They remained in that cage for 24 hours when two males, one from each of the 16 genetic groups of the diallel and a standard tester (a male of the C57 × SJL hybrid group) were placed together in a standard cage containing only a .5-gm piece of standard lab chow. Testing lasted for 20 minutes. About eight pairs representing each genetic group were tested, for a total of 123 pairs. The behavior of mice in this situation was observed and recorded using the behavioral categories and time measures used in the intermale study. In addition, several behaviors relating specifically to food possession were measured: food possession ratio (time the nonstandard mouse possessed the food); and food exchanges by take-aways, attempted take-aways, and uncontested drops. After each test, both males were reweighed.

Data analysis was completed as before with a modified Hayman (1954) procedure. Figure 4.6 illustrates the results on the measure of latency to aggression. Inspection of the inbred values: C, D, B, and S reveals large differences in the length of time before fighting began with the BALB strain averaging over 700 seconds and the DBA mice slightly over 200 seconds. Inspection of the hybrid values indicates that some hybrid means fell about halfway between their parent strain values, whereas other hybrids resemble one parent strain more than the other. The genetic analysis of these data reveal that only one component, the additive (a), even approaches significance ($p < .10$).

A comparison of the latencies to aggression in the intermale and food competition situations reveals two interesting points. First, in partial agreement with Fredericson's work (1950), the latencies to aggression of aggressive mice were lengthened in the presence of food, although in less aggressive mice, latencies were shortened. Overall, food deprivation and the presence of food and another mouse reduced the range of latency to aggression from about 1340 seconds in the intermale situation to about 550 seconds in the food competition. Second, although the rank order of the inbred strain mean values changed from the intermale to the food competition situation, the basic picture of genetic architecture of no-directional dominance variance and some additive variance was unchanged.

Perhaps a more important measure of behavior in a food competition situation is food possession. The measure reported here is the ratio of time the nonstandard mouse possessed the food to the total time that food was possessed by either mouse. Figure 4.7 illustrates food possession ratios for all 16 genetic groups. Of interest here is that the C57 × SJL hybrid, standard male was somewhat more successful in food possession than the 50% one would expect if that hybrid were precisely at the midpoint of the 16 genetic groups of the diallel in food possession ability. Even though the standard male hybrid was more successful, two inbred strains, C57 and BALB, possessed the food more when tested against the stan-

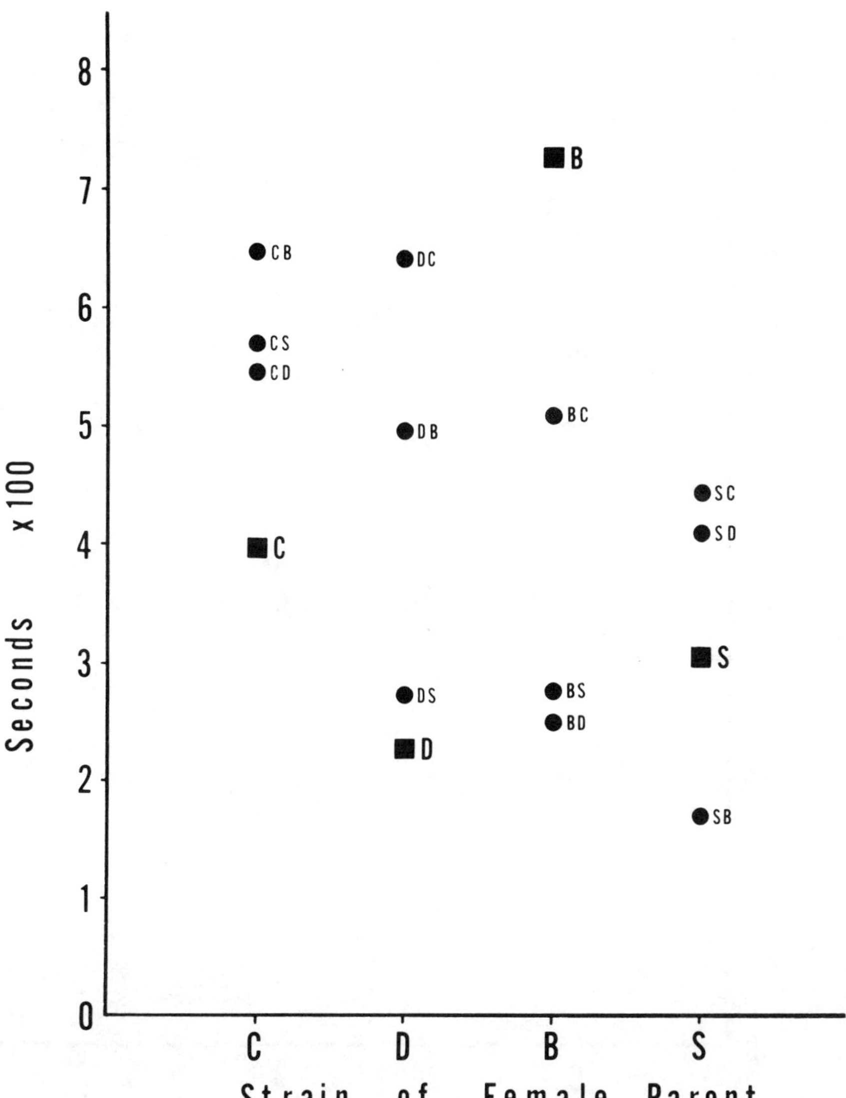

FIG. 4.6. Mean latencies to aggression in the food competition situation. Hybrid group scores are arrayed above the strain of their female parent.

dard male. Furthermore, a pattern of hybrid vigor did not emerge here as inbred parent lines often outperformed their hybrids.

Table 4.3 presents the genetic analysis on the measure of food possession. A clear reversal of previous results is apparent in this table, as general dominance is

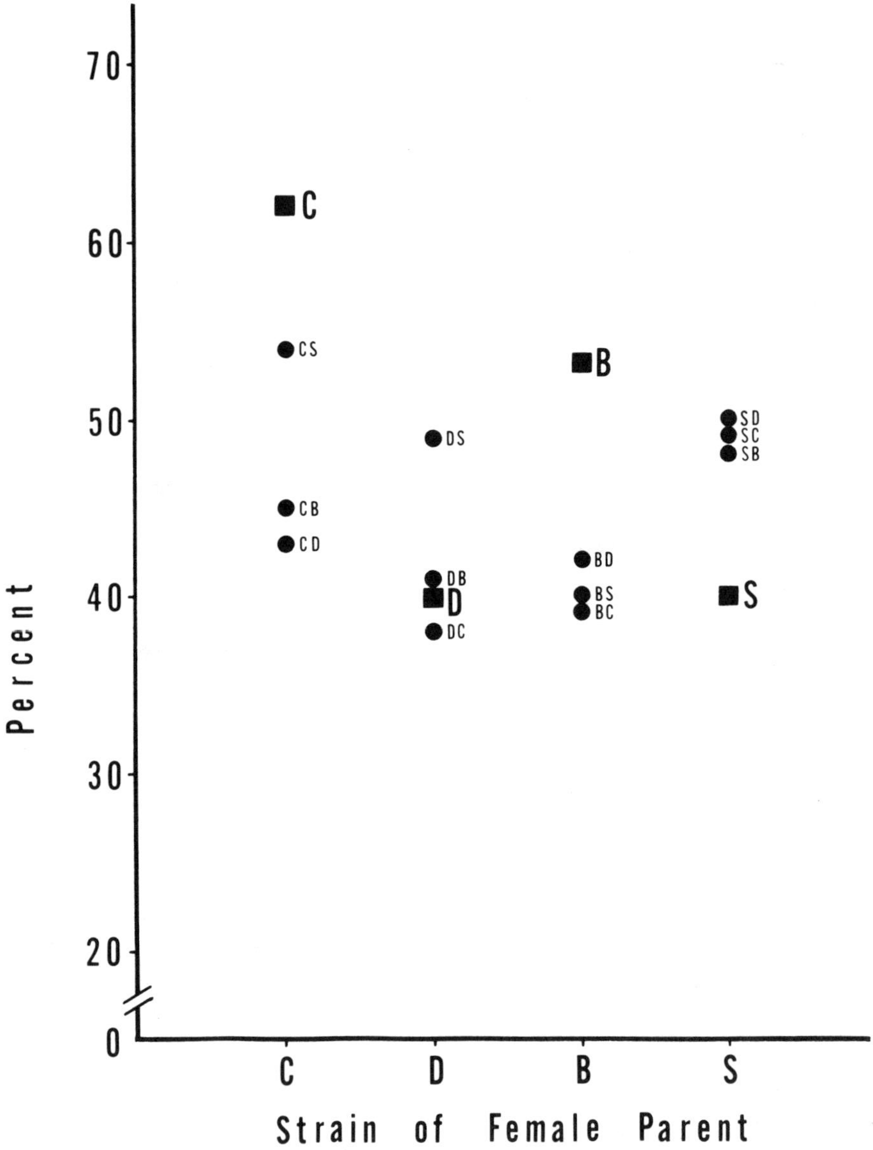

FIG. 4.7. Percentage of time the nonstandard male possessed food during food competition. Hybrid group scores are arrayed above the strain of their female parent.

TABLE 4.3
Genetic Analysis of Food Possession

Source	*MS*	*df*	*F Ratio*	*p Value*
a	.0051	3	2.52	NS
b	.0075	6	19.28	$<.05$
b_1	.0047	1	12.24	$<.05$
b_2	.0119	3	30.84	$<.01$
b_3	.0021	2	5.46	$<.10$
c	.0020	3	5.24	$<.10$
d	.0004	3		
Within				

an important contributor to variability in this behavior. More specifically, the directional dominance component (b_1) reaches significance and accounts for more of the genetic variability than does the additive component. These results, interpreted with the aid of biometrical theory, indicate that food possession is a fitness character when a mouse is food deprived and is in the presence of another deprived mouse.

Further support for this conclusion comes from the data on the measures: take-aways, attempted take-aways, and uncontested drops. All three measures show a pattern of results like that pictured in Fig. 4.8, which depict the results of take-aways. This pattern is clearly one of hybrid vigor because hybrids are taking away food much more often than are the inbred groups when all are tested against common opponents. As expected, the genetic analysis of these behaviors supports the illustration, namely large and significant b_1 effects and small and nonsignificant additive components.

The results of this study are complex. A further description of the data presented here plus an analysis of the relationships between food deprivation, food possession, and aggression appears elsewhere. However, it is clear at this point that the genetic results of behaviors measured in the food competition situations show that high levels of aggression have not been selected for, but rather that intermediate levels of aggression are advantageous. Furthermore, behaviors that directly relate to possessing food and taking it away from a competitor have undergone strong positive directional selection.

Nest Defense. The third situation I choose to study involves the responses of a female mouse with a 3-day-old litter to the intrusion of a strange male mouse. This situation, like food competition, is likely to occur in nature and provides the opportunity for a variety of behaviors.

A number of studies have shown that lactating female mammals will attack intruders, presumably to protect their offspring from harm. Much of the work on this topic has explored the hormonal basis of nest defense, in mice in particular. For example, Noirot, Goyens, and Buhot (1975) showed that the strength of nest

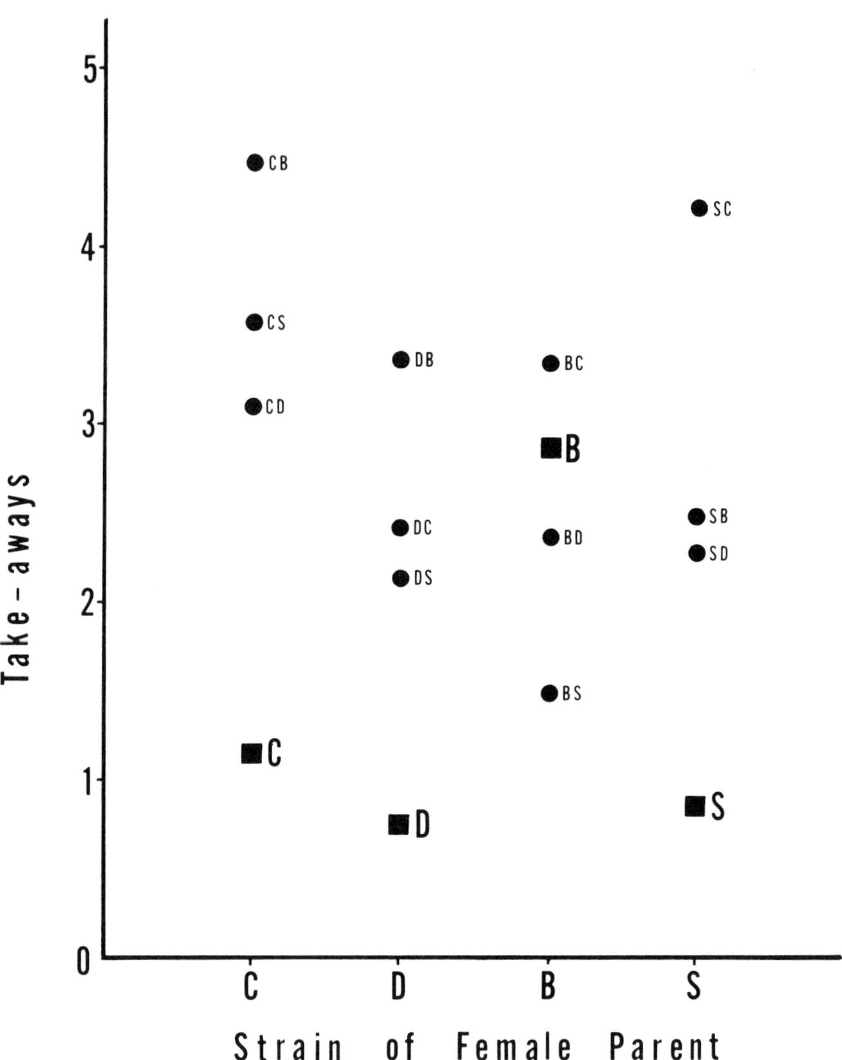

FIG. 4.8. Mean food take-aways/pair in the food competition situation. Hybrid group scores are arrayed above the strain of their female parent.

defense was inversely related to the time since pup birth. Along similar lines, Gandelman (1972) demonstrated that lactating mice would attack male and female intruders, and that a significant decrease in defense occurred after the pups were 14 days old. Nest defense would seem to be important for the survival of offspring, as Gandelman and vom Saal (1977) have shown that male mice will kill pups they find when intruding into a nest.

These studies have investigated hormonal effects on female aggression. However, the genetic contribution to nest defense has not been examined. The purpose of the present study is to examine the genetic architecture of female responses to an intruder male and examine the relationships between female behaviors and pup survival.

The mice used in this study were 214 females, about 13 for each genetic group of the diallel and an equal number of "strange male" intruders, the hybrid result of a cross between A/J females and C57BL/6J males. Between the age of 45 and 55 days of age, a male and female pair from each of the 16 genetic groups were mated and placed in standard lab cages where they remained until a litter of pups was born. At that time, the male was removed and the pups counted and returned to the nest. On the third postpartum day, a female's cage containing nest and pups was placed in a quiet room under low illumination. An intruder male was placed into the cage without disrupting the nest, and behavioral measurement begun. Each observational session lasted for 20 minutes. In all cases, pups were counted and checked for physical injury following the observation, and in half of those tested, the cage with female, litter of pups, and intruder remained undisturbed for 24 hours following observation. For the other half of the cases, all animals were removed after testing and the female's estrous stage was determined by a smear of vaginal cells. As in the previously described studies, behavioral categories were used to quantify the observation: chasing, fighting, attack, social grooming, genital sniffing, tail lashing, nosing, squeaking and, rushing. The last category was observed in females during pilot studies and was counted when a female ran toward and squeaked at an intruder male.

As in the previous two studies, the data were analyzed with the modified Hayman (1954) procedure. Table 4.4 presents the results of the genetic analyses

TABLE 4.4
Summary of Genetic Analyses of Female Behaviors in Nest Defense Situation with Intruder

Measure	*Probability Associated with Source of Variation*					
	a	b	b_1	b_2	b_3	c
Rush	.10	.01	—	.01	.01	.05
Chase	–	–	–	–	–	–
Fighting	.01	–	–	–	–	–
Attack	.01	–	–	–	–	–
Social grooming	.10	–	–	–	–	–
Genital sniffing	–	–	–	–	.10	.10
Tail lashing	.05	–	–	–	–	–
Defense posture	.05	–	–	–	–	–
Nosing	.05	.05	.05	–	–	–
Squeaking	–	–	–	–	–	–

FIG. 4.9. Behaviors that occur in nest defense. Description of behaviors is in the text.

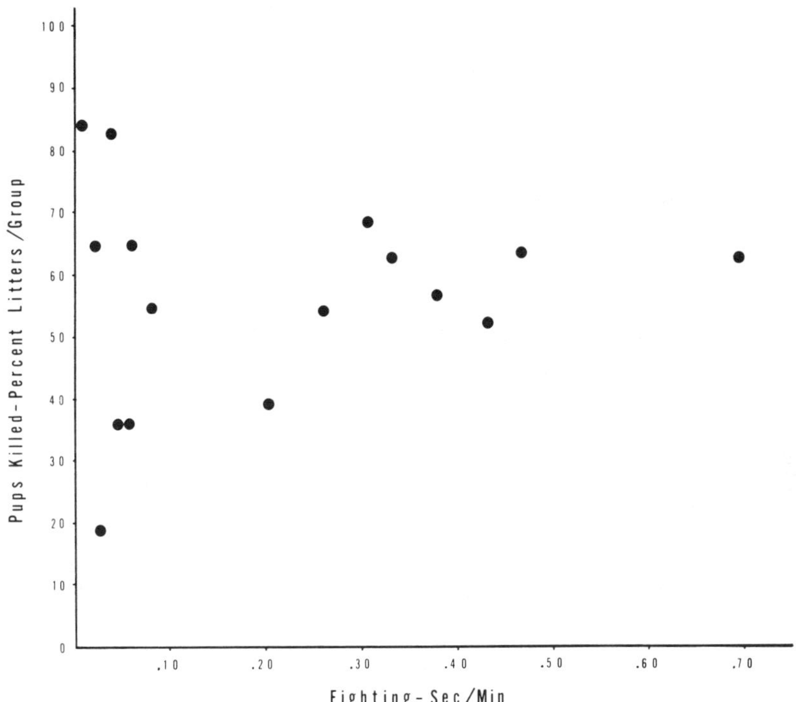

FIG. 4.10. Scatterplot of fighting and the percentage of litters per genetic group in which pups were killed.

of all behavioral categories. With the exception of nosing, variation in behaviors is primarily associated with the additive source. Interpreted through biometrical genetic theory, aggressive behaviors in this situation have not undergone directional selection and thus high levels of aggression have not provided an evolutionary advantage.

Figure 4.9 illustrates some behaviors that occurred frequently in the nest defense situation. In Part a, a female is seen investigating her nest. In the corner opposite the nest, a male intruder is wounded and exhibiting defense posture as the result of attacks by the female. In photograph b, the defending female is again examining her nest, this time, however, despite attacks by the female on the intruder male, the intruder has attacked and killed several pups. Pup killing occurred in about 50% of the observations made. In Part c, a female is seen eating the body of one of her dead pups. Pup killing seemed to occur regardless of the amount or intensity of aggression exhibited by the resident female.

Figure 4.10 illustrates the relationship between the amount of fighting by females and the litters in each genetic group in which pups were killed. A Pearson product moment correlation coefficient for these data yielded an *r*

= .05. The lack of a relationship between fighting and pup survival is consistent with and provides independent confirmation of the results of the genetic analysis.

The findings that maternal aggression against an intruder was not a fitness character and that such behavior against an intruder was ineffective in preventing infanticide are somewhat surprising. However, as Svare (this volume) and Paul, Gronek, and Politch (1980) point out, maternal aggression may not have the protective function that has been assumed. Future studies should examine the specific role of female aggression in nest defense and identify the reasons for infanticide committed by intruding males.

SUMMARY AND CONCLUSIONS

The three studies described in this chapter were designed to examine the genetic architecture and thus the Darwinian fitness of aggressive behavior in situations of varying complexity and naturalness. A positive relationship between agression and fitness had traditionally been assumed and in some cases supported (DeFries & McClearn, 1970). However, a finding common to all three studies, intermale aggression, food competition, and nest defense, was that high levels of aggression have not been under directional selection pressure. In terms of biometrical genetics, high levels of aggression are not positively related to fitness. Rather, in intermale aggression, an intermediate level of aggression is advantageous. In food competition, behaviors related to obtaining and keeping food are fit, and in nest defense, aggression is unrelated to pup survival.

These conclusions are in agreement with work presented elsewhere in this volume. Lagerspetz and Lagerspetz report a successful bidirectional selection for intermale aggression and Ebert reports the same result for interfemale aggression. Such selection results depend on the presence of additive genetic variability in their founding populations. Additive variation characterized the F_1 generations in all three of the studies I presented. My conclusions are also in substantial agreement with those of Hewitt and Broadhurst. On the basis of a number of studies they examined, they concluded that in simple encounters between dyads of mice, intermediate levels of aggression have been an advantage.

Although it is satisfying to agree with colleagues, many unanswered questions remain on the relationship between aggression and Darwinian fitness. I plan further studies on that relationship. In one line of research, the stimulus conditions under which intruder males commit infanticide will be examined. In another, I will continue to employ diallel methods to study aggression in more complex and natural social situations.

ACKNOWLEDGMENTS

I am grateful to the Department of Psychology of Miami University and to William Paterson College for support while I wrote this account of my research. I am indebted to

Karen Glovinski Rogalski, Lynn Hahn, John McGraw, and Susan Schwartz for assistance in data collection.

REFERENCES

Allee, W. C., & Ginsburg, B. E. Recent experience and aggressiveness in male mice: A study in social dominance. *Anatomical Record,* 1941, *81,* 50.

Broadhurst, P. L. The experimental approach to behavioral evolution. In J. R. Royce, & L. P. Mos (Eds.), *Theoretical advances in behavior genetics.* Germantown, Md.: Sijthoff & Noordhoff, 1979.

Broadhurst, P. L., & Jinks, J. L. What genetic architecture can tell us about the natural selection of behavioral traits. In J. H. F. van Abeelen (Ed.), *The genetics of behavior.* Amsterdam: The North-Holland Publishing Co., 1974.

Brown, R. Z. Social behavior, reproduction, and population changes in the house mouse (*Mus musculus*). *Ecological Monographs,* 1953, *23,* 217–240.

Bruell, J. H. Behavioral heterosis. In J. Hirsch (Ed.), *Behavior-genetic analysis.* New York: McGraw-Hill Book Co., 1967.

DeFries, J. C., & McClearn, G. E. Social dominance and Darwinian fitness in the laboratory mouse. *The American Naturalist,* 1970, *104,* 408–411.

Fredericson, E. The effects of food deprivation upon competitive and spontaneous combat in C57 black mice. *Journal of Psychology,* 1950, *29,* 89–100.

Fuller, J. L., & Hahn, M. E. Problems in the genetics of social behavior. *Behavior Genetics,* 1976, *6,* 391–406.

Gandelman, R. Induction of pup killing in female mice by androgenization. *Physiology and Behavior,* 1972, *9,* 101–102.

Gandelman, R., & vom Saal, F. S. Exposure to early androgen attenuates androgen-induced pup killing in male and female mice. *Behavioral Biology,* 1977, *20,* 252–260.

Hahn, M. E., & Haber, S. B. The inheritance of brain weight in male mice: A diallel analysis. *Behavior Genetics,* 1978, *8,* 251–260.

Hahn, M. E., & Haber, S. B. The inheritance of agonistic behavior in male mice: A diallel analysis. *Aggressive Behavior,* 1982, *8,* 19–38.

Hayman, B. I. The theory and analysis of diallel crosses. *Genetics,* 1954, *39,* 789–809.

Henderson, N. D. Dominance for large brains in laboratory mice. *Behavior Genetics,* 1979, *9,* 45–49.

Horn, J. M. Aggression as a component of relative fitness in four inbred strains of mice. *Behavior Genetics,* 1974, *4,* 373–381.

Lagerspetz, K. M. J. Genetic and social causes of aggressive behavior in mice. *Scandinavian Journal of Psychology,* 1961, *2,* 167–173.

Levine, L. Studies on sexual selection in mice. I. Reproductive competition between albino and black–agouti males. *American Naturalist,* 1958, *92,* 21–26.

Levine, L., Barsal, G. E., & Diakow, C. A. Interaction of aggressive and sexual behavior in male mice. *Animal Behavior,* 1965, *13,* 272–280.

Manosevitz, M. Behavioral heterosis: Food competition in mice. *Journal of Comparative and Physiological Psychology,* 1972, *79,* 46–50.

Mather, K., & Jinks, J. L. *Biometrical genetics.* Ithaca, N.Y.: Cornell University Press, 1971.

Noirot, E., Goyens, J., & Buhot, M. C. Aggressive behavior of pregnant mice toward males. *Hormones and Behavior,* 1975, *6,* 19–29.

Paul, L., Gronek, J., & Politch, J. A. Maternal aggression in mice: Protection of young is a by-product of attacks at the home site. *Aggressive Behavior,* 1980, *6,* 19–29.

Scott, J. P. Genetic differences in the social behavior of inbred strains of mice. *Journal of Heredity,* 1942, *33,* 11–15.

Scott, J. P. Differences in the social organization of mice caused by differences in social behavior (fighting in males). *Genetics,* 1943, *28,* 88–89.

Scott, J. P. An experimental test of the theory that social behavior determines social organization. *Science,* 1944, *99,* 42–43.

Wynne-Edwards, V. C. *Animal dispersion in relation to social behavior.* London: Oliver & Boyd, 1962.

5 Genes and Aggression

Kirsti M. J. Lagerspetz
Åbo Akademi

Kari Y. H. Lagerspetz
University of Turku

THE LIMITATIONS OF HUMAN BEHAVIOR GENETICS

Because the traditional methods of genetic research cannot be applied to the study of human behavior, we still know little about the inheritance of behavioral characteristics in humans. In fact, research on the inheritance of human behavioral traits will probably always be limited methodologically for reasons that, although obvious, deserve mention.

First, the main method of genetic research, matings, cannot be used experimentally. This severely hampers the development of human genetics—in the areas of both somatic and behavioral research.

Second, the other important method of genetic research, familial comparisons, is also not suitable, as such, for the study of the inheritance of behavioral traits, for several reasons. The length of the generation for the object of study is the same as that for the research worker. Hence, the researcher must either rely on historical sources to estimate the prevalence in earlier generations of the characteristic under study, or hand over to successors the task of completing the studies he or she has begun. Historical documents, moreover, seldom give information about personality characteristics, as aggressiveness, for example. Furthermore, compared with measurements of somatic characteristics, the results of measurements of behavioral characteristics are to a much greater extent dependent on the method used. The different methods for measuring aggressiveness, for instance, do not correlate highly with each other. To date no studies have been conducted in which the aggressiveness of relatives in several generations has been measured with the same, reliable aggression test.

There are studies showing that the same kind of aggressive behavior, like assault and battery, is found in several generations of the same family (Carroll, 1977). But such a result does not, in itself, imply that either the behavior or the disposition for the behavior is inherited. On the contrary, results of this type can be presented and regarded as evidence for the power of environmental influences: (1) imitation of the behavior of the parents by their children; (2) attitudes toward violence in ''subcultures''; and (3) transmission from one generation to the next of disturbed social relations within the family. For with aggressiveness, we have a large body of psychological and psychiatric knowledge about environmental factors that typically result in children growing up to become aggressive personalities (a summary of these is given by Johnson, 1972, pp. 124–126). Thus, if we find family resemblance in aggressiveness, we are not entitled to regard it as a proof of heredity.

Because learning plays a primary role in the development of human behavior, an estimation of the amount of hereditary determination of such behavior is much more difficult and uncertain than a corresponding estimation in animal behavior or in the development of somatic characteristics, whether in animals or humans. Further, the fact that the cultural and social environments for different groups of humans are different, but quite uniform within the groups, causes a combination of genetic and learning effects that is likely to distort the results of population genetic research. Although presently there is a growing awareness of these pitfalls of behavior-genetic research, we still lack full agreement about the elements in this area, as evidenced by the recent debate on the heredity of intelligence (Eysenck & Kamin, 1981).

In regard to aggressiveness, virtually nothing is known about its heredity in humans, after attempts to localize the genes of aggressiveness in the Y chromosome seem to have failed. However, as Scott (1981) points out, emotional differences in humans as well as in other mammals may be more dependent on heredity than intellectual ones. Hence, one would also expect to find in humans a hereditary variation of the disposition for aggressiveness.

Admittedly, there have been sophisticated attempts to evade the restrictions of human behavior genetics, such as, for example, the application of biometrical genetics to human behavior (Fulker, 1974). In such research, twin studies and studies of adopted children can be helpful tools (see for instance Kaplan, 1976). These efforts do not compensate, however, for the fact that rigorous research techniques cannot be used with humans.

Because human behavior genetics is stymied by so many methodological limitations, interest has turned to using other mammals as experimental objects. This places a double burden on the research in animal behavior genetics. Attending to its responsibilities as a branch of science in its own right, it must also answer the challenge from genetics and from psychology to offer sensible and detailed models to be used in the generalizations from animal experiments to a general theory of behavior.

Typically, the geneticists who study hereditary effects, and the ethologists and psychologists who study social and other environmental effects, have been different people. The result has been an insufficient integration of these two approaches in the scientific explanation of the origin and in the development of behavior. Although the hereditary and environmental aspects have been integrated in some excellent articles (for instance Manning, 1976; Scott, 1977, 1981), the discussion on this subject has, in the sociobiological approach, remained at a very general and sometimes speculative level.

In the sociobiology debate, behavior genetics is in a key position on the borderline between biology and social science. After all, genes cannot influence social behavior in any other way than through individuals.

SELECTIVE BREEDING

One of the most important methods in animal behavior genetics is selective breeding. If selective breeding for a characteristic is successful, it is in itself proof that hereditary factors play a role in the interindividual variation of that characteristic. The aim of selective breeding is to obtain lines that differ from each other only with respect to the characteristic for which the selection is made, and in no other respect.

For instance, strains that are selectively bred for high and low aggressiveness will show random variation in those characteristics inherited through genes that are not closely linked with the genes for aggressiveness. In selective breeding, inbreeding should be avoided because it will lead to the development of sublines that differ from each other in other characteristics as well, not only in those for which the selection has been made.

Selectively bred strains offer an opportunity to study correlational relationships between the trait selected for and other behavioral or physiological properties. Such study can yield information about the mechanisms underlying the development of the trait.

Using selectively bred strains in psychological research also offers a unique opportunity for studying the effects of environment on individuals of a known hereditary disposition. For instance, if the strain is selectively bred for aggressiveness, the offspring of the strain can be predicted to become aggressive, as long as no special interventions are made. By studying the effects, for example, of early environmental variables on such offspring, information can be obtained about the possibilities and the limits of environmental influences on aggressiveness.

THE MEASUREMENT OF AGGRESSION IN MICE

The animal's level of aggressiveness in our research has been tested in individual encounters with so-called standard opponents (Lagerspetz, 1964). These are group-caged, nonaggressive males that have been found in pretests to never have attacked another male. The behavior of the experimental mouse is rated according to a 7-point scale on which 1 indicates the lowest and 7 the highest degree of aggression (Lagerspetz, 1964). The properties of the scale were investigated and the scale steps were found to be sufficiently equal to allow application of parametric statistical methods.

In addition to the rating on the scale, the aggression of the animals has also been indicated by numbers of bites, bites hard enough to draw blood, and bouts of tail rattling per minute. These separate behavior units are seen by some research workers (van Oortmerssen & Bakker, 1981) as more unambiguous indicators of aggression.

When we speak of the aggressiveness level of the animals, we refer to the average aggression scores they have obtained in at least two, but often in several tests with standard opponents, performed in a testing cage without shavings.

TA and TNA Strains

There is a substantial body of evidence from studies dealing with mammalian species such as mice, rats, and dogs, that show that a hereditary variation underlies the disposition for aggressiveness. These studies have been reviewed elsewhere (Lagerspetz & Lagerspetz, 1974). The most widely studied species is the mouse. Most data have been obtained by comparing results achieved with strains, often inbred, that have been developed for other purposes. However, some experiments with selective breeding for high and low aggressiveness have also been conducted (Ebert & Hyde, 1975; Lagerspetz, 1964; van Oortmerssen & Bakker, 1981).

The mouse strains TA and TNA, selectively bred for aggressiveness and nonaggressiveness, respectively, have been maintained in Turku, Finland, since the start of their breeding in 1959. In addition, the intermediate parental strain

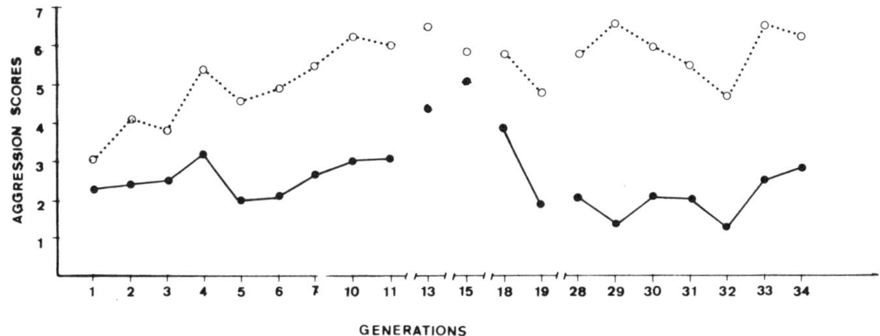

FIG. 5.1. Mean aggression scores of the males in the parental and the successive selection generations of the two strains. Open circles = TA strain; black dots = TNA strain.

has also been maintained. Research performed with these strains has been reported previously (for instance Lagerspetz, 1961, 1964, 1969, 1979; Lagerspetz & Lagerspetz, 1971, 1974, 1975), and some new results are reported here.

Figure 5.1 shows the mean aggression scores of the TA and TNA strains during successive generations. Already, in the second generation of selection, mean scores differed significantly, a difference that has persisted ever since, except in the case of generation S_{15}. Generations 12 through 15 of the TNA strain, but not of the TA strain, were affected by an infectious disease (the strains were kept in separate rooms). Selective breeding for nonaggressiveness in the TNA mice could not be carried out during this period, the main objective being to keep the strain alive. This is reflected in the high aggression scores of generation S_{15} in the TNA strain.

Female Aggressiveness

The selection for matings in TA and TNA strains has been made only on the basis of the male aggression scores, because the females failed to display aggressive behavior (Lagerspetz, 1964). The females of the aggressive TA strain do, however, carry genes determining a disposition for aggressiveness, although their effect is manifested only in the presence of androgen. Lagerspetz and Lagerspetz (1974) treated the females of both strains with testosterone propionate neonatally and in adulthood. As adults, the TA females were aggressive, but the TNA females were not. Because the females do not have a Y chromosome, the genes determining aggression cannot be located on that chromosome. The literature on this subject has been somewhat conflicting, and evidence has been presented that suggests that in some strains the genes that influence aggressiveness might be situated in the Y chromosome (Maxson, 1981).

Female mice of some strains can be aggressive without testosterone treatment, and this aggressiveness has a hereditary basis, as demonstrated by Ebert and Hyde (1975). These authors carried out a study in which a wild mouse population was selectively bred for aggressiveness. Selection was based only on the aggression scores of the females. Aggressiveness of the males did not follow the selection (Hyde & Ebert, 1976). In the study by van Oortmerssen and Bakker (1981), female aggressiveness was also not affected by a selection exerted on the males.

To see whether the females of the TA and TNA strains might exhibit some aggressiveness after 35 generations of selection under normal conditions and without testosterone treatment, we tested the females for aggressiveness in 1981. The females of neither strain displayed any biting or tail rattling in the presence of either a nonestrous female or a male standard opponent. Experiments are in progress to determine whether TA females show maternal or predatory aggression.

The female mice in the study by Hyde and Sawyer (1979) showed a strain difference between high and low lines for maternal, but not for predatory aggression. It is also worth mentioning that in S_6, females of the TA and TNA strains showed no difference in dominance behavior over food (Lagerspetz, 1964, pp. 95–96).

Crossbreeding of TA and TNA Strains

With the establishment of the TA and TNA strains by selective breeding it was clearly demonstrated that genes exist in male mice that were necessary for the appearance of aggressive behavior. In 1977–1979, we carried out a crossbreeding experiment with a partial replication—starting with S_{28} and S_{30} as parental generations. The results of these experiments have been analyzed with respect to the heritability of aggressiveness in male mice of the strains studied and the minimum number of genetic loci involved. The biometrical genetic analysis also yielded information about the general applicability of the additive-dominance model of this particular case.

Some words of caution are in order here. We have shown earlier that a few encounters with a more aggressive opponent reduces the overt aggressive behavior of the male mouse previously rated as aggressive to a minimal level. When reared in groups, neither TA nor TNA mice behave aggressively in test situations. Gene-based aggression becomes apparent only after social isolation of from 1 to 6 weeks (Lagerspetz & Lagerspetz, 1971, Table 5.1). This implies that the effects of environmental social influences can mask such hereditary social behavior as aggression. Reasoning from observed behavior to its genetic basis presupposes, therefore, either an unvarying, well-defined environment or an environment whose variations can be proven to be truly random. In experiments, it is easier to realize the former.

Figure 5.2 shows the distributions of the mean aggression scores for the populations of male mice in the first crossbreeding experiment; Fig. 5.3 shows the corresponding distributions for the partial replication.

Genetics describes matings and their outcome. Reasoning from the qualities of the offspring to the qualities of the genes of the parents must be iterative. There are many possible models of inheritance. The demonstrated applicability of a model lends support to the reasoning from effects to causes.

The model of inheritance we used was the additive-dominance model. It poses certain criteria for inheritance and also for the scales used in the measurement of the effects seen in the parents and their offspring. These tests of the expected relationships have been termed "scaling tests" by Mather (1949; Mather & Jinks, 1977). They have also been discussed by Bruell (1962) and by Whitney, McLearn, and DeFries (1970).

We performed three scaling tests of Mather (1949) on the raw score values of aggression tests, as well as on the square root and logarithmic transformations of these values. The raw score values satisfied all three equations of Mather, whereas the square root and logarithmic transformations failed to satisfy the third

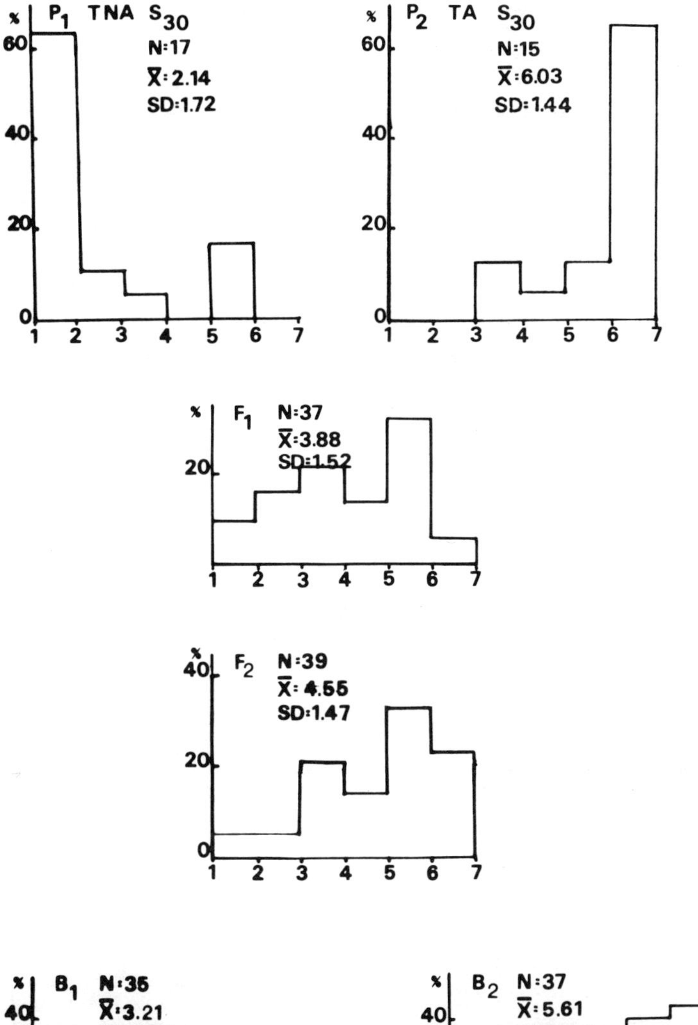

FIG. 5.2. Distributions of the mean aggression scores of the males in the parental generations (TNA and TA), in the crossbred generations F_1 and F_2, and in the back crosses B_1 and B_2. 1 = lowest, and 7 = highest aggression score.

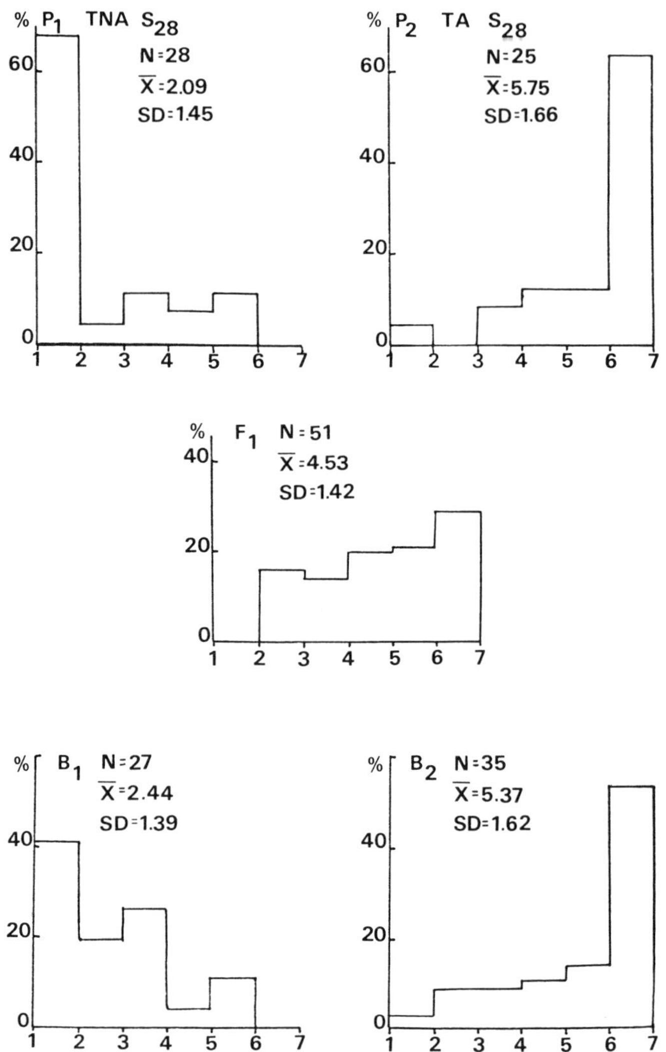

FIG. 5.3. Distribution of the mean aggression scores of the males in the parental generations (TNA and TA), in the crossbred generation F_1, and in the back crosses B_1 and B_2. 1 = lowest, and 7 = highest aggression score.

equation. In addition, the variances of the raw score values did not differ significantly in the nonsegregating populations (P_1, P_2, and F_1), which corroborated their suitability for further calculations.

At the suggestion of Dr. John K. Hewitt we also performed the joint scaling test (Hewitt, 1981; Mather & Jinks, 1977) on our data from crossbreeding. The unweighted least squares solution calculated from the means of the raw scores of the six generations gave, for the chi-square of the goodness of the fit of the model, a value of .447 ($df = 3$). This shows that the additive-dominance model was applicable to our material. The estimates of the model parameters from the unweighted solution were: $\hat{m} = 4.256$, $[\hat{d}] = 2.036$, $[\hat{h}] = .034$.

From these results we tried first to estimate the heritability of aggressiveness by using the formula of Whitney et al. (1970). Environmental variance (V_E) was estimated as the mean of the variances of the nonsegregating generations; the summated additive effect (a) was estimated either from parental or from backcross means. The former estimation gave a heritability value of .44, the latter a value of .54. The corresponding heritability estimates from the replication were .42 and .65, respectively. These values are, apparently, overestimates. From data on our selective breeding of the TA and TNA strains, McClearn & DeFries (1973) had estimated the heritability to be .36.

Both the estimation of the minimum number of loci involved and the estimation of heritability according to the procedures suggested by Mather and Jinks (1977) and Hewitt (1981) are based on the variances of all the usual six families in crossbreeding experiments. In our experiment, the variance of F_2 was smaller than the variances of the nonsegregating populations and hence smaller than V_E. This is not unusual in experiments in behavior genetics. It may result either from sampling errors or scaling problems, as pointed out by Whitney et al. (1970); but it may also reflect clear dominance and the small number of loci affecting the characteristic studied (Eriksson, 1971). In our particular case the small variance of F_2 rendered impossible the estimation of either heritability—by the methods selected—or the minimum number of loci involved.

Activity and Aggression

A positive correlation (.76) was found in generation S_3 between aggressiveness and revolving drum activity (Lagerspetz, 1964, pp. 83–85), as well as between aggressiveness and open-field activity (.46) (Lagerspetz, 1964, p. 78). In generation S_3 the two strains also differed significantly in the extent of ambulation in the open field, the animals of the TA strain being the more active.

In 1982, a replication experiment to determine the difference in activity levels between the two strains was carried out in generation S_{35}. The seven males from the TA strain that had scored the highest (7) on the aggressiveness scale in tests with standard opponents, and the seven males from the TNA strain that had scored the lowest (1) were studied. Their activity was tested with an Animex activity meter, Type S, in which recordings are made electromagnetically. (For a description of this apparatus see Svensson & Thieme, 1969.) The sensitivity was set at 19μA. The animals were 5 months old and had lived in isolation since weaning. The tests were performed in daylight between noon and 4:00 P.M. One test trial lasted 10 minutes. The mean Animex values were 577.00 (SD = 124.89) for the TNA and 1042.71 (SD = 74.43) for the TA animals. The difference was significant at the .01 level (two-tailed *t*-test, $t = 3.10$, $df = 12$). This result substantiated our earlier observation of a positive relationship between aggressiveness and activity.

It has been shown, however, that different devices for measuring activity do not always measure the same behavioral trait. For instance, van Abeelen's (1975) two strains, selectively bred for high and low open-field activity, did not differ with respect to activity in the home cage. De Fries, Wilson, and McClearn (1970) reported that their high and low lines, also bred selectively for open-field activity, differed on some measures of exploratory activity (arena, crossing a barrier, and hole-in-a-wall tests), but not in activity in a Y maze, climbing a staircase, the emergence test, or in two wheel-running tests (De Fries et al. 1970, p. 209). In all tests, however, the animals of the high line tended to score higher than the animals of the low line.

To determine whether the greater activity of the aggressive strain pertains to more exploratory behavior as well, we designed an "enriched environment" test. The apparatus consisted of a plastic case, 55 × 31 × 43 cm in size, which contained play or exercise devices: a running wheel, 18 cm in diameter and 10 cm in breadth, made of steel wire grid with a 1-cm space between the wire strides; a climbing staircase with five stairs hanging from a perch; five rings 4 cm in diameter, linked together into a chain that hung from a perch to the ground; and a climbing tree, 20 cm high, with eight branches; the two perches hung 20 cm, and a third hung 31 cm above the field. A recording was made each time an animal climbed up on a device and each time it turned the wheel. The animals had free access to all the devices. Each animal was tested separately for 10 minutes.

The eight males from the aggressive and eight from the nonaggressive strains that had the highest and lowest scores, respectively, were tested again. At the time of testing the animals were 5½ months old. The testing conditions were the same as for the Animex activity tests.

In this test, the TA animals were again the more active. Their mean score for all activities counted together, 25.52 (SD = 21.52), differed significantly ($p < .001$, $t = 5.12$, $df = 14$) from that of the TNA animals, 9.63 (SD = 5.42). The running wheel was the most popular of the devices available. The nonaggressive mice never climbed up on the perches.

The difference in the activity level between the strains is thus also shown in more flexible explorative activity of the TA animals. This difference might be associated with the more frequent defecation in open-field tests by the nonaggressive mice (Lagerspetz, 1964), which can be taken as a sign of fearfulness.

CONCLUSION

The present results substantiate the observation that, at least in mice, there prevails a hereditarily determined variation in aggressiveness. The genes for aggressiveness are autosomal but their effects are manifested only in the presence of testosterone. These genes show a Mendelian segregation.

In several types of experiments, the aggressive animals were more active than the nonaggressive ones. It has previously been observed that aggressive mice are less fearful, learn a maze better, have a greater water intake (Lagerspetz, 1964), and have higher epinephrine content in the adrenals and a lower serotonin content in the forebrain (Lagerspetz, Tirri, & Lagerspetz, 1968). Aggressive behavior is known to be associated, moreover, with physiological signs of high arousal and with intense orthosympathetic stimulation. As noted previously (Lagerspetz, 1964), the higher activity level of the aggressives, together with the aforementioned correlates of aggressiveness, is consistent with the view that aggressiveness is associated with a general tendency to a high sympathetic tone.

The genetic effects of aggressiveness are demonstrable only when the animals are caged individually. Research on TA and TNA strains has demonstrated that social experiences can alter their level of aggressiveness (Lagerspetz, 1969, 1979; Lagerspetz & Sandnabba, 1982). It might be concluded, then, that the phenotypic variation in aggressiveness that we see in nature often does not correspond to the underlying genetic variation.

We stated at the beginning of this chapter that animal experiments can be used to generate ideas and to spur thinking in research on the inheritance of behavioral and personality characteristics in humans. Can we then make any generalizations about aggressiveness on the basis of the results presented here? We venture to say a guarded yes.

Overt aggressive behavior is, socially and culturally, quite different in humans from what it is in other mammals. In the great majority of societies, physical aggression is not considered "normal" under most circumstances. To be overtly violent a human being must have a personality structure and a value system that tolerate violent behavior. From social, clinical, and developmental psychology we know a good deal about the kinds of social circumstances likely to produce a violent or aggressive personality. Any explanation of aggressiveness in humans must take into account all attendant social variables.

The capacity to learn plays a substantially greater role in the development of all human behavior than it does in that of other animals. If social learning—as has been shown—can reduce or enhance aggressiveness in mice, how much greater is not the effect of such learning on the development of aggressiveness in humans?

For the sake of speculation, it seems possible that the human equivalent of the hereditary distribution of aggressiveness, described here, might be the distribution of a tendency to emotional reactivity, perhaps to high versus low orthosympathetic tone. The differences among people in this respect are not likely to appear as differences in overtly aggressive behavior but rather, may be manifested in other ways, perhaps as a background for so-called temperamental differences.

ACKNOWLEDGMENTS

The authors are obliged to Béatrice Kvist, *licentiate of philosophy,* for assistance in the experiments. The research was supported by the Council of Social Sciences, Academy of Finland.

REFERENCES

Bruell, J. H. Dominance and segregation in the inheritance of quantitative behavior in mice. In E. L. Bliss (Ed.), *Roots of behavior.* New York: Harper & Brothers, 1962.

Carroll, J. C. The intergenerational transmission of family violence: The long-term effects of aggressive behavior. *Aggressive Behavior,* 1977, *3,* 289–299.

De Fries, J. C., Wilson, J. R., & McClearn, G. E. Open-field behavior in mice: Selection response and situational generality. *Behavior Genetics,* 1970, *1,* 195–211.

Ebert, P. D., & Hyde, J. S. Selection for agonistic behavior in wild female *Mus musculus. Behavior Genetics,* 1975, *6,* 291–304.

Eriksson, K. Inheritance of behaviour towards alcohol in normal and motivated choice situations in mice. *Annales Zoologici Fennici,* 1971, *8,* 400–405.

Eysenck, H. J., & Kamin, L. *Intelligence: The battle for the mind.* London: Pan Books, 1981.

Fulker, D. W. Applications of biometrical genetics to human behaviour. In J. H. F. van Abeelen (Ed.), *The genetics of behaviour.* Amsterdam: Elsevier North Holland, 1974.

Hewitt, J. K. *The design and analysis of crossbreeding studies in animal behavior genetics.* Eleventh Annual Meeting of the Behavior Genetics Association, June 18th, 1981, Purchase, N.Y. (Mimeographed).

Hyde, J. S., & Ebert, P. D. Correlated response in selection for aggressiveness in female mice. I. Male aggressiveness. *Behavior Genetics,* 1976, *6,* 421–427.

Hyde, J. S., & Sawyer, T. F. Correlated characters in selection for aggressiveness in female mice. II. Maternal aggressiveness. *Behavior Genetics,* 1979, *9,* 571–577.

Johnson, R. N. *Aggression in man and animals.* Philadelphia: Saunders, 1972.

Kaplan, A. R. (Ed.), *Human behavior genetics.* Springfield, Ill.: Charles C Thomas, 1976.

Lagerspetz, K. M. J. Genetic and social causes of aggressive behaviour in mice. *Scandinavian Journal of Psychology,* 1961, *2,* 167–73.

Lagerspetz, K. M. J. Studies on the aggressive behaviour in mice. *Annales Academiae Scientiarum Fenniae,* 1964, Series B, *131,* 1–131.

Lagerspetz, K. M. J. Aggression and aggressiveness in laboratory mice. In S. Garattini & E. B. Sigg (Eds.), *Aggressive behavior: Proceedings of the Symposium on the Biology of Aggressive Behavior, Milan.* Amsterdam: Excerpta Medica, 1969.

Lagerspetz, K. M. J. Modification of aggressiveness in mice. In S. Feshbach & A. Frączek (Eds.), *Aggression and behavior change: Biological and social processes.* New York: Praeger Publishers, 1979.

Lagerspetz, K. M. J., & Lagerspetz, K. Y. H. Changes in the level of aggressiveness of mice as results of isolation, learning, and selective breeding. *Scandinavian Journal of Psychology,* 1971, *12,* 241–48.

Lagerspetz, K. M. J., & Lagerspetz, K. Y. H. Genetic determination of aggressive behavior. In J. H. F. van Abeelen (Ed.), *Behavioural genetics.* Amsterdam: North Holland, 1974.

Lagerspetz, K. M. J., & Lagerspetz, K. Y. H. The expression of the genes of aggressiveness in mice: The effect of androgen on aggression and sexual behaviour in females. *Aggressive Behavior,* 1975, *1,* 291–96.

Lagerspetz, K. M. J., & Sandnabba, K. The decline of aggressiveness in male mice during group caging as determined by punishment delivered by the cage mates. *Aggressive Behavior*, 1982, *8*, 319–334.

Lagerspetz, K. Y. H., Tirri, R., & Lagerspetz, K. M. J. Neurochemical and endocrinological studies of mice selectively bred for aggressiveness. *Scandinavian Journal of Psychology*, 1968, *9*, 157–160.

Manning, A. The place of genetics in the study of behavior. In P. P. G. Bateson & R. A. Hinde (Eds.), *Growing points in ethology*. Cambridge, Eng.: Cambridge University Press, 1976.

Mather, K. *Biometrical genetics: The study of continuous variation*. London: Methuen, 1949.

Mather, K., & Jinks, J. L. *Introduction to biometrical genetics*. London: Chapman and Hall, 1977.

Maxson, S. C. The genetics of aggression in vertebrates. In P. F. Brain, & D. Benton (Eds.), *The biology of aggression*. The Netherlands: Sijthoff/Noordhoff, 1981.

McClearn, G. E., & DeFries, J. C. *Introduction to behavioral genetics*. San Francisco: Freeman, 1973.

Scott, J. P. Social genetics. *Behavior Genetics*, 1977, *7*, 327–346.

Scott, J. P. The evolution of function in agonistic behavior. In P. F. Brain & D. Benton (Eds.), *Multidisciplinary approaches to aggression research*. Amsterdam: Elsevier/North-Holland Biomedical Press, 1981.

Svensson, T. W., & Thieme, G. An investigation of a new instrument to measure motor activity of small animals. *Psychopharmacologia*, 1969, *14*, 157–163.

van Abeelen, J. H. F. Genetic analysis of behavioural responses to novelty in mice. *Nature*, 1975, *254*, 239–241.

van Oortmerssen, G. A., & Bakker, T. C. M. Artificial selection for short and long attack latencies in wild *Mus musculus domesticus*. *Behavior Genetics*, 1981, *11*, 115–126.

Whitney, G., McClearn, G. E., & DeFries, J. C. Heritability of alcohol preference in laboratory mice and rats. *Journal of Heredity*, 1970, *61*, 165–169.

6 Selection for Aggression in a Natural Population

Patricia D. Ebert
Niagara University

Until recently, virtually all research on mouse aggression has involved studies of intermale aggression based on domesticated heterogenous lines and inbred strains of mice. Within the past 10 years, however, other kinds of aggression in the mouse, such as maternal (Gandelman, 1972; Hahn, this volume; Svare, 1979, this volume) and predatory (Butler, 1973), have received attention. Another kind of aggression, interfemale aggression, has also been identified (Ebert, 1972, 1976) and has been the subject of behavior-genetic analysis using artificial selection (Ebert, 1975; Ebert & Hyde, 1976; Hyde & Sawyer, 1980).

Interfemale aggression was first discovered in wild-trapped mice housed at Bowling Green State University. There are two main advantages for the behavior geneticist in using subjects coming from such natural populations (Bruell, 1970). First, one would expect to find even greater genetic variability in wild populations than in stocks of mice that have been subjected to the pressures of domestication over hundreds of generations. Second, assumptions concerning the adaptivity of a particular behavior can be made with greater confidence, because it is assumed that subjects from wild populations would be more representative of the natural selection processes experienced in the evolutionary history of the species.

The preceding three chapters contain several excellent examples of how behavior-genetics methodology can be used to study aggression in the mouse. The authors of these chapters seem to be in general agreement concerning several basic aspects of mouse aggression: (1) the evolution of the species *Mus musculus* has favored the maintenance of genes involved in the expression of at least moderate levels of aggression; and (2) a considerable amount of genetic variability exists among the various inbred strains of mice and among individuals of heterogeneous populations. Aggression, therefore, must serve some positive or adaptive function for the species under some, but not all conditions (Hahn, this volume; Hewitt & Broadhurst, this volume; Lagerspetz & Lagerspetz, this volume).

The research on mouse aggression has also shown that aggressive behaviors are influenced by numerous environmental and physiological factors. This rather common finding is not exclusive to research on mice and has led researchers to question whether aggression is a unitary behavioral trait. An alternative conceptualization of aggression is that it describes behaviors that are similar in appearance, especially to the casual observer, but actually are discrete traits, each independently controlled by its own genetic and neural mechanisms. Kenneth Moyer (1976), a strong proponent of this latter view, has attempted to provide a comprehensive taxonomy of kinds of aggression. He identifies predatory, intermale, fear-induced, maternal, irritable, and sex-related aggression in this taxonomy.

The present chapter begins with an examination of the differences in aggression between wild and domestic mice, including the discovery of interfemale aggression in wild mice. Then, an artificial selection study for interfemale aggression is described, as is auxillary research using the selected lines. Included in this research are studies on intermale, maternal, and predatory aggression. Finally, the relationships among different kinds of mouse aggression and the adaptivity of aggression for the species are discussed.

AGGRESSION IN WILD MICE

Wild Mice as Laboratory Subjects

In the fall of 1970, J. P. Scott, who was then my graduate advisor, suggested that by observing various kinds of animal behavior, we first year students would be better able to clarify our own areas of research interest. Consequently, Terry Pettijohn, Pat Legget, and I began trapping small animals in the Bowling Green, Ohio area and bringing them back into the laboratory for observations. Wild *Mus musculus*, the same species of mouse found domesticated in the laboratory, were the easiest animals to trap and would breed readily in captivity. Thus, a colony of laboratory-bred wild mice was established.

Although wild-trapped mice and their descendants fare well in captivity, their behavior is very different from that of domestic lines and strains. Specifically, wild mice engage in much more running, jumping, and biting-when-handled behavior, as first noted by Dawson (1932) and later confirmed by observations of our Bowling Green colony and by other researchers working with wild mice in different parts of the United States during the 1970s. For example, James Connor and Roy Smith have separately published several studies involving various lines of wild mice that are all descendants of 16 breeding pairs trapped in a Philadelphia pasta factory. Connor (1975) used latency to recapture as one of his tests to differentiate wild from domestic mice and to measure the effects of inbreeding. Smith (1972) compared wilds to inbreds on a variety of standard laboratory tasks and found that only the wild mice were likely to display jumping in an open field. Plomin and Manosevitz (1974), using mice trapped in Texas and Colorado, also report much jumping in the open-field test.

The behavior of the wild mice does not seem to be easily modified by daily handling of the mouse pups from birth. In an unpublished study on the development of wild mice, Terry Pettijohn and I found that at 12 or 13 days of age the wild mice became extremely difficult to handle as they would bite the hand or forceps that held them and suddenly jump away. At 17 days of age, daily handling of the mouse pups was discontinued because they were biting the handlers enough to draw blood.

Comparing Wild and Domestic Mice for Aggressiveness

Because the behavior of the wild mice was so different from that of domestic mice, I decided to compare them in a fairly typical laboratory test of intraspecific aggression (Ebert, 1972, 1976). Casual observation had shown that both wild males and wild females would readily engage in fighting behavior, and it was my hypothesis that wild mice would be more likely to fight than domestic mice even when tested under conditions commonly used to elicit intermale aggression in domestic mice.

Both males and females of second- and third-generation wild mice and C57BL/6 and BALB/c inbred mice were tested. In order to maximize the probability of attack occurring within a short period of time, and that an attack be instigated by just one of the mice, I used the technique of pairing a mouse that had been isolated for 30 days with a mouse that had been housed with same-sex littermates for the same period of time. Table 6.1 shows the number of mice attacking on 2 consecutive days of testing. The hypothesis that wild mice are more aggressive than domestic was confirmed. Wild males fought more than the inbred males and the wild females; wild females fought more than inbred females.

The finding that wild males are more aggressive than inbred males has been confirmed by James Connor (1975), who obtained similar results using a slightly different testing procedure. However, the discovery of fighting in 25% of the female mice was more of a surprise because the existing research on domestic mice at that time generally indicated that females simply did not fight (Scott, 1966). Having discovered a supposedly nonexistent behavior, I wanted to determine whether this interfemale aggression was influenced by the same genetic mechanisms as intermale aggression.

TABLE 6.1
Number of Pairs of Mice that Actually Fought*

Genotype	*Males* Day 1	*Males* Day 2	*Females* Day 1	*Females* Day 2
Wild	15	19	5	5
BALB/c	7	9	0	0
C57BL/6	1	2	0	0

*Results are from 20 paired encounters.
Note: From "Agonistic Behavior in Wild and Inbred *Mus musculus*" by P. D. Ebert, *Behavioral Biology*, 1976, *18*,291-294. Copyright 1976 by Academic Press, Inc. Reprinted by permission.

SELECTION FOR INTERFEMALE AGGRESSION

The artificial selection study is a proven method for studying the inheritance of a behavioral trait (e.g., DeFries & Hegmann, 1970). Consequently, Janet Hyde and I designed a program of artificial selection for interfemale aggression and decided to attempt selection for four generations in order to determine whether or not there was a measurable genetic basis for this trait (Ebert, 1975; Ebert & Hyde, 1976). It seemed reasonable to assume that selection would be successful, as the influence of genetics on intermale aggression had been so well established (Scott, 1966). Not only were inbred strains known to differ with respect to this behavior, but Kirsti Lagerspetz (1964; Lagerspetz & Lagerspetz, this volume) had successfully selected aggressive and nonaggressive lines of male albino mice.

The use of a wild population as a foundation for a selection program has much merit because the large amount of genetic variability found in wild mouse populations (Bruell, 1970) would mean a great capacity for response to the pressures of artificial selection. Previous selection studies on mice had used either randombred domestic lines or lines derived from crosses of two or more inbred strains of mice as their foundation stock (DeFries & Hegmann, 1970; Lagerspetz, 1964).

Subjects

In order to obtain a foundation stock for the selection program on interfemale aggression, I trapped a second group of wild *Mus musculus* during September, October, and November of 1972. Trapping was done in two different rural locations near Bowling Green, Ohio. These two locations were far enough apart to ensure sampling from at least two different demes and so to increase the genetic variability of the foundation population. Offspring of some of the wild-trapped mice, usually those of females who were pregnant when trapped, were also included as part of the foundation stock. Of the 30 breeding pairs of mice constituting the foundation population, 14 of the females and 23 of the males were wild trapped; 16 of the females and 7 of the males were born in the laboratory. The 23 mice born in the laboratory represented eight different litters. It is interesting to note that females were more difficult to trap than males. Plomin and Manosevitz (1974) also reported trapping fewer wild females than males.

Genetic Design

Figure 6.1 shows the schematic of the selection design. The Parental Generation consisted of the 73 female offspring born to the foundation population of wild mice. The 30 breeding pairs in the foundation population produced 73 female offspring of wild mice. These 73 mice were all tested for agonistic behavior and, of these, 60 were chosen to become the mothers of the First Selected Generation (S1). Mice that scored high in aggression were assigned to either replicate 1 or 2 of the high lines; that is, to H1 or H2. Mice that scored low in aggression were assigned to either replicate 1 or 2 of the low lines (L1 or L2). Twenty of the remaining mice were assigned to control lines (C1 or C2). Only one female per litter was assigned to a particular line, in order to maintain as much within-line genetic variability as possible. These females were then randomly mated to male offspring of the foundation population with the restriction that no sib matings be made.

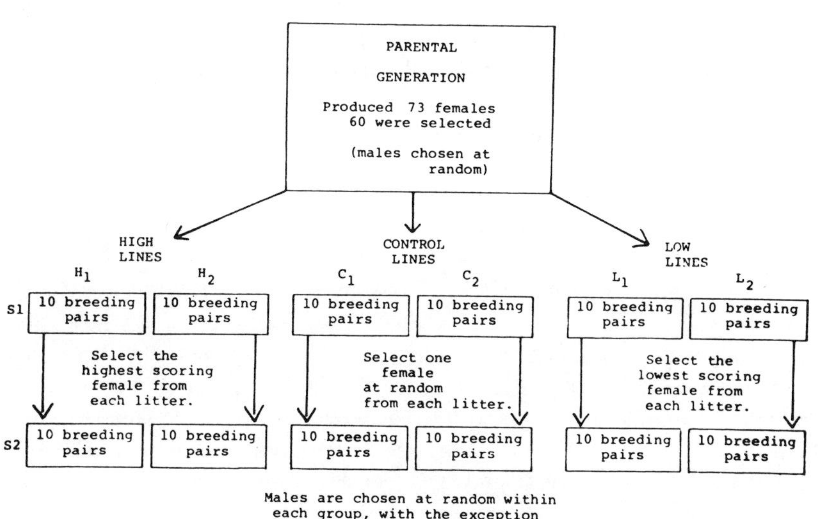

FIG. 6.1. Schematic of the selection procedure. (From "Selection for Agonistic Behavior in Wild Female *Mus musculus*," by P. D. Ebert & J. S. Hyde. *Behavior Genetics*, 1976, *6*, 291–304. Copyright 1976 by Plenum Publishing Corporation. Reprinted by permission.)

There are many advantages of using this type of selection design (DeFries, 1967; DeFries & Hegmann, 1970). The use of replicated lines permits the comparison of variability between lines selected in the same direction over the same number of generations. If both lines demonstrate similar response to selection pressure, then one's confidence in the estimate of heritability is enhanced. Also, the existence of correlated characters can be confirmed when replicated lines selected in the same direction are employed. If the relationship between the selected trait and the character can be demonstrated in both lines, this relationship is less likely to be fortuitous.

The use of nonselected control lines enables the investigator to determine whether or not selection for high and low levels of a trait has been successful. If high and low lines simply diverge from each other without any reference to a nonselected control line, it is impossible to sort out variability produced by environmental fluctuation or to assess the symmetry of the response. An asymmetrical response to selection would indicate that it is easier to select in one direction than in the other, because response to selection would be faster and the limits of selection would be reached sooner in that direction.

This design also employs within-family selection. That is, the number of breeding pairs within a line remains constant over the selected generations. Each breeding pair contributes one male and one female offspring to the next generation. Therefore, after the S1 generation, subsequent selected generations for the high lines consisted of the highest scoring female from each litter paired with a male from the same line that was not a sib. In a similar manner, the lowest scoring females were assigned to the subsequent selected generations for the low lines. For the control lines, a female was chosen at random from each litter. Males in the low and control lines were assigned in the same manner as in the high lines. Extra males and females from some of the larger litters in all lines were saved and mated (although sib matings were not done) so that the lines could be expanded to 10 families again if any of the originally assigned pairs failed to reproduce.

The within-family selection design serves to control for maternal (or paternal) effects because each breeding pair contributes equally to the next generation. This design also minimizes inbreeding, which is very important because response to selection pressure should ultimately be greater if the amount of genetic variability within a line is kept as large as possible. The combination of within-family selection and single-sex selection in the present design leads to an inbreeding coefficient estimate of 1.25% per generation (Falconer, 1960).

Testing Procedure

After weaning at 28 days of age, females were housed in isolation for another 28 days. At the end of this isolation period, the mice were tested in their home cages on 2 consecutive days. The wire cage top was removed and replaced with a

TABLE 6.2
Rating Scale

Value	*Definition*
1	Occasional nosing, very little contact
2	Frequent nosing, moderate contact
3	Frequent, vigorous nosing
4	Following and biting
5	Attack, including wrestling and biting

Plexiglass cover. A C57BL/6J female of approximately 5 weeks of age was placed in the cage opposite the wild mouse. The use of the inbred mouse insured that any fighting would be instigated by the wild mouse.

If an attack occurred within 7 minutes, the latency to attack was recorded and the test was terminated. If no attack occurred, the trial was terminated at the end of the 7 minutes. At the end of the trial, the wild mouse was rated from 1 to 5 on an aggression scale similar to that used by Lagerspetz (1964). The rating scale is presented in Table 6.2. The criterion for selection was each mouse's rating-scale score summed over the 2 testing days. Therefore, the range of possible scores for each mouse was 2 to 10.

Actual attacking occurred on at least 1 day in 21% of the Parental mice. This finding is in good agreement with the previous study comparing wilds to inbreds, in which 25% of the wild females attacked.

Selection through S4

The means of the aggression rating-scale scores for all six lines plotted over four selected generations are shown in Fig. 6.2. By the Fourth Selected Generation, the high and low lines have significantly diverged from each other in the expected directions, and there is little evidence of an asymmetrical response to selection in this generation, as the control lines are intermediate between the highs and lows. Thus, selection appears to have been effective in producing lines of wild female mice that differ in their levels of aggressiveness.

In order to determine whether interfemale aggression was related to the weight of the mice, each mouse was weighed at the end of a test trial. Figure 6.3 shows the mean weights for all six lines over the first four selected generations. Weight does not appear to be a correlated character of interfemale aggression because the order of the lines for weight does not correspond to their order for agonistic behavior. The decrease in weight for all six lines in the Third Selected Generation probably represents environmental fluctuation. Confidence in this assumption has been increased through the use of replicated and control lines.

The relationship between maternal competence and interfemale aggression was examined at this point in the selection study. When females are found to be less aggressive than males in a species such as *Mus musculus,* this sex difference

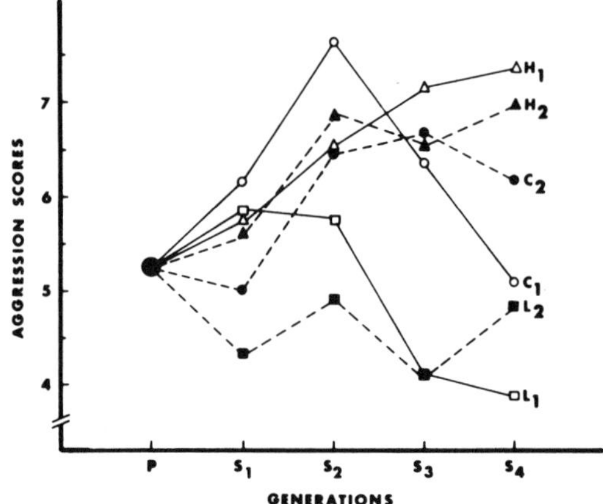

FIG. 6.2. Mean aggression rating scores for the six lines over four selected generations. (From "Selection for Agonistic Behavior in Wild Female *Mus musculus,*" by P. D. Ebert & J. S. Hyde. *Behavior Genetics,* 1976, *6,* 291–304. Copyright 1976 by Plenum Publishing Corporation. Reprinted by permission.)

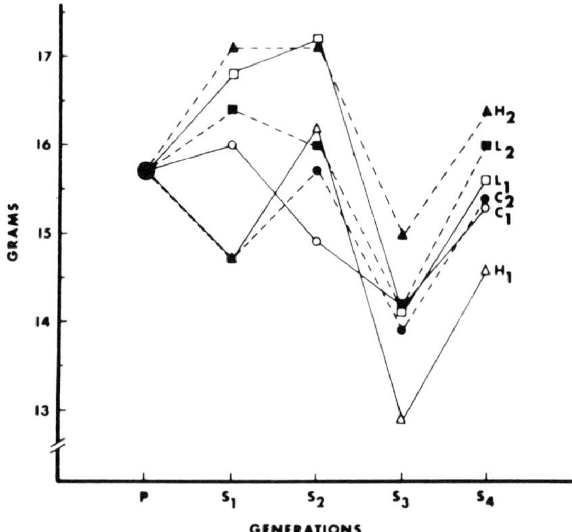

FIG. 6.3. Mean weights in grams at testing for the six lines over four selected generations. (From "Selection for Agonistic Behavior in Wild Female *Mus musculus,*" by P. D. Ebert & J. S. Hyde. *Behavior Genetics,* 1976, *6,* 291–304. Copyright 1976 by Plenum Publishing Corporation. Reprinted by permission.)

is frequently assumed to be related to female reproductive function. That is, high levels of aggressiveness are assumed to be incompatible with maternal behavior. Implicit in this assumption is the belief that aggression is a unitary concept and that an organism behaving aggressively in one situation will behave aggressively in others. Therefore, the high-line mothers in the selection study might be expected to behave aggressively toward their pups. In order to assess maternal competence in the Third and Fourth Selected Generations, several indices were used. These included litter survival rate, pup weight at 7 days of age, and mean litter size. There were no line differences for any of these (Ebert, 1975; Ebert & Hyde, 1976). Consequently, it does not appear that interfemale aggression affects maternal competence. The ratio of male to female pups was also analyzed for the six lines in the Third and Fourth Selected Generations, and, again, no line differences were found. Recent research (vom Saal & Bronson, 1980) has indicated that intrauterine position can affect the aggressiveness of females in that female fetuses that develop between two male fetuses have higher levels of circulating testosterone and tend to be more aggressive than females developing between females. It does not appear, however, that this mechanism was responsible for the increase of interfemale aggression found in the high lines, as an increase in the proportion of males born to high-line females would be necessary in order to increase the probability that a female fetus would be positioned between two males.

Selection Through S11

After the female offspring of the Fourth Selected Generation were tested in the summer of 1974, I left Bowling Green. Janet Hyde decided to continue the selection program and, with the assistance of Tom Sawyer, carried it out over 11 selected generations (Hyde & Sawyer, 1980). Selection was discontinued after the 12th generation because fertility problems began occurring in later generations. These problems were somewhat surprising, as the within-family selection design results in minimal inbreeding. Inbreeding, of course, would be expected to reduce fertility due to the presence of recessive lethal genes in wild-trapped populations. For example, Connor (1975) was successful in maintaining only five strains of wild mice of an original number of ten, after seven generations of inbreeding.

Domestic stocks of mice appear to have fewer fertility problems when they are used in breeding programs (Lagerspetz & Lagerspetz, this volume). Future behavior-genetics research using wild-trapped mice is certainly feasible and desirable, but the design of a breeding program should take into account the possibility of encountering fertility problems at some point in the program.

The results of selection over 11 generations are presented in Fig. 6.4. Separation of the lines has continued through the 11th generation. There has been no overlap of high and low lines since the First Selected Generation. Interestingly,

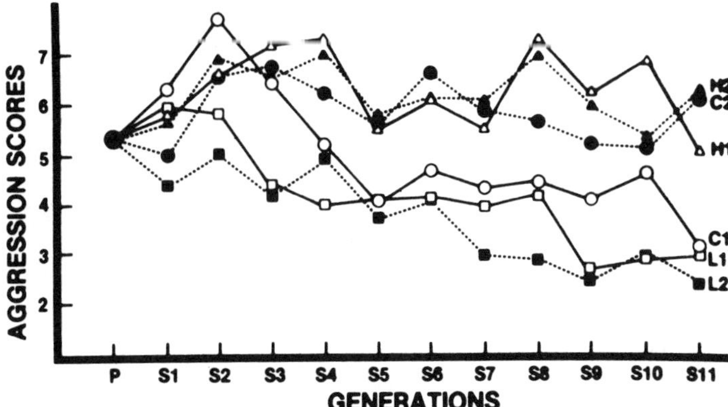

FIG. 6.4. Mean aggression rating scores for the six lines over 11 selected generations. (From "Selection for Agonistic Behavior in Wild Female Mice," by J. S. Hyde & T. F. Sawyer. *Behavior Genetics*, 1980, *10*, 349–359. Copyright 1980 by Plenum Publishing Corporation. Reprinted by permission.)

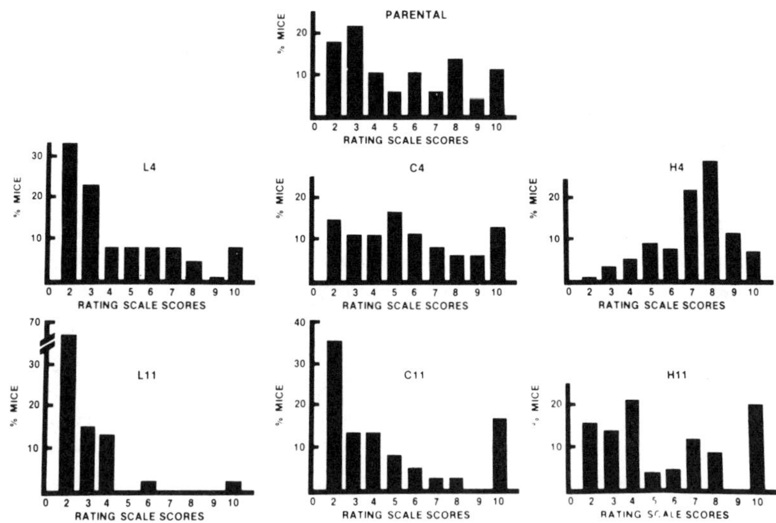

FIG. 6.5. Distributions of rating scale scores for high, control, and low lines (replicated combined) in the parental, S_4 and S_{11} generations. (From "Selection for Agonistic Behavior in Wild Female Mice," by J. S. Hyde & T. F. Sawyer. *Behavior Genetics*, 1980, *10*, 349–359. Copyright 1980 by Plenum Publishing Corporation. Reprinted by permission.)

there are many more instances of overlap between high and control lines. In other words, there seems to be some evidence of an asymmetrical response to selection that was not apparent after the first four generations. Maximum response to selection seems to have been reached by S7 for L2 and by S9 for L1. It is unclear whether the high lines have yet reached maximum response. Figure 6.5 shows the percentages of mice receiving each rating-scale score in the Parental, S4, and S11 generations for the combined replicate lines. These data also support the notion that the low lines have reached selection limits by the 11th generation. The response to selection for high levels of aggression can also be seen in this figure although the high lines display more variability than the low lines. The nonselected control lines remain quite variable.

Heritability

Heritability in the narrow sense is the estimate of the proportion of the total variance of a trait that can be accounted for by the additive genetic variance or the average effects of genes. At the beginning of the selection program, a heritability estimate of .17 was calculated from the regression of S1 daughters' aggression scores on their mothers' aggression scores. Artificial selection over several generations allows for the calculation of realized heritabilities (Falconer, 1960).

Table 6.3 shows the realized heritabilities for the two high lines and the two low lines calculated following S4 and following S8. The estimate based on the regression of daughters' scores on mothers' scores was not a good predictor of realized heritability except for the high lines after the Eighth Selected Generation. Results for S8 support the finding of faster response to selection for low levels of aggression, although it is puzzling that this difference in realized heritabilities between high and low lines was not apparent after the Fourth Selected Generation.

TABLE 6.3
Realized Heritabilities

	Line			
Realized heritability	*H1*	*H2*	*L1*	*L2*
P to S_4	0.64	0.44	0.47	0.21
P to S_8	0.12	0.14	0.34	0.46

Note: From "Selection for Agonistic Behavior in Wild Female Mice" by J. S. Hyde and T. F. Sawyer, *Behavior Genetics*, 1980, *10*, 349-359. Copyright 1980 by Plenum Publishing Corporation. Reprinted by permission.

Asymmetrical Response to Selection

Hyde and Sawyer (1980) speculated that genetic homeostasis might have been responsible for the faster response to selection for low levels of aggression. That is, artificial selection for high levels of female aggression may have been resisted by natural selection pressures keeping genes related to fitness at certain frequencies. However, as mentioned earlier, there did not seem to be any line differences in fitness, at least in terms of maternal competence. Also, the fertility problems encountered in the later generations were found in both high and low lines.

The finding of faster response to selection for low levels of aggression could also be explained by the existence of directional dominance effects. If dominant genes are more likely to be associated with high levels of aggressiveness, a faster response to selection in the direction of low aggressiveness would be expected, assuming that initial gene frequencies were about .5. The reason for this effect is that low aggressive mice would have more homozygous loci, or be more likely to breed "true," whereas high aggressive mice would have more heterozygous loci and would consequently produce more variable offspring.

Traits having directional dominance would also show inbreeding depression in the direction of the recessive alleles. Therefore, if genes determining low levels of aggressiveness are recessive, then inbreeding should result in reduced levels of aggression. This finding is precisely what James Connor reported (1975) when he compared random-bred wild mice to inbred wild mice on proportion of time spent attacking an intruder mouse. After 10 generations of inbreeding, at which point about 80% of all loci are homozygous, Connor found that the level of aggressiveness of the inbred wild mice was comparable to the level of aggressiveness in domestic inbred strains of mice. Both male and female mice were tested in the inbred and random-bred wild groups. No sex differences are reported. This finding seems to support the hypothesis that directional dominance effects could explain the asymmetrical response to selection for agonistic behavior as measured by the rating-scale scores. Other authors in this volume, however, do not find any evidence of directional dominance effects for aggression in domestic stocks of mice.

Although the results of selection based on the rating-scale scores seem consistently to indicate an asymmetrical response to selection, this response is less apparent when the percentages of mice actually attacking are considered.

Table 6.4 shows the percentages of mice actually attacking in each of the selected lines in each generation. This table confirms the fact that a substantial increase in the number of mice attacking has occurred in the high lines, as well as a decrease in attacking in the low lines. In fact, these data seem to show a fairly symmetrical response to selection, although there still seems to be considerable variability in the high lines. Much variability is also seen in the control lines, as would be expected.

TABLE 6.4
Percentage of Animals Attacking in Each of the Selection Lines in Each Generation*

	Line (%)					
Generation	*H1*	*H2*	*C1*	*C2*	*L1*	*L2*
S1	21	10	40	16	25	9
S2	17	14	40	25	27	17
S3	23	15	27	42	11	10
S4	19	19	21	36	15	13
S5	8	19	5	15	0	4
S6	27	30	16	44	10	21
S7	21	38	18	38	15	0
S8	48	43	18	32	8	0
S9	47	50	24	29	0	4
S10	69	33	32	31	6	9
S11	36	58	6	45	5	0

*Twenty-one percent of the parental generation for the selection program attacked.
Note: From "Selection for Agonistic Behavior in Wild Female Mice" by J. S. Hyde and T. F. Sawyer, *Behavior Genetics,* 1980, *10*, 344-359. Copyright 1980 by Plenum Publishing Corporation. Reprinted by permission.

Estrous Cycle Effects

When the selection program was begun, the only attempt to control for any cyclical fluctuations in female aggressive behavior that might be related to the estrous cycle was to test the mice on 2 days, and to test them only during the light part of the laboratory light–dark cycle. It was assumed that the mice would be least likely to be in estrus during this time. Also, preliminary investigation seemed to indicate that the isolated female mice remained in diestrus for exceptionally long periods of time, possibly due to an absence of pheromonal cues from mature male mice. However, Hyde and Sawyer (1977) have reported the results of a systematic investigation of the relationship between estrous cycle fluctuations and female aggressiveness. Figure 6.6 shows their results based on high and control females in the Eighth Selected Generation. Significant fluctuations in rating-scale scores were found, with scores being higher during proestrus and metestrus, and lower during estrus and diestrus.

Hyde and Sawyer also analyzed cyclic fluctuations in the various component behaviors of the aggression rating scale. Cyclic fluctuations following the same pattern as the overall rating-scale scores were found for frequency of nosing, frequency of vigorous nosing, and total time of vigorous nosing. However, no significant cyclic fluctuations were found for following, tail rattling, or biting attacks. Consequently, estrous fluctuation may have introduced greater variability in determining the rating-scale scores of 1, 2, and 3, which are defined in terms of nosing frequency and vigor, than in scores of 4 or 5, which do not

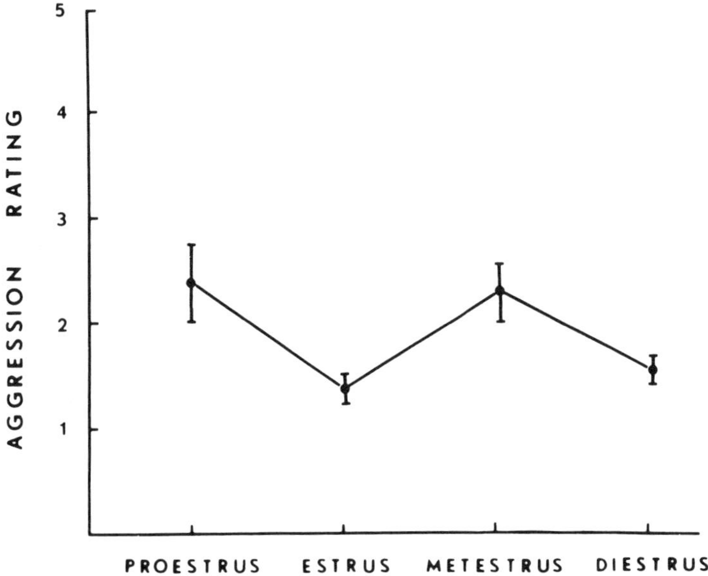

FIG. 6.6. Fluctuations in mean aggression ratings over the estrous cycle. (From "Estrous Cycle Fluctuations in Aggressiveness of House Mice," by J. S. Hyde & T. F. Sawyer. *Hormones and Behavior,* 1977, *9,* 290–295. Copyright 1977 by Academic Press, Inc. Reprinted by permission.)

depend on these behaviors. It is interesting that actual attacking does not seem to fluctuate with the estrous cycle.

Isolation Effects

As mentioned earlier, mice were isolated 28 days prior to testing. It was assumed that this isolation period would enhance aggression because this effect has been

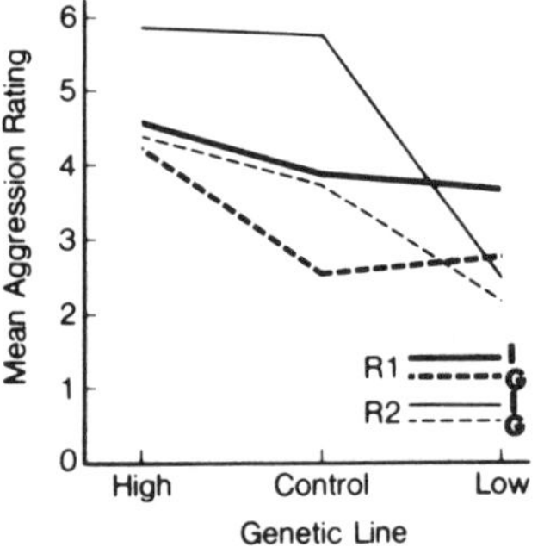

FIG. 6.7. Mean aggression ratings of high-, control-, and low-line females, housed either in isolation or groups (I, isolated; G, group housed; R1, replicate 1; R2, replicate 2). (From "Selection for Agonistic Behavior in Wild Female Mice," by J. S. Hyde & T. F. Sawyer. *Behavior Genetics,* 1980, *10,* 349–359. Copyright 1980 by Plenum Publishing Corporation. Reprinted by permission.)

well documented (Sigg, Day, & Colombo, 1966; Valzelli, 1969) for male mice. Hyde and Sawyer (1980) reported the results of a study done to assess the effects of isolation versus group housing in mice coming from the Ninth Selected Generation. Figure 6.7 shows the results for replicate 1 (H1, C1, and L1) and replicate 2 (H2, C2, and L2). Isolated mice were consistently more aggressive than the group-housed mice, whereas the line differences were still significant and in the expected order. There were no significant line-by-housing interactions. These results suggest that isolation may produce physiological changes in female mice similar to those produced in males.

OTHER KINDS OF AGGRESSION AS CORRELATED CHARACTERS

Intermale Aggression

Because the selected behavior was phenotypically indistinguishable from intermale aggression, it was expected that intermale aggression would be a correlated character of interfemale aggression. In the Fifth Selected Generation, males were tested under conditions identical to those described for females, with the exception that a C57BL/6J male mouse served as the intruder mouse (Hyde & Ebert, 1976). The results of this study did not support the hypothesis. Although significant line differences were found for replicate 2 (H2, C2, and L2), these lines did not follow the predicted order because the controls were higher than the high lines. Thus, there was no strong evidence that male aggression was a correlated

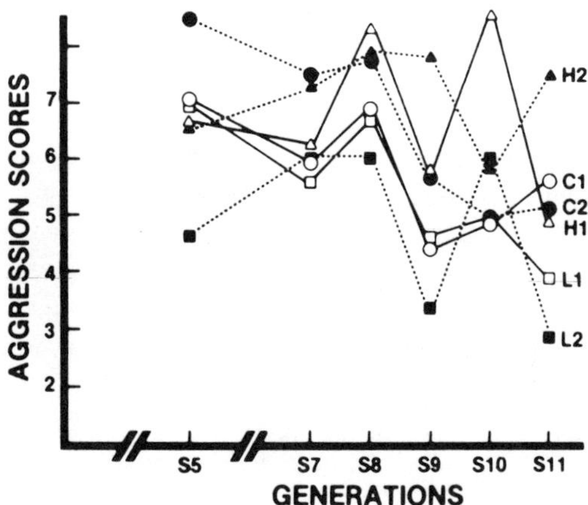

FIG. 6.8. Mean aggression ratings for males in the six selection lines. (From "Selection for Agonistic Behavior in Wild Female Mice," by J. S. Hyde & T. F. Sawyer. *Behavior Genetics*, 1980, *10*, 349–359. Copyright 1980 by Plenum Publishing Corporation. Reprinted by permission.)

character of female aggression. When all six lines were rank ordered, the Spearman correlation coefficient comparing males and females was equal to only .20.

Because the lack of an apparent relationship between male and female aggression seemed so surprising, Hyde and Sawyer (1980) investigated it further. Figure 6.8 shows the results from S5 as well as the results of males tested in generations S7 to S11. There is still no consistent evidence of a strong relationship between intermale and interfemale aggression, although there is little overlap of highs and lows, and significant separation of the lines in the expected order was occasionally found when replicates were analyzed separately.

This lack of a relationship between male and female aggression was recently confirmed by van Oortmerssen and Bakker (1981). Through artificial selection, these researchers were able to establish a line of wild mice characterized by shorter attack latencies than an unselected control line. Selection was performed only on males. When females were tested in the 11th and 12th generation, no differences between selected and control lines were found.

Maternal Aggression

As mentioned previously, maternal aggression in the mouse has received much recent attention. Because this kind of aggression exclusively involves females and seems likely to have an adaptive function for the species, Hyde and I decided to determine whether maternal aggression was a correlated character of interfemale aggression. The procedure used to test for maternal aggression was similar to that used in the selection program. The only major differences were the presence of the litter in the cage at the time of testing and the testing of each female every other day from 2 until 20 days postpartum. A C57BL/6J female once again served as the intruder mouse.

When maternal aggression was examined in mice born in the Fifth Selected Generation, the results were suggestive, but they did not conclusively demonstrate line differences (Hyde & Sawyer, 1979; Hyde, Sawyer, & Ebert, 1976). However, when the lines were tested for maternal aggression in the Tenth Selected Generation (Hyde & Sawyer, 1979), the results were quite conclusive, as shown in Fig. 6.9. Because each mean represents only 1 day of testing, the results are plotted on the 5-point rating scale. These results demonstrate that maternal aggression is a correlate of interfemale aggression, as the separation of lines is quite good and in the expected directions.

Predatory Aggression

In order to determine whether interfemale aggression is related to another kind of aggression in Moyer's (1976) classification scheme, Yvonne Green and I tested descendants of the H1, C1, and L1 lines of mice for predatory aggression (Ebert & Green, in preparation). Ten males and ten females from each of the three lines

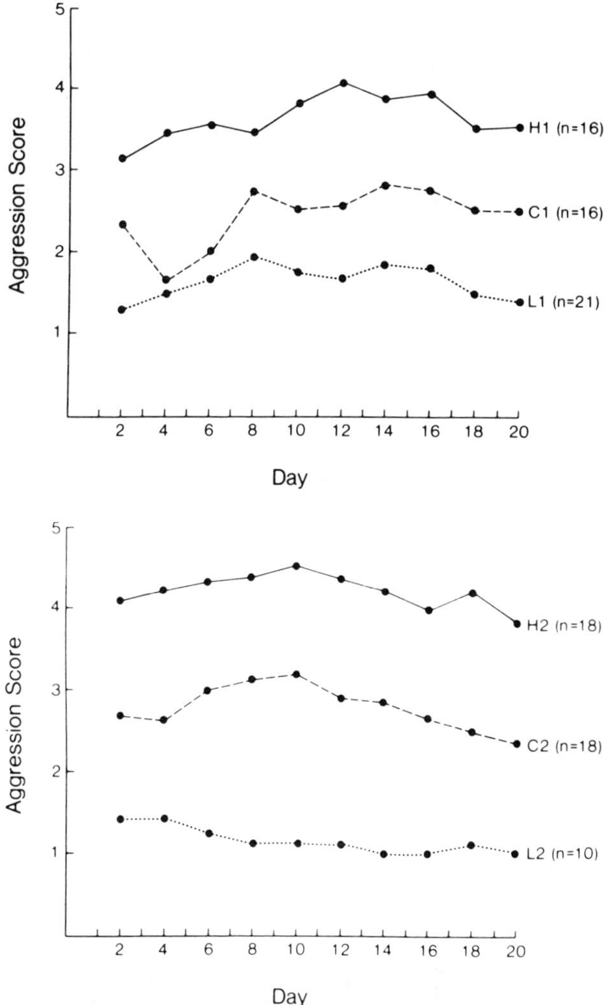

FIG. 6.9. Maternal aggression ratings for high, control, and low lines in S_{10}. (From "Correlated Characters in Selection for Aggressiveness in Female Mice. II. Maternal Aggressiveness," by J. S. Hyde & T. F. Sawyer. *Behavior Genetics*, 1979, *9*, 571–577. Copyright 1979 by Plenum Publishing Corporation. Reprinted by permission.)

served as subjects. Mice were tested for 2 consecutive days and were not food or water deprived prior to testing. Testing consisted of placing the mouse in the test cage for an acclimation period of 30 minutes and then dropping a live cricket (*Acheta domesticus*) into the cage. The experimenter timed the latency to attack the cricket, an attack being defined as pouncing on, biting, and/or tearing the cricket with the forepaws, and timed the latency to begin eating the cricket. The trial ended 5 minutes after eating was first observed, or after 30 minutes had elapsed, whichever came first.

This methodology, similar to that used by Butler (1973), was successful in producing at least one attack in 70% of the mice and at least one instance of eating in 38.8% of the mice. Figure 6.10 shows the results for the attack latencies in all three lines over the 2 days of testing. Scores from males and females are combined. An analysis of variance on these data yielded a significant main effect only for the factor of days ($F(1, 54) = 4.19$, $p < .05$). Latency to attack decreased from Day 1 to Day 2. There were no interaction effects.

Figure 6.11 shows the results for the eating latencies. Scores for males and females are again combined. An analysis of variance yielded a significant main effect for lines ($F(2, 54) = 6.50$, $p < .01$). However, *post hoc* comparisons of means indicated that latencies to eat were shorter for control line mice than for either high or low line mice.

Significant correlations between Day 1 and Day 2 for both attacking and eating were found ($r = .758$, attacking; $r = .659$, eating; $p < .01$ for both). The correlation between attacking and eating latencies for all subjects on both days was also significant ($r = .67$, $p < .01$). However, this correlation was somewhat lower than anticipated because Butler (1973) had found a correlation coeffi-

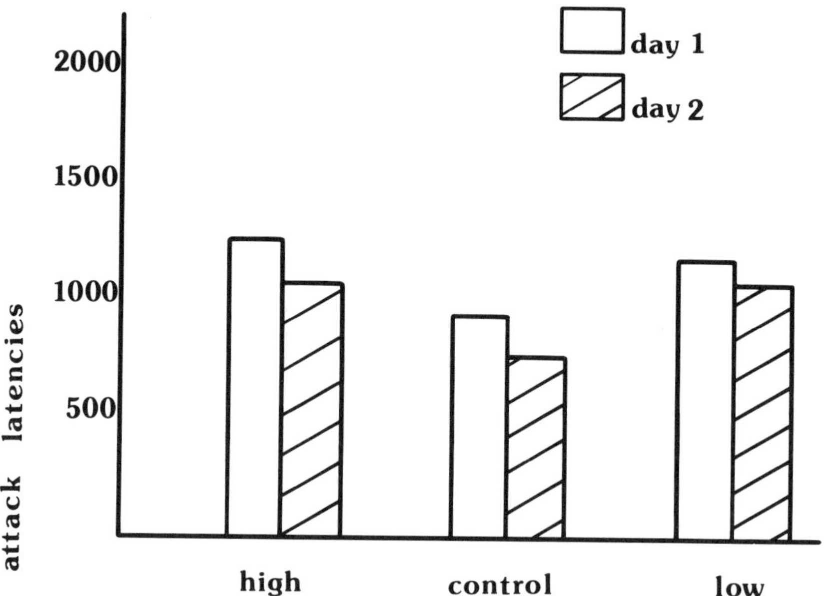

FIG. 6.10. Mean latencies to attack in seconds for high-, control-, and low-line mice.

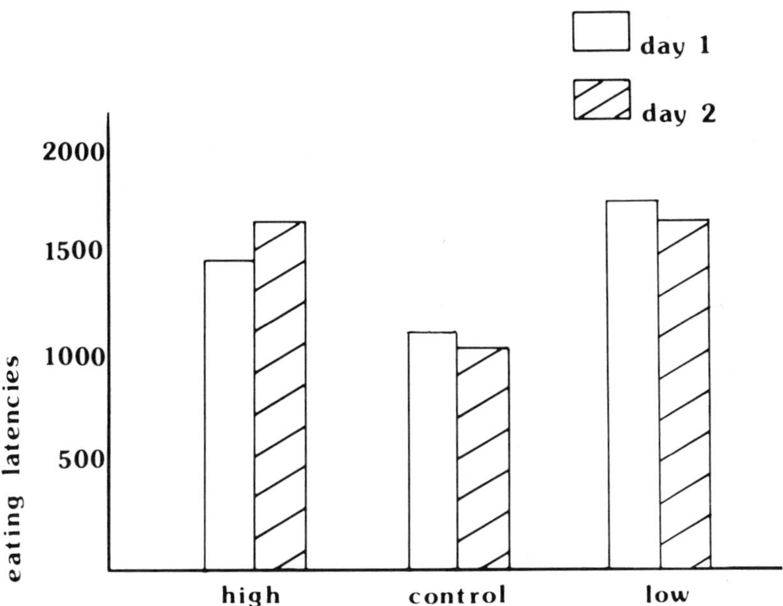

FIG. 6.11. Mean latencies to eat in seconds for high-, control-, and low-line mice.

TABLE 6.5
Number of Mice Attacking and Eating on Both Test Days

Sex	High	Control	Low
	Line		
	Attacking		
Males			
Day 1	5	5	5
Day 2	5	7	5
Females			
Day 1	3	7	4
Day 2	6	7	8
	Eating		
Males			
Day 1	3	5	1
Day 2	3	6	2
Females			
Day 1	2	6	1
Day 2	2	5	1

Note: There were ten mice in each group.

cient of .988 for these two behaviors. Apparently, selection for both high and low levels of aggression has resulted in some dissociation of attacking and eating behaviors.

Comparisons of lines and sexes in terms of numbers of individuals actually attacking or eating also yielded no line or sex differences, as shown in Table 6.5.

The results of this study very clearly indicate an absence of a relationship between interspecific aggression and predatory aggression in either females or males. These results also support the conclusions drawn by other researchers who have compared male and female domestic mice on predatory aggression (Brain & Al-Maliki, 1978; Butler, 1973) and those of investigators who have compared predatory aggression to intraspecific aggression (Brain & Al-Maliki, 1978; Lynds, 1980).

IS AGGRESSION A UNITARY TRAIT?

Much evidence does exist to support the conclusion that intraspecific aggression is an independent trait from predatory aggression (Brain & Al-Maliki, 1978; Ebert & Green, in preparation; Lynds, 1980). The two traits seem to involve different genetic mechanisms and have quite dissimilar eliciting-stimulus situations and response topographies. The adaptive functions of these two behavioral traits are also likely to be independent from each other, with predatory behaviors being exclusively linked with ingestive behavior. If one can extrapolate these conclusions to humans, it seems unreasonable to assume that such intraspecific aggression as homicide and violent assault are related to an evolutionary history involving hunting as a major food gathering activity. Therefore, if there is a genetic basis to intraspecific aggression in humans, it probably did not evolve as a result of selection for predatory behaviors.

Intermale and interfemale aggression also do not seem to be correlates of each other (Hyde & Ebert, 1976; Hyde & Sawyer, 1980; van Oortmerssen & Bakker, 1981). This fact indicates that different groups of genes are probably involved in the expression of these two traits. This lack of a strong correlational relationship, however, does not mean that no common genes are involved, as the absolute absence of a relationship has not been established either. For example, St. John and Corning (1973), using four inbred strains of mice, found that males and females within a particular strain behaved more similarly to each other than to mice from other strains when tested for aggression in a situation typically used to elicit "maternal" aggression.

There are some important implications of these results for future selection studies in that a finding of phenotypic similarity in the behavior of males and females does not necessarily mean that the trait is influenced by exactly the same group of genes in both sexes. Studies in which the sexes are simultaneously selected may actually be producing changes in the frequencies of two independent groups of genes.

The finding of a relationship between interfemale and maternal aggression (Hyde & Sawyer, 1979; Hyde et al., 1976) indicates that some kinds of aggression may be influenced by the same genetic mechanisms. Because interfemale and maternal aggression are elicited by different sets of external stimuli and physiological conditions, these findings seem to contradict Moyer's (1976) contention that various kinds of aggression form discrete categories and are controlled by separate physiological and, by implication, genetic mechanisms.

The relationship of these two types of aggression may also explain the virtual disappearance of interfemale aggression from domestic stocks of mice. A common laboratory breeding technique is to group house a single male mouse with several mature females. Under these conditions, breeders would favor females that were low in both interfemale and maternal aggression. As already indicated, this selection procedure would not have much effect on the aggressiveness of domesticated male mice.

The studies discussed in the present chapter indicate that there is not a simple answer to the question of whether or not aggression is a unitary trait. Clearly, it is not when intraspecific and predatory aggression are compared. The relationships among various kinds of intraspecific aggression need to be elucidated by further research. As seen in the present chapter, the selection program is an ideal tool for assessing the relationships among aggressive behaviors elicited by various environmental and physiological antecedent conditions.

ADAPTIVE FUNCTIONS OF AGGRESSION IN NATURAL POPULATIONS

Predatory aggression is fairly easy to elicit in both wild and domestic stocks of mice. Mice will readily attack and eat such insects as crickets and locusts when given the opportunity to do so in the laboratory (Brain & Al-Maliki, 1978; Butler, 1973; Ebert & Green, 1982). Analyses of stomach contents of wild-trapped mice have indicated that their diets include insects (Berry, 1968). Therefore, predatory aggression in the mouse has probably served the highly adaptive function of food-gathering.

At first glance maternal aggression would seem to have the equally obvious adaptive function of protecting the young from intruders. However, recent research has shown that the situation is somewhat more complex. Although Svare (1979, this volume) has demonstrated that suckling and exteroceptive stimuli from the young are necessary for the onset and maintenance of maternal aggression, Paul, Gronek, and Politch (1980) have found that the presence of the young is not a factor in determining whether a lactating female will attack an intruder. Further, Paul et al. also found that when the intruder actually was allowed to attack the pups, maternal aggression decreased, and maternal cannibalism of the pups increased. Hahn (this volume) also does not find maternal aggression to be very successful in protecting the pups from being killed by intruders.

Nevertheless, it seems quite likely that a lactating female's attacks on an intruder of the homesite would be effective in expelling the intruder in a situation where the mice were not confined in a small space. The research of Hahn and Paul et al. certainly indicates that the presence of an intruder carries a real threat to the survival of a litter.

Thus, maternal aggressiveness has probably been a highly adaptive trait in the evolutionary history of the mouse. Although maternal aggression is frequently found in domestic stocks of mice, the domestication process may have favored less aggressive genotypes due to the breeding practice described earlier.

A considerable amount of genetic variability for maternal aggressiveness seems to have been present in our wild-trapped mice, as Hyde and Sawyer (1979) found such pronounced separation of lines for the trait. This finding of genetic variability for the trait may indicate that different environmental conditions may favor different levels of maternal aggression, and that natural populations retain the ability to adapt to a variety of conditions.

If we can assume that maternal aggression is an important, potentially positive trait for a mouse population, then the importance of its correlate, interfemale aggression, the selected trait, comes into question: Does interfemale aggression serve some adaptive function in a natural population, or is its relationship to maternal aggression simply fortuitous? It is likely that under certain environmental conditions, interfemale aggression might serve to increase the spatial distances among sexually mature females. This distancing or spreading effect might increase the probability that a female would mate with an unrelated male, thus decreasing the amount of inbreeding within a population. It would also encourage the colonization of adjacent geographical locations. New demes may be founded by an individual pregnant female (Bruell, 1970). In fact, the physiological condition of pregnancy has been shown to increase aggressiveness in certain domestic stocks of mice (Buhot-Aversent & Goyens, 1981).

Under certain environmental conditions such as an abundant, but localized food source, however, it would be more advantageous for breeding females to behave unaggressively. Anderson (1961) observed that in a feral population of mice, home ranges were aggressively defended by most mature females, although in especially favorable habitats, females would associate in groups of up to five. Butler (1980), using laboratory-bred wild mice in seminatural enclosures, also found that females would aggressively defend their territories, especially from intruding females. Consequently, natural selection may have favored moderate levels of interfemale aggressive behavior, with considerable genetic variability for the trait. Conditions favoring low levels of interfemale aggression would probably also favor relatively lower levels of maternal aggression.

The foregoing description of the genetics of aggression in wild female mice is very similar to what has been reported for domestic male mice. However, domestic male mice have been shown to be considerably less aggressive than wild males in studies using fairly standard laboratory techniques for inducing aggression (Connor, 1975; Ebert, 1972, 1976). It may be that the importance of intermale aggression in the evolutionary history of the mouse has actually been underestimated due to the use of domestic stocks in most laboratory research. Intermale aggression seems to influence the formation and maintenance of such social structures as territories and dominance hierarchies (Scott, 1966). Although dominance hierarchies are readily formed when males of domestic stocks are housed together, studies in which territory formation has been reported have generally used wild mice or F_1 hybrids of wild and domestic mice (Anderson & Hill, 1965; Butler, 1980). Butler (1980) has suggested that the size of a mouse population is related to its social structure in that territory formation will be found when the population is large. The domestication process has undoubtedly favored animals tolerant of living together in small, fairly dense groups. Domestic stocks of mice are, consequently, less aggressive and more likely to form dominance hierarchies or live together peacefully than to form territories.

Further evidence for the importance of intermale aggression for the species was reported by van Oortmerssen and Bakker (1981), who were quite unsuccessful in selecting for long attack latencies in their laboratory-bred population of wild mice. Failure to produce long attack latency lines seemed to be due to the inability of the less aggressive males to impregnate females, suggesting that a certain amount of male aggressiveness is a part of species fitness. The inbreeding depression for aggression found in Connor's (1975) study also suggests the same conclusion, as genes producing less fitness are usually recessive (Falconer, 1960).

As discussed previously in this chapter, van Oortmerssen and Bakker (1981) found no differences between their short attack latency line and their control line for female aggressiveness, thus confirming our finding of an absence of a relationship between intermale and interfemale aggression. This finding presumably indicates that environmental conditions may differentially affect the adaptiveness of aggression for males and females.

CONCLUDING REMARKS

Although I have stressed the adaptive functions of aggression for mouse populations in this chapter, I must also state that I strongly concur with the views of the other authors of this volume who have chosen to emphasize the modifiability of aggressive behavior in the individual. Clearly, the past learning history and the immediate social environment of an organism are powerful determinants of aggressive behavior. My own observations of laboratory-reared wild mice have confirmed that these animals can live together very peacefully in rather crowded conditions for long periods of time if they are housed together as pups or juveniles. Also, it was our laboratory practice to leave breeding pairs together after the pups were born, and I frequently observed instances of males retrieving pups to the nest and even sitting on the nest. This tender paternal behavior is certainly in sharp contrast to Hahn's findings concerning the attacks of intruder male mice. If we are ever to understand completely the antecedents of aggressive and peaceful behaviors, it will be necessary to unravel the complex interactions of genetic, physiological, and environmental factors.

REFERENCES

Anderson, P. K. Density, social structure, and nonsocial environment in house-mouse populations and the implications for regulation of numbers. *Transactions of the New York Academy of Sciences,* 1961, *23,* 477–451.

Anderson, P. K., & Hill, J. L. *Mus musculus:* Experimental induction of territory formation. *Science,* 1965, *145,* 177–178.

Berry, R. J. The ecology of an island population of the house mouse. *Journal of Animal Ecology,* 1968, *37,* 445–470.

Brain, P. F., & Al-Maliki, S. A comparison of "intermale fighting" in "standard opponent" tests and attack directed towards locusts by "TO" strain mice: Effects of simple experimental manipulations. *Animal Behaviour,* 1978, *26,* 723–737.

Bruell, J. H. Behavioral population genetics and wild *Mus musculus.* In G. Lindzey & D. D. Thiessen (Eds.), *Contributions to behavior genetic analysis: The mouse as prototype.* New York: Appleton–Century–Crofts, 1970.

Buhot-Averseng, M. C., & Goyens, J. Effects of cohabitation with another female on aggressive behavior in pregnant mice. *Aggressive Behavior,* 1981, *7,* 111–121.

Butler, K. Predatory behavior in laboratory mice: Strain and sex comparison. *Journal of Comparative Psychology,* 1973, *85,* 243–249.

Butler, R. G. Population size, social behaviour, and dispersal in house mice: A quantitative investigation. *Animal Behaviour,* 1980, *28,* 78–85.

Connor, J. L. Genetic mechanisms controlling the domestication of a wild house mouse population (*Mus musculus* L.). *Journal of Comparative and Physiological Psychology,* 1975, *89,* 118–130.

Dawson, W. M. Inheritance of wildness and tameness in mice. *Genetics,* 1932, *17,* 296–326.

DeFries, J. C. Quantitative genetics and behavior: Overview and perspective. In J. Hirsch (Ed.), *Behavior genetic analysis.* New York: McGraw-Hill Book Company, 1967.

DeFries, J. C., & Hegmann, J. P. Analysis of open-field behavior. In G. Lindzey & D. D. Thiessen (Eds.). *Contributions to behavior genetic analysis: The mouse as prototype.* New York: Appleton–Century–Crofts, 1970.

Ebert, P. D. *Agonistic behavior in wild and inbred mice.* Unpublished master's thesis, Bowling Green State University, August 1972.

Ebert, P. D. *Selection for agonistic behavior in wild female Mus musculus.* Unpublished doctoral dissertation, Bowling Green State University, March, 1975.

Ebert, P. D. Agonistic behavior in wild and inbred *Mus musculus. Behavioral Biology,* 1976, *18,* 291–294.

Ebert, P. D., & Green, Y. V. *Predatory aggression in lines of wild mice selected for interfemale aggression*. Manuscript in preparation.

Ebert, P. D., & Hyde, J. S. Selection for agonistic behavior in wild female *Mus musculus*. *Behavior Genetics*, 1976, *6*, 291–304.

Falconer, D. S. *Introduction to quantitative genetics*. New York: The Ronald Press Company, 1960.

Gandelman, R. Mice: Postpartum aggression elicited by the presence of an intruder. *Hormones and Behavior*, 1972, *3*, 23–28.

Hyde, J. S., & Ebert, P. D. Correlated response in selection for aggressiveness in female mice. I. Male aggression. *Behavior Genetics*, 1976, *6*, 421–428.

Hyde, J. S., & Sawyer, T. F. Estrous cycle fluctuations in aggressiveness of house mice. *Hormones and Behavior*, 1977, *9*, 290–295.

Hyde, J. S., & Sawyer, T. F. Correlated response in selection for aggressiveness in female mice. II. Maternal aggression. *Behavior Genetics*, 1979, *9*, 571–577.

Hyde, J. S., & Sawyer, T. F. Selection for agonistic behavior in wild female mice. *Behavior Genetics*, 1980, *10*, 349–359.

Hyde, J. S., Sawyer, T. F., & Ebert, P. D. *Correlated characters in selection for aggressiveness in female mice:* II. Maternal aggressiveness. Unpublished manuscript, 1976.

Lagerspetz, K. M. J. Studies on the aggressive behavior of mice. *Annales Academiae Scientiarum Fennicae*, (B), 1964, *131*, 1–131.

Lynds, P. G. Intermale fighting and predatory behavior in house mice: An analysis of behavioral content. *Aggressive Behavior*, 1980, *6*, 139–147.

Moyer, K. E. *The psychobiology of aggression*. New York: Harper & Row, 1976.

Paul, L., Gronek, J., & Politch, J. A. Maternal aggression in mice: Protection of young is a by-product of attacks at the home site. *Aggressive Behavior*, 1980, *6*, 19–29.

Plomin, R. J., & Manosevitz, M. Behavioral polytypism in wild *Mus musculus*. *Behavior Genetics*, 1974, *4*, 145–157.

Scott, J. P. Agonistic behavior of mice and rats: A review. *American Zoologist*, 1966, *6*, 683–701.

Sigg, E. B., Day, C., & Colombo, C. Endocrine factors in isolation-induced aggressiveness in rodents. *Endocrinology*, 1966, *78*, 679–684.

Smith, R. H. Wildness and domestication in *Mus musculus:* A behavioral analysis. *Journal of Comparative and Physiological Psychology*, 1972, *79*, 22–29.

St. John, R. S., & Corning, P. A. Maternal aggression in mice. *Behavioral Biology*, 1973, *9*, 635–639.

Svare, B. Maternal aggression in mice: The non-specific nature of the exteroceptive maintenance by young. *Aggressive Behavior*, 1979, *5*, 417–424.

Valzelli, L. Aggressive behaviour induced by isolation. In S. Garattini & E. B. Sigg (Eds.), *Aggressive behaviour*. Amsterdam: Excerpta Media Foundation, 1969.

van Oortmerssen, G. A., & Bakker, T. C. M. Artificial selection for short and long attack latencies in wild *Mus musculus* domesticus. *Behavior Genetics*, 1981, *11*, 115–126.

vom Saal, F. S., & Bronson, F. H. Sexual characteristics of adult female are correlated with their blood testosterone levels during prenatal development. *Science*, 1980, *208*, 597–599.

7 Psychobiological Determinants of Maternal Aggressive Behavior

Bruce Svare
State University of New York at Albany

INTRODUCTION

Historically, the subjects selected for study in aggression research have been male mammals (for the most part rodents). It has been only recently that the scope of this research has expanded to include studies of female agonistic behavior. The reasons for our neglect of female aggressive behavior are manifold but probably are rooted in our chauvinistic assumptions about male dominance and superiority over females in competitive situations. Regardless, it is now well known that under certain reproductive conditions, female mammals become intensely aggressive and will attack and defeat conspecific males. The purpose of the present review is to describe and interpret our data base with respect to one form of aggression in female rodents, that being maternal defense. This behavior, which is observed during pregnancy and lactation, undoubtedly functions to protect the young but also may be involved in other important dimensions of social organization. Although more is known about this aspect of female aggressive behavior than about the factors governing other types of female aggression (i.e., spontaneous interfemale), we know far less about maternal defense than we do about aggression in the male.

Requisite to a psychobiological analysis is an exploration of how both molar and molecular events may be influencing the exhibition of this behavior. With this in mind, I examine experiential, genetic, neuroendocrine, and biochemical influences on this behavior in mice, rats, and hamsters. Moreover, I explore from a sociobiological perspective the importance of this behavior for both groups and individuals. Finally, I provide directions and tactics for future research in this area.

DESCRIPTIVE AND ENVIRONMENTAL FACTORS

Response Topography

In mice, the topography of maternal defense during lactation is qualitatively and quantitatively different from that observed during pregnancy. In the postpartum period, aggression is characterized by immediate attacks (latencies usually are less than 10 sec), with biting directed primarily toward the flanks and neck of the intruder (Svare & Gandelman, 1973). The duration of most attacks is around 5–10 sec. In a 30-min test period, most of the attacks are concentrated in the first 3–5 minutes with little fighting seen thereafter (Green, 1978; Svare, Betteridge, Katz, & Samuels, 1981). This is due in part to the fact that postpartum attacks appear to induce almost immediate submission on the part of intruder males and females; counterattacks are rarely observed in opponent animals (Green, 1978; Svare et al., 1981). It is interesting to note that only one factor seems to separate the topography of postpartum defense from that of intermale aggression, that being the latency to engage in the behavior. Males typically investigate each other for several minutes prior to the first attack, whereas postpartum females, as noted previously, attack immediately (Lynds, 1976a). In contrast to the intense attacks observed during the postpartum period, aggression during pregnancy is more subtle and is characterized by lunges without physical contact along with occasional biting attacks (e.g., Hedricks & Daniels, 1981; Mann & Svare, in press). Threats of this nature in the wild may be every bit as effective as actual attack in warding off potential predators.

Maternal aggression in pregnant and lactating rats appears to be more deliberate than the defensive behavior of lactating mice (Erskine, Barfield, & Goldman, 1978; Erskine, Denenberg, & Goldman, 1978; Price & Belanger, 1977). After several minutes of mutual exploration, attacks consisting of rapid lunges toward the neck or back region of the opponent are followed by kicking, biting, and scuffling. Hip throws, in which the female orients herself to the side of the intruder and thrusts one rear leg toward him, also are characteristic of most bouts. Opponent rats become immediately submissive and little fighting is observed beyond the first 15 minutes of the test session.

The topography of maternal aggression in the hamster is similar to that described for the rat (Wise, 1974). Pregnant hamsters take longer to begin attacking than postpartum animals (4 min as opposed to 1 min). Aggression consists of episodes of chasing and pouncing in which the female rapidly pursues the opponent, jumps on his back with her front paws, and bites the intruder in the back. It is unclear at this time as to whether these behaviors are qualitatively and/or quantitatively different from the aggression observed during the virgin state. With the exception of a short period of estrus, the female hamster is aggressive during all reproductive states.

Stimulus Factors Eliciting Aggression

The elicitation of maternal aggression in rodents is influenced by the sex, age, reproductive status, and degree of familiarity with the opponent.

The sex and hormonal status of the intruder have been found to influence maternal aggression in some studies but not in others. For example, lactating Rockland–Swiss (R–S) mice attack adult male and female intruders with equal intensity (Svare & Gandelman, 1973; Svare et al., 1981). On the other hand, CD-1 postpartum female mice attack intact males more vigorously than do virgin or lactating females (Rosenson & Asheroff, 1975). Gonadectomized animals of either sex are rarely attacked by CD-1 dams, and late lactating (postpartum days 16–20) female intruders are attacked more frequently than early lactating (postpartum days 3–8) animals. Pregnant mice also are differentially aggressive depending on the sex and reproductive status of the intruder (Goyens & Noirot, 1977). Male intruders are attacked more severely than any type of female opponent. Late pregnant animals exhibited little aggression toward late pregnant intruders, more to early pregnant ones, and were most aggressive toward virgin female intruders. In the same study, early pregnant animals were less aggressive toward all types of intruders. The basis of the stimulus control exhibited by pregnant and postpartum animals in the aforementioned studies is not understood at this time but may reside in the differing hormonal conditions of the intruder. Because hormonal status influences pheromone production and the elicitation of other forms of aggression (Lee & Ingersoll, in press), it is intuitive that pheromone-based olfactory cues also modulate the elicitation of maternal aggression. However, we are not aware of any research that has directly examined this possibility.

In mice and rats, age of the intruder influences postpartum aggression. Male and female mice between 25 and 65 days of age are attacked with equal intensity by lactating R–S mice (Svare et al., 1981); 1- to 10-day-old intruders are retrieved or ignored, whereas 14- to 20-day-old opponents are intensely attacked (Svare & Gandelman, 1973). The presence of body hair may be one factor that elicits postpartum aggression in mice, as hairless 14-day-old intruders are rarely attacked (Svare & Gandelman, 1973). Other stimuli such as body size and olfactory cues have not been systematically explored. In lactating rats, 35- and 45-day-old male intruders are attacked more intensely than 55- and 110-day-old males (Erskine, Denenberg, & Goldman, 1978). The basis of this differential responsiveness is also unknown.

Finally, one report indicates that unfamiliar animals are attacked more intensely than familiar animals. Lactating R–S mice are nonaggressive toward males that have been housed in the females' cage and separated by a wire mesh partition between Days 2 and 10 of lactation, whereas strange males are vigorously attacked (Svare & Gandelman, 1973). The recognition of strange and familiar intruders by lactating mice may be controlled by an olfactory cue. Opponents doused with "strange" conspecific urine are attacked more vigorously than opponents coated with "familiar" urine (Lynds, 1976b).

Experiential Factors

Pregnancy. In albino mice, aggressive behavior increases with advancing pregnancy with peak levels of the behavior observed from midpregnancy (Day 10) onward (Hedricks & Daniels, 1981; Mann & Svare, in press; Noirot, Goyens, & Buhot, 1975) (See Fig. 7.1). Aggression during pregnancy is a good predictor of postpartum agonistic behavior. Animals rated as highly aggressive during pregnancy tend also to exhibit high levels of the behavior during lactation, whereas nonaggressive pregnant animals exhibit less fighting behavior during the postpartum period (Mann & Svare, in press). This suggests that the mechanism(s) controlling postpartum and pregnancy-induced aggression might be one and the same. It is interesting to note that when animals are simultaneously pregnant and lactating, a condition that apparently is the norm for mice in the wild, aggression is as intense as in animals that are just lactating (Al-Maliki, Brain, Childs, & Benton, 1980; Mann & Svare, in press). Finally, housing a pregnant female mouse with another pregnant animal elevates aggression during gestation (Buhot-Averseng & Goyens, 1981). To our knowledge, no research has been conducted to examine the possible physiological mechanism involved.

The peak period of aggression in the pregnant hamster is around the 10th day of gestation (hamsters have a 16-day gestation period) (Wise, 1974). Pregnant rats also exhibit some aggression toward the end of pregnancy (between Gestation Days 18 and 22) (Erskine et al., 1978) but the incidence of the behavior at earlier gestational periods has not been reported for this species.

Lactation. For mice, rats, and hamsters, aggression declines with advancing lactation. Peak frequencies of attacks and bites and short latencies to the first attack are observed on Day 9 in the lactating rat (Erskine, Barfield, & Goldman, 1978) and during the first 5 postpartum days in the hamster (Wise, 1974). In the mouse, aggression is highest between Days 3 and 8, declines between Days 9 and 14, and is very low between Days 15 and 21 of the postpartum period (Gandelman, 1972; St. John & Corning, 1973; Svare et al., 1981; Svare & Gandelman, 1973) (See Fig. 7.2). Because the decline in aggression with advancing lactation can be retarded by daily litter replacement with newborns (Svare, 1977), changes in the frequency and/or duration of nursing episodes may be important. Surprisingly little research has been conducted to explore this possibility.

When tested for aggression on six successive lactation periods or until they ceased to remate, R–S mice exhibited an increase across the first three lactation

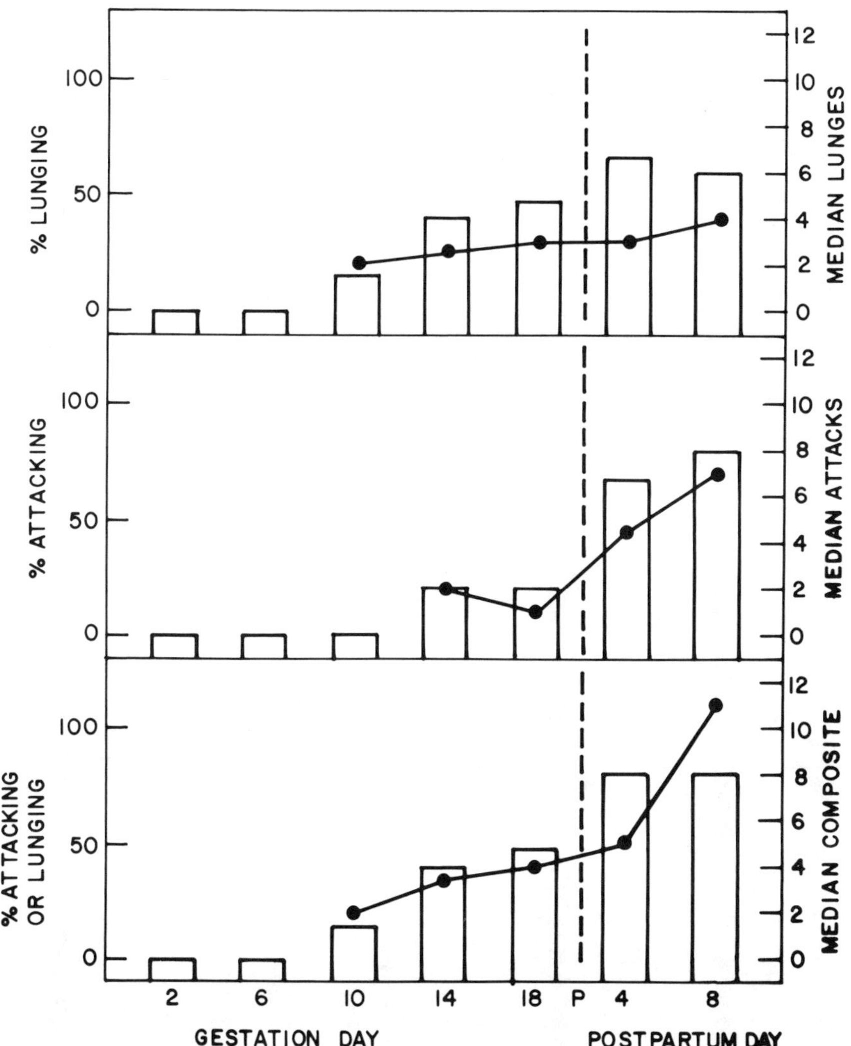

FIG. 7.1. The maternal aggressive behavior of pregnant Rockland–Swiss female mice toward adult male intruders as a function of advancing gestation. Separate groups of animals were examined for aggressive behavior on Gestation Day 2, 6, 10, 14, or 18. For comparison to postpartum aggression, separate groups of animals also were tested in a similar manner on Lactation Day 4 or 8. The histograms represent percentages, whereas lines represent median scores. (Mann & Svare, in press).

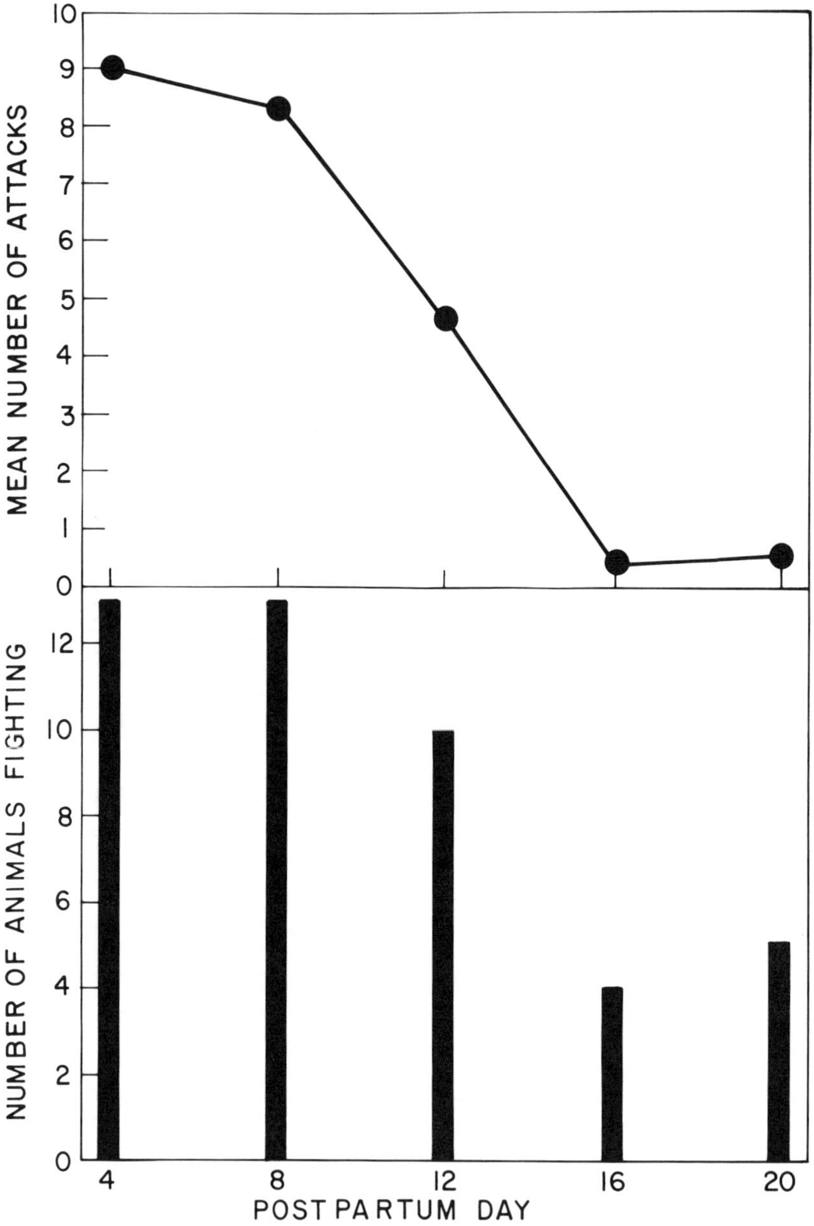

FIG. 7.2. The maternal aggressive behavior of lactating female mice toward adult male intruders as a function of advancing lactation. Three-minute tests for aggression were conducted at 4-day intervals on Days 4, 8, 12, 16, and 20 of lactation. The top half of the figure represents the average number of attacks, whereas the bottom half represents the number of animals exhibiting aggression. (N = 13). (From Svare, Betteridge, Katz, & Samuels, 1981).

periods followed by a decline during later lactations (Svare & Gandelman, 1976a). The fighting behavior displayed by multiparous animals was not due simply to previous fighting experience, because some multiparous animals exhibited aggression when tested for the first time on the sixth lactation period. Perhaps changes in the intensity of aggression with successive lactations are due to alterations in the exhibition of other maternal behaviors or to age-related changes in the secretion of other hormones.

Experiential and situational factors modulate the decline in fighting with advancing lactation. For example, lactating female mice that are repeatedly tested for aggressive behavior from days 2–22 postpartum continue to exhibit the behavior at higher levels than females tested only once at various times during lactation (Green, 1978). Also, isolation during pregnancy promotes postpartum aggression (Green, 1978). Pregnant females paired with a male prior to parturition are less aggressive following delivery of young than females housed in isolation (Green, 1978; Al-Maliki et al., 1980). However, unlike intermale aggression, maternal aggression is not promoted by early postweaning isolation (Svare et al., 1981). Finally, when compared to animals tested for aggression in the home cage, testing in a neutral arena reduces postpartum defense (Al-Maliki et al., 1980; Paul, Gronek, & Politch, 1980; Svare et al., 1981). The extent to which neuroendocrine factors might be playing a role in these situationally and experientially induced alterations in postpartum aggression is unknown but their role in similar aspects of intermale aggressive behavior has been well established (Leshner, 1979).

Role of the Young. The presence of young is instrumental for both the initiation and the maintenance of postpartum defense in rats and mice. This dimension of maternal aggression has been well researched and a number of reviews have recently been published (Svare, 1977, 1981; Svare & Mann, 1983).

A number of lines of evidence show that suckling stimulation from young is essential for the postpartum onset of maternal aggression. Female rats and mice that are thelectomized (nipples removed) prior to parturition and continuously fostered young following delivery, and females whose young are removed following parturition fail to become maternally aggressive (Gandelman & Simon, 1980; Gandelman & Svare, 1974; Svare & Gandelman, 1976b).

Virgin rats and mice, which lack the nipple growth that normally occurs during pregnancy, fail to exhibit fighting behavior following long-term exposure to foster young (Erskine, Barfield, & Goldman, 1980a; Gandelman & Simon, 1980; Svare & Gandelman, 1976b). However, they can be induced to exhibit postpartumlike aggressive behavior by exposing them to a hormone regimen that induces nipple growth (daily estrogen and progesterone injections for 19 days) followed by suckling stimulation from foster young (Gandelman & Simon, 1980; Svare & Gandelman, 1976c). Also, hormone-primed virgin female rats and mice, like pregnant and normal parturient animals, are relatively nonaggressive prior to suckling exposure and fail to exhibit aggression following either the removal of young or thelectomy combined with the fostering of young (Gandelman & Simon, 1980; Svare & Gandelman, 1976c). Finally, aggressive behavior is present in pregnant animals hysterectomized and fostered young at a time when nipple growth is adequate for suckling to take place (i.e., after Gestation Day 11). Conversely, the behavior is not evident in animals hysterectomized and fostered young at a time during gestation when nipple growth is inadequate for suckling to take place (i.e., on or before Gestation Day 11) (Svare, Mann, & Samuels, 1980).

The initiation of maternal aggression in mice and rats is dependent on the duration, but not the temporal onset of postpartum suckling. It takes at least 48 hours of continuous suckling stimulation for the initiation of the behavior (Svare & Gandelman, 1976b). Animals receiving less than 48 hours of suckling exposure fail to become maternally aggressive. However, the time at which suckling commences during the postpartum interval is not important. Mice receiving suckling exposure for the first time as much as 3 weeks following parturition and rats receiving such exposure for the first time 9 days following delivery exhibit an onset and intensity of fighting behavior that is identical to that of animals receiving suckling exposure immediately following parturition (Erskine, Barfield, & Goldman, 1980a; Svare et al., 1980).

The presence of young is also essential for the maintenance of maternal aggressive behavior. Five hours, but not 1 hr, of pup removal during early lactation (Postpartum Day 6) eliminates postpartum aggression in the mouse (Gandelman, 1972; Svare, 1977; Svare & Gandelman, 1973). If the young are replaced for as little as 5 min following 5 hr of pup removal, the behavior is restored. In the rat, removal of the litter 4 hr prior to aggression testing on either Day 9 or 10 of lactation results in significant decreases in fighting levels (Erskine, Barfield, and Goldman, 1978).

Direct physical contact between the dam and her young is not a prerequisite for the short-term maintenance of the behavior in mice. Placement of the dam's entire litter or a single pup behind a double wire mesh partition in the home cage maintains the behavior at a level indistinguishable from mothers in direct contact with their young (Svare & Gandelman, 1973). Also, when placed behind the partition, unfamiliar 6-, 13-, and 20-day-old pups, but not 30-day-old mice, maintain the behavior as effectively as the dam's own young (Svare, 1979). These adaptations probably function to ensure the protection and survival of unfamiliar young as well as pups that inevitably become separated from the nest and other littermates.

NEUROENDOCRINE FACTORS

Perinatal Hormone Influences

It is well documented that various aspects of female behavior are normally influenced by hormonal status during perinatal life. Studies of female sexual behavior, for example, show that estrogen-induced lordotic responding in rats is elevated by the prenatal administration of the aromatase inhibitor ATD or the antiandrogen flutamide (Gladue & Clemens, 1978). Several reports suggest that maternal aggression may also be modulated by the perinatal hormone environment.

In mice, restraint stress during pregnancy reduces the number of maternal attacks displayed by female offspring during their first lactation (Politch & Herrenkohl, 1979). Because adrenocorticotrophic hormone (ACTH) and glucocorticoids are greatly elevated following stress, it has been suggested that increased pituitary–adrenal hormones during prenatal life are responsible for the reported reductions in maternal aggression. In support of that hypothesis, it recently has been shown that prenatal exposure to prednisone, a synthetic glucocorticoid, significantly reduces the proportion of mice exhibiting maternal aggression in adulthood (Reinisch, Simon, & Gandelman, 1980). How prednisone produces these deficits is unknown at present, but it is well known that it is both mildly androgenic and can depress estrogen-binding alpha-fetoprotein (AFP).

Prenatal androgen exposure also has been implicated in the display of maternal aggression in mice. Female mice positioned between two males (i.e., 2M female) in utero are more maternally aggressive than females located between two females (i.e., 0M female). The significantly higher level of aggression in 2M animals as compared to 0M animals was limited to interactions with female intruders and was not evident when male opponents were used. During fetal life, 2M females are exposed to higher levels of testosterone (T) in serum and amniotic fluid than 0M females (vom Saal & Bronson, 1980). Elevating perinatal T by exogenous administration (2.0 μg/day on Days 12, 14, and 16 of fetal life) increases the number of attacks displayed by lactating Rockland–Swiss female mice (Mann & Svare, unpublished observations). Thus, female aggressive behavior, like male aggression, may be influenced by the early perinatal hormone environment.

Postnatal Adult Hormone Influences

Hormonal Determinants During Pregnancy. As noted earlier, aggression exhibited during pregnancy shows a gradual rise with advancing gestation. If this change in aggressive behavior is related to corresponding changes in the secretory patterns of endocrine glands, especially the ovaries, then one would expect to see elevated aggressive behavior in virgin females made pseudopregnant. In one study, female mice made pseudopregnant by exposure to a vasectomized male were as aggressive as pregnant animals (Noirot et al., 1975). In a more recent report (Hedricks & Daniels, 1981), however, pseudopregnant mice were no different from virgin females with respect to any major aspect of aggressive behavior. Regardless of the physiological mechanism involved in pregnancy-induced aggression, it apparently is unresponsive to suckling stimulation. Exposure to young during pregnancy does not promote the onset or elevate the intensity of the behavior in R–S mice (Mann & Svare, in press). Clearly, we know little about this aspect of maternal aggression and more research is critically needed to understand more fully the mechanisms responsible for pregnancy-induced agonistic responding.

Hormonal Determinants During Lactation. As noted earlier, suckling stimulation is a prerequisite for the establishment of postpartum aggression in mice and rats. Stimulation of the teats promotes rapid changes in the release of many lactation-promoting hormones from the pituitary gland (Mena, Pacheco, Whitworth, & Grosvenor, 1980; Nicoll, 1974). Suckling-induced changes in ovarian and adrenal hormones are not important for the behavior in mice, as ovariectomized and adrenalectomized animals continue to exhibit maternal aggression identical to that of sham-operated animals (Svare & Gandelman, 1976c; unpublished observations). Because the pituitary hormone prolactin (PRL) is very sensitive to changes in suckling stimulation and has been implicated in lactation and other aspects of parental care (Zarrow, Gandelman, & Denenberg, 1971), many investigators (Beach, 1948) have felt that this hormone is the most likely candidate for involvement in the maternal aggressive behavior displayed by mice. This issue is still controversial. However, recent data now clearly show that PRL is not involved in the maternal aggression displayed by rats and house mice. The findings are reviewed in the following.

High levels of circulating PRL and aggression are evident during early and mid-lactation, whereas levels of both the hormone and behavior are low during late lactation (Sinha, Selby, & Vanderlaan, 1974; Svare & Gandelman, 1973). However, examination of correlations between the hormone and the behavior in individual animals fails to reveal any systematic relationships. In postpartum mice, maternal aggression and circulating levels of PRL were measured in separate groups of parturient animals on Postpartum Day 0 (the day of delivery), 6, 12, or 18. The results showed that there was little correspondence between circulating levels of the hormone and behavior (Broida, Michael, & Svare, 1981). On Postpartum Day 0, the dams rarely fought but circulating PRL was at its highest level. Aggression was highest on Postpartum Days 6 and 12 and significantly declined between Postpartum Days 12 and 18. Importantly, however, plasma PRL declined well in advance of a decline in aggression, because a significant reduction in levels of the hormone was observed between Postpartum Days 6 and 12. Also, there was no significant correlation between circulating PRL and the intensity of fighting behavior.

Another tactic for exploring the role of PRL in postpartum aggression is to inject specific PRL inhibitors (i.e., ergot drugs). In one study (Mann, Michael, & Svare, 1980), parturient mice received a daily dose of .5 mg of ergocornine or bromocryptine for 8 days and were examined for circulating PRL, lactation, and aggression behavior toward a male intruder. The findings showed that drug-treated dams did not lactate, in spite of receiving fresh foster young on a daily basis, and the animals exhibited a sevenfold and twofold reduction respectively in plasma PRL. Aggression, however, was indistinguishable from that of oil-treated controls, suggesting that PRL may be unnecessary for the behavior. To the contrary, however, an older report shows that ergot drug treatment does reduce the postpartum aggressive behavior of hamsters. Twice daily injections of .5 mg ergocornine for 3 days inhibits the behavior in recently parturient female hamsters, whereas PRL replacement therapy reverses the trend (Wise & Pryor, 1977).

A better way to test whether or not PRL is involved in maternal defense is to examine the fighting behavior of parturient animals whose pituitary gland has been removed (hypophysectomy). In one study (Mann, Broida, Michael, & Svare, 1980), postpartum mice were hypophysectomized prior to any exposure to suckling stimulation. Following the receipt of suckling stimulation from foster young, the hypophysectomized animals exhibited normal levels of postpartum aggression in spite of marked deficiencies in circulating PRL (See Table 7.1). Similarly, in rats, hypophysectomy performed on Postpartum Day 5 in that species reduces circulating PRL but does not disrupt maternal aggression (Erskine, Barfield, & Goldman, 1980b).

Yet another tactic for exploring PRL involvement in postpartum defense is to elevate levels of the hormone by injections or pituitary grafts. PRL injections promote aggression in ovariectomized–adrenalectomized virgin peromyscus mice (Gleason, Michael, & Christian, 1981) and virgin female hamsters made hyperprolactinemic with ectopic pituitary grafts exhibit elevated levels of aggression (Buntin, Cantanzaro, & Lisk, 1981).

TABLE 7.1
Maternal Aggressive Behavior and Plasma Prolactin (PRL) Levels of Parturient Rockland–Swiss Albino Female Mice that were Hypophysectomized (HYPOX), Sham-Operated (SHAM), or Nonoperated (NOC) (From Mann, Broida, Michael, & Svare, 1980)[a]

Group	*Proportion (and %) Fighting*	*Mean (± S.E.M.) Latency (in Test Days) to Exhibit Fighting*	*Mean (± S.E.M.) Number of Tests Fighting*	*Mean (± S.E.M.) Number of Attacks*	*Mean Plasma Prolactin (ng/ml) Levels*
NOC	14/24 (.58)	2.6 ± 0.3	2.3 ± 0.3	2.6 ± 0.6	159.4 ± 46.2
SHAM	19/32 (.59)	2.3 ± 0.3	2.7 ± 0.3	3.9 ± 0.5	124.5 ± 28.6
HYPOX	15/22 (.68)	1.7 ± 0.2	2.8 ± 0.3	2.9 ± 0.5	5.3 ± 1.3

[a]Surgery was performed within 8 days following parturition. To prevent any suckling-induced rise in PRL release prior to surgery, the animals delivered their young through double wire mesh partitions inserted in the floors of the cages just prior to delivery. Beginning on Postpartum Day 9, the animals were fostered five 2–8-day-old replete pups on a daily basis for 9 days. Three-minute tests for aggression against an adult male intruder were conducted every other day beginning on Postpartum Day 12 for a total of four tests.

In spite of the positive effects of PRL in the aforementioned studies, the question remains as to whether or not postpartum aggression or spontaneous interfemale aggression (i.e., non-lactation-induced) was being explored. Regardless, the findings clearly show that PRL is not involved in rat and house mouse maternal aggression. More comparative data is needed before we can make definitive conclusions concerning the extent to which PRL mediates maternal aggression.

PEPTIDES AND NEUROTRANSMITTERS

In addition to influencing the hormonal status of the parturient animal, it is well known that suckling stimulation alters other aspects of brain biochemistry. In particular, suckling is known to alter profoundly the turnover rates of hypothalamic monoamines and catecholamines (cf. Tindall, 1978) and specific agonists and antagonists of these systems would be expected to alter maternal defense. For example, turnover rates of serotonin (5-HT) dramatically increase with suckling stimulation (cf. Tindall, 1978) and experimental evidence strongly links serotonergic function to rodent sexual and aggressive behavior (e.g., Meyerson, Palis, & Sietnieks, 1979). Interestingly, preliminary findings (Mann & Svare, unpublished observations) show that a daily dose of 400 mg/kg of the serotonin antagonist D-L-parachlorophenylalanine (*p*-CPA) significantly reduces the proportion of lactating R–S animals exhibiting aggression. *p*-CPA in the aforementioned study was administered on 6 consecutive days during early lactation with behavioral testing 90 minutes following the injection on Days 4, 5, and 6 of the treatment period. If 5-HT is involved in the suckling-induced onset of the behavior in mice, then one would expect that other manipulations of the serotonergic system should modulate postpartum aggression. Testosterone propionate (TP) and estradiol benzoate (EB), steroids known to depress 5-HT functioning, reduce fighting behavior in lactating mice after short-term treatment (as little as 3 injections of .5 μg EB or 500 μg TP [Svare, 1980; Svare & Gandelman, 1975]). Finally, intraventricular injection of 6-hydroxydopamine (6-OHDA), a drug that depletes catecholamines (CA), increases the proportion of postpartum Sprague–Dawley rats exhibiting maternal aggression (Sorenson & Gordon, 1975). It is interesting to note that CAs normally are inhibited following suckling stimulation (Tindall, 1978). These findings tentatively suggest involvement of 5-HT and CAs in maternal aggression.

Examination of other prototypical drugs and their effects on either postpartum or pregnancy-induced aggression has been very limited. In one study (Brain & Al-Maliki, 1979), administration of the frequently used antidepressant, lithium chloride (LiCl), depressed intermale aggressive behavior but had no effect on postpartum aggression in T.O. albino mice. This would suggest that maternal defense is very different from other forms of aggressive behaviors with respect to mechanism(s) of control.

GENETIC FACTORS

Outbred Rockland–Swiss (R–S) mice exhibit large individual variation in the exhibition of postpartum aggression. Roughly 50–70% of lactating R–S females exhibit postpartum aggression, whereas the remainder are nonaggressive (Svare & Gandelman, 1973). Of those animals that are aggressive, the intensity of fighting behavior can range anywhere from 1 to over 20 attacks in a single 3-min test session during early lactation. This individual variability in aggressive behavior is remarkably consistent even when animals are examined for the behavior on six successive litters; highly aggressive animals maintain high levels of the behavior, whereas nonaggressive animals rarely become "fighters" (Svare & Gandelman, 1976a). It is clear, then, that genotype should account, in part, for some of the observed variability in the behavior. Work with inbred and selectively bred animals supports this assumption.

Lactating DBA/2 and BALB female mice are known to exhibit high levels of maternal aggression, whereas C57BL/6 and C3H mice rarely exhibit the behavior (St. John & Corning, 1973). The strain difference in maternal aggression evident in DBA/2 and C57BL/6 mice does not appear to be related to maternal environmental or experiential factors (Broida & Svare, 1982). Reciprocally crossed animals exhibit DBA/2-like levels of high maternal aggression and cross-fostered animals perform true to their genotype. Also, the strain difference is not altered by additional reproductive experience, because multiparous animals continue to exhibit patterns of aggressive behavior consistent with their genotype. These findings apparently suggest that inherent biological differences among the strains may be responsible for differences in aggressive behavior. It is interesting to speculate that differences in neuroendocrine and/or neurotransmitter functions may be responsible.

Another strategy that ultimately may help us to understand the biological mechanisms involved in maternal aggression is the use of selectively bred mice. In wild female *Mus musculus* selectively bred for spontaneous interfemale aggressive behavior, the exhibition of postpartum aggression was also differentially affected by the selection process (Ebert, this volume; Hyde & Sawyer, 1979). Thus, maternal defensive behavior is a correlated character of spontaneous female aggression. An examination of possible physiological correlates has not yet been conducted.

BIOLOGICAL FUNCTIONS OF MATERNAL AGGRESSION

Although most researchers agree that maternal aggression functions to protect the offspring, there is little scientific support for this notion in the literature. For example, when tested in an extended cage apparatus (Erskine et al., 1978), lactating female rats are not effective in preventing access of the intruder to the litter. In tests where the intruder had the opportunity to avoid contact with the mother and her litter by fleeing to another part of the cage, most of the intruders spent more time in the nest than the mothers. Also, cannibalization of the litters by the intruder frequently occurred, and the number of attacks by the females was not correlated with either the number of times the intruder moved in and out of the nest or the amount of time the intruder spent in the nest. In similar studies with mice (Green, 1978; Paul et al., 1980), maternal attacks were ineffective in preventing pup cannibalism by intruding males. Moreover, attacks on the young actually decreased maternal aggression and increased cannibalism of pups by dams. An undesirable aspect of the aforementioned studies is the fact that forced cohabitation was an unnatural feature. Perhaps the only valid way to explore the biological function of maternal aggression is to examine the behavior in the wild. Nevertheless, these findings have suggested to some that the biological function of maternal aggression is not protection, as has been traditionally assumed (Paul et al., 1980).

The display of maternal aggression in rodents may serve other functions that heretofore have been neglected. Although there is little information of a systematic nature to support or refute the claim, anecdotal observations suggest that maternal aggression may play an important role in regulating population size. For example, in studies of freely growing but confined populations of house mice, several researchers (Brown, 1953; Christian & LeMunyan, 1958; Southwick, 1955) noted that maternal behavior, including aggression, broke down under conditions of high population density, thus permitting nest encroachment, cannibalism of young, and reduction of population size. In contrast to this, however, the hypothesis has been advanced that heightened maternal aggression would be expected in high population densities in order to disperse individuals to adjacent unoccupied territories (Svare, 1977). Speculation must be bolstered by data however, and at this time there is little research to support either position.

If the display of maternal aggression is adaptive, then one might expect the exhibition of the behavior to be heritable and positively correlated with some aspects of reproductive performance. Work reviewed earlier (Broida & Svare, 1982; St. John & Corning, 1973), as well as research reported in this volume (see chapters by Hahn and by Ebert), clearly suggest that postpartum aggression is under genetic control. This conclusion awaits further classical genetic experimentation for additional proof. In addition, other work suggests that the behavior may be related to reproductive performance. In freely growing populations of *Mus musculus,* high-ranking female mice were responsible for almost all offspring produced (Lloyd & Christian, 1969). Also, lactating mice that exhibited high overall levels of aggression tended to produce litters with more young than did animals exhibiting lower overall levels of aggression (Svare & Gandelman, 1976a).

DIRECTIONS FOR FUTURE RESEARCH

We can identify at least three research tactics that should help us in the future to explore the psychobiological basis of maternal aggression. First, basic psychopharmacological work is needed in order to elucidate further the biochemistry of this behavior. The data base already available for intermale aggression should aid researchers in their selection of drugs, doses, and treatment regimes. Second, the use of inbred and selectively bred animals, with their natural genetic variation in neuroendocrine and neurotransmitter function, provides a useful tool for exploring the biological basis of maternal aggressive behavior. Genetic analyses as tools for understanding physiological mechanisms have already been used to great advantage by those studying other aspects of social behavior. Third, comparative studies are critically needed in order to establish whether or not the present findings in rodents are generalizable across the so-called phylogenetic scale. These strategies ultimately will provide us with a more thorough analysis of this little studied dimension of aggressive behavior.

ACKNOWLEDGMENTS

This review was written while the author was supported by a Research Grant from the Harry Frank Guggenheim Foundation, Grant BNS80–08546 from NSF, and by Grant AG01319 from NIA. The stimulation provided by John Broida, Ron Gandelman, Craig Kinsley, Martha Mann, Sandy Michael, and Owen Samuels is gratefully acknowledged.

REFERENCES

Al-Maliki, S., Brain, P. F., Childs, G., & Benton, D. Factors influencing maternal attacks on conspecific intruders by lactating female TO strain mice. *Aggressive Behavior,* 1980, *6,* 103–117.

Beach, F. A. *Hormones and behavior.* Harper: New York, 1948.

Brain, P. F., & Al-Maliki, S. Effects of lithium chloride injections on rank-related fighting, maternal aggression, and locust-killing responses in naive and experienced TO strain mice. *Pharmacology, Biochemistry, and Behavior,* 1979, *10,* 663–669.

Broida, J., Michael, S. D., & Svare, B. Plasma prolactin levels are not related to the initiation, maintenance, and decline of postpartum aggression in mice. *Behavioral and Neural Biology,* 1981, *32,* 121–125.

Broida, J., & Svare, B. Postpartum aggression in C57BL/6J and DBA/2J mice: Experiential and environmental influences. *Behavioral and Neural Biology,* 1982, *35,* 76–83.

Brown, R. Z. Social behavior, reproduction, and population changes in the house mouse. *Ecological Monographs,* 1953, *23,* 217–240.

Buhot-Averseng, M. C., & Goyens, J. Effects of cohabitation with another female on aggressive behavior in pregnant mice. *Aggressive Behavior,* 1981, *7,* 111–121.

Buntin, J. D., Cantanzaro, C., & Lisk, R. D. Facilitatory effects of pituitary transplants on intraspecific aggression in female hamsters. *Hormones and Behavior,* 1981, *15,* 214–225.

Christian, J. J., & LeMunyan, C. D. Adverse effects of crowding on reproduction and lactation of mice and two generations of their progeny. *Endocrinology,* 1958, *63,* 517–529.

Erskine, M., Barfield, R. J., & Goldman, B. D. Intraspecific fighting during late pregnancy and lactation in rats and effects of litter removal. *Behavioral Biology,* 1978, *23,* 206–218.

Erskine, M., Barfield, R. J., & Goldman, B. D. Postpartum aggression in rats: II. Dependence on maternal sensitivity to young and effects of experience with pregnancy and parturition. *Journal of Comparative and Physiological Psychology,* 1980, *94,* 495–505. (a)

Erskine, M., Barfield, R. J., & Goldman, B. D. Postpartum aggression in rats: I. Effects of hypophysectomy. *Journal of Comparative and Physiological Psychology,* 1980, *94,* 484–494. (b)

Erskine, M., Denenberg, V. H., & Goldman, B. D. Aggression in the lactating rat: Effect of intruder age and test arena. *Behavioral Biology,* 1978, *23,* 52–66.

Gandelman, R. Mice: Postpartum aggression elicited by the presence of an intruder. *Hormones and Behavior,* 1972, *3,* 23–28.

Gandelman, R., & Simon, N. G. Postpartum fighting in the rat: Nipple development and the presence of young. *Behavioral and Neural Biology,* 1980, *28,* 350–360.

Gandelman, R., & Svare, B. Pregnancy termination, lactation, and aggression. *Hormones and Behavior,* 1974, *5,* 397–405.

Gladue, B. A., & Clemens, L. G. Androgenic influences on feminine sexual behavior in male and female rats: Defeminization blocked by prenatal antiandrogen treatment. *Endocrinology,* 1978, *103,* 1702–1709.

Gleason, P. E., Michael, S. D., & Christian, J. J. Prolactin-induced aggression in female peromyscus leucopus. *Behavioral and Neural Biology,* 1981, *33,* 243–248.

Goyens, J., & Noirot, E. Intruders of differing reproductive status alter aggression differentially in early and late pregnant mice. *Aggressive Behavior,* 1977, *3,* 119–125.

Green, J. A. Experiential determinants of postpartum aggression in mice. *Journal of Comparative and Physiological Psychology,* 1978, *92,* 1179–1187.

Hedricks, C., & Daniels, C. E. Agonistic behavior between pregnant mice and male intruders. *Behavioral and Neural Biology,* 1981, *31,* 236–241.

Hyde, J. S., & Sawyer, T. F. Correlated response in selection for aggressiveness in female mice. II. Maternal aggression. *Behavior Genetics,* 1979, *9,* 571–577.

Lee, C. T., & Ingersoll, D. W. Pheromonal influences on aggressive behavior. In B. Svare (Ed.), *Hormones and aggressive behavior.* Plenum: New York, 1983.

Leshner, A. I. Kinds of hormonal effects on behavior: A new view. *Neuroscience and Biobehavioral Reviews,* 1979, *3,* 69–73.

Lloyd, J. A., & Christian, J. J. Reproductive activity of individual females in three experimentally freely growing populations of house mice (*Mus musculus*). *Journal of Mammalogy,* 1969, *50,* 49–59.

Lynds, P. G. *A comparison of the behavioral components of postpartum intermale aggression in wild housemice.* Paper presented at Nebraska Academy of Sciences Meeting, 1976. (a)

Lynds, P. G. Olfactory control of aggression in lactating female housemice. *Physiology and Behavior,* 1976, *17,* 157–159. (b)

Mann, M., Broida, J., Michael, S. D., & Svare, B. *Prolactin is not necessary for maternal aggression in mice.* Paper presented at International Society for Developmental Psychobiology meeting, Cincinnati, Ohio, 1980.

Mann, M., Michael, S. D., & Svare, B. Ergot drugs suppress plasma prolactin and lactation but not aggression in parturient mice. *Hormones and Behavior,* 1980, *14,* 319–328.

Mann, M., & Svare, B. Factors influencing pregnancy-induced aggression in mice. *Behavioral and Neural Biology,* in press.

Mena, F., Pacheco, P., Whitworth, N., & Grosvenor, C. Recent data concerning the secretion and function of oxytocin and prolactin during lactation in the rat and rabbit. *Frontiers in Hormone Research,* 1980, *6,* 217–250.

Meyerson, B. J., Palis, A., & Sietnieks, A. Hormone–monoamine interaction and sexual behavior. In C. Beyer (Ed.), *Endocrine control of sexual behavior*. New York: Raven, 1979.

Nicoll, C. Physiological actions of prolactin. In E. Knobil & W. H. Sawyer (Eds.), *Handbook of Physiology* (Vol. 4). Washington: American Physiological Society, 1974.

Noirot, E., Goyens, J., & Buhot, M. C. Aggressive behavior of pregnant mice toward males. *Hormones and Behavior,* 1975, *6,* 9–17.

Paul, L., Gronek, J., & Politch, J. A. Maternal aggression in mice: Protection of young is a by-product of attacks at the home site. *Aggressive Behavior,* 1980, *6,* 19–29.

Politch, J. A., & Herrenkohl, L. Prenatal stress reduces maternal aggression in mice offspring. *Physiology and Behavior,* 1979, *23,* 415–418.

Price, E. O., & Belanger, P. L. Maternal behavior of wild and domestic stocks of Norway rats. *Behavioral Biology,* 1977, *20,* 60–69.

Reinisch, J. M., Simon, N. G., & Gandelman, R. Prenatal exposure to prednisone permanently alters fighting behavior of female mice. *Pharmacology, Biochemistry, and Behavior,* 1980, *12,* 213–216.

Rosenson, L. M., & Asheroff, A. K. Maternal aggression in CD-1 mice: Influence of the hormonal condition of the intruder. *Behavioral Biology,* 1975, *15,* 219–224.

St. John, R. S., & Corning, P. A. Maternal aggression in mice. *Behavioral Biology,* 1973, *9,* 635–639.

Sinha, Y. N., Selby, F. W., & Vanderlaan, W. P. Relationship of prolactin and growth hormone to mammary function during pregnancy and lactation in the C3H/ST mouse. *Journal of Endocrinology,* 1974, *61,* 219–229.

Sorenson, C. A., & Gordon, M. Effects of 6-hydroxydopamine on shock-elicited aggression, emotionality, and maternal behavior in female rats. *Pharmacology, Biochemistry, and Behavior,* 1975, *3,* 331–335.

Southwick, C. H. Regulatory mechanisms of house mouse populations: Social behavior affecting litter survival. *Ecology,* 1955, *36,* 627–634.

Svare, B. Maternal aggression in mice: Influence of the young. *Biobehavioral Reviews,* 1977, *1,* 151–164.

Svare, B. Maternal aggression in mice: The nonspecific nature of the exteroceptive maintenance by young. *Aggressive Behavior,* 1979, *5,* 417–424.

Svare, B. Testosterone propionate inhibits maternal aggression in mice. *Physiology and Behavior,* 1980, *24,* 435–439.

Svare, B. Maternal aggression in mammals. In D. J. Gubernick & P. Klopfer, (Eds.), *Parental care in mammals*. New York: Plenum, 1981.

Svare, B., Betteridge, D., Katz, D., & Samuels, O. Some situational and experiential determinants of maternal aggression in mice. *Physiology and Behavior,* 1981, *26,* 253–258.

Svare, B., & Gandelman, R. Postpartum aggression in mice: Experiential and environmental factors. *Hormones and Behavior,* 1973, *4,* 323–334.

Svare, B., & Gandelman, R. Postpartum aggression in mice: Inhibitory effect of estrogen. *Physiology and Behavior,* 1975, *14,* 31–36.

Svare, B., & Gandelman, R. A longitudinal analysis of maternal aggression in mice. *Developmental Psychobiology,* 1976, *9,* 437–446. (a)

Svare, B., & Gandelman, R. Postpartum aggression in mice: The influence of suckling stimulation. *Hormones and Behavior,* 1976, *7,* 407–416. (b)

Svare, B., & Gandelman, R. Suckling stimulation induces aggression in virgin female mice. *Nature,* 1976, *260,* 606–608. (c)

Svare, B., & Mann, M. Hormonal influences on maternal aggression. In B. Svare (Ed.), *Hormones and aggressive behavior*. New York: Plenum, 1983.

Svare, B., Mann, M., & Samuels, O. Mice: Suckling stimulation but not lactation important for maternal aggression. *Behavioral and Neural Biology,* 1980, *29,* 453–462.

Tindall, J. S. Neuroendocrine control of lactation. In B. L. Larson (Ed.), *Lactation: A comprehensive treatise* (Vol. 4). New York: Academic, 1978.

vom Saal, F. S., & Bronson, F. H. Sexual characteristics of adult females correlates with their blood testosterone levels during development in mice. *Science,* 1980, *208,* 597–599.

Wise, D. A. Aggression in the female golden hamster: Effects of reproductive state and social isolation. *Hormones and Behavior,* 1974, *5,* 235–250.

Wise, D. A., & Pryor, T. L. Effects of ergocornine and prolactin on aggression in the postpartum golden hamster. *Hormones and Behavior,* 1977, *8,* 30–39.

Zarrow, M. X., Gandelman, R., & Denenberg, V. H. Prolactin: Is it an essential hormone for maternal behavior in the mammal? *Hormones and Behavior,* 1971, *2,* 343–354.

NEURAL ASPECTS

8 Ethopharmacology of Aggression, Defense, and Defeat

Klaus A. Miczek
Tufts University

HISTORICAL BACKGROUND

The search for the neural processes mediating aggression has a venerable history and has generated a formidable research literature. In the past 25 years, the neuroanatomical and neurochemical hypotheses on the control mechanisms for aggression have paralleled each other in many respects and have started to converge. The initial anatomical studies focused on circumscribed brain loci that appeared to be critical for the occurrence of certain aggressive behaviors. The use of microelectrodes for excitation of discrete clusters of cell bodies or, alternatively, the ablation technique were instrumental in the development of the hypothesis of neural centers that exclusively control a specific behavior such as eating, drinking, copulating, and also fighting and killing. For example, the pioneering studies by Hess (1948) delineated a zone around the perifornical nucleus in the cat hypothalamus from which affective defensive responses could be evoked.

In the 1960s, the discovery of new neural degeneration and histochemical methods, and the concurrent application of electrical stimulation and lesion techniques implicated several telencephalic, limbic, and mesencephalic structures in the neural processes mediating aggressive behaviors. The significant role of limbic and mesencephalic processes in cat aggression and flight was demonstrated early on, for example, by de Molina and Hunsperger (1962) and Wasman and Flynn (1962). A series of elegant degeneration studies in the cat began to analyze the complex neural networks for affective defense and predatory attack (see for review Flynn, Smith, Coleman, & Opsahl, 1979). These observations forced abandonment of the "subcortical phrenology."

Parallel with the development of neuroanatomical work, initial efforts describing neurotransmitter coding of behavior attempted to link the control mechanism for a specific behavioral response to the activity of a transmitter substance at synapses in discrete brain regions. Spurred by early discoveries such as that of Grossman (1960) that found acetylcholine and norepinephrine directly applied to the lateral hypothalamus of sated rates, and evoked drinking and feeding respectively, thus, the hypothesis for a neurochemical code of behavior emerged (Miller, 1965). In contrast to research on neurotransmitter coding of ingestive behavior, similar efforts to identify "aggressive monoamines" (Eichelman & Thoa, 1973) were considerably less successful. Attempts to link acetylcholine activity in the lateral hypothalamus of rats to predatory killing or, alternatively, to refer to serotonin as the "civilizing neurohumor" (i.e., reduced functioning in serotonin-containing neurons may lead to the uncontrollable release of undesirable activities such as sex and aggression) remained isolated and were met with skepticism.

The past decade has seen a broader proposal emerge, namely the multitransmitter control of aggressive behavior initially positing two substances in opposite functional roles. For example, such simplistic "neurochemical dualism" viewed dopamine as activator and serotonin as inhibitor of aggression. More recently, additional neurohumors were implicated in various proposals for a neurochemical profile of aggression (Daruna, 1978; Eichelman, 1979; Karczmar, Richardson, & Kindell, 1978; Krsiak, Solcova, Tomasikova, Dlohozkova, Kosar, & Masek, 1981; Pradhan, 1975; Reis, 1974).

LABORATORY PARADIGMS FOR AGGRESSION IN ANIMALS

Before presenting an outline and critique of the major current concepts on neurotransmitter control of aggression, it may be useful to examine some of the methodological and theoretical contributions of the behavioral analysis of aggression. In the past decade a cavalier attitude has developed among neuroscientists toward a precise, accurate, and sensitive analysis of behavior, and aggression is no exception. General conclusions from recent literature reviews are seriously tempered by conceptual and methodological problems, the most significant of which appears to be the lack of a satisfactory definition of aggressive behavior patterns.

It has long been recognized that aggression is not a unitary behavioral phenomenon, but instead includes a range of behavior patterns. It is still not clear whether to categorize different aspects of aggression according to the situations in which the behavior occurs, the functions it serves, or the behavioral topography that it displays. Most laboratory studies of brain mechanisms and aggression have been guided by pragmatical considerations. Experimental protocols have been developed that generate some kind of violent behavior in a selected animal species, each considered a distinctive "model" of aggression. For example, fighting is assessed in pairs of mice after prolonged isolated housing (isolation-induced aggression), the defensive upright postures are tallied in rats exposed to electric pulses to the feet (shock-induced aggression), aggressive packing toward a target is counted in pigeons subjected to nonreinforcement (extinction- or frustration-induced aggression), rats are selected for their propensity to kill a mouse (predatory aggression), or affective defensive reactions are evoked by electrical stimulation of a discrete brain structure (brain-stimulation-elicited aggression). At present, the causative and controlling variables for various aggressive behaviors are poorly understood, in particular the impact of aversive environmental events.

In Table 8.1 the major paradigms for the study of aggression in laboratory animals are given. In addition to describing the stimulus conditions and the type

TABLE 8.1
Major Paradigms for the Study of Aggression in the Laboratory

Paradigm, Species	*Stimulus Situation*	*Behavioral Topography*	*Biological Function*
Isolation-induced aggression, mostly in mice	Prolonged isolated housing before confrontation with another isolate or group-housed animal in a test cage or home cage of the isolate	Complete agonistic behavior pattern; isolates attack, threaten, pursue opponent	Territorial defense or compulsive, abnormal, pathological behavior
Pain-elicited or shock-induced aggression, mostly in rats	Pairs of animals are exposed to pulses of electric shock delivered through grid floor	Defensive reactions, including upright postures, bites toward face of opponent, audible vocalizations	Some similarity to reaction toward predator or toward large opponent
Brain-lesion-induced aggression in rats, cats	Destruction of neural tissue, and subsequent social or environmental challenges	Defensive reactions; biting	Brain disease
Brain-stimulation-induced aggression, in cats, rats, monkeys	Electrical excitation of neural tissue, mostly in diencephalon and mesencephalon, but also in other, limbic or cerebellar areas	Defensive reactions accompanied by autonomic arousal; predatory attack and kill	Defense against attacker Predation

(continued)

TABLE 8.1 (*Continued*)

Paradigm, Species	*Stimulus Situation*	*Behavioral Topography*	*Biological Function*
Predatory aggression, mostly in rats, cats	Presence of prey, food deprivation	Stalking, seizing, killing, consuming (?)	Food source; "killer instinct"
Frustration- or extinction-induced aggression, mostly in pigeons	Conditioning history; operant behavior under control of a reinforcement schedule; omission or prolonged intermittency of reinforcement	Attack bites or pecks, threat displays towards suitable object or conspecific	Competition for resources (?)
Resident–intruder aggression in most animals, in both sexes	Confrontation with an unfamiliar adult member of the species	Full species-specific repertoire of agonistic behavior, including attack, threat by resident, and defense, submission, flight by intruder	Territorial or group defense (?)
Maternal aggression, mostly in rodents	Lactating female, in the presence of litter, confronting an intruder male	Species-specific repertoire of attack and threat behavior toward intruder	Defense of young
Intragroup aggression, mostly in monkeys, mice, and rats	Formation or maintenance of a social group	Species-specific repertoire of communicative signals (displays, odors, sounds) between group members of different social rank. Low level and intensity of agonism.	Social cohesion and dispersion

Note: Adapted in part from Miczek & DeBold, 1982.

of aggressive behavior, the possible biological function of the behavior is mentioned; entries in this last column are obviously speculative, and it is this aspect of the frequently used laboratory paradigms that is most suspect. Most earlier laboratory paradigms of aggression suffer because they are only vaguely related to aggression outside the laboratory, and because their relationship to human aggression has not been established. The more recent emphasis on biologically relevant situations and types of aggressive and defensive behavior patterns represents a significant departure from the past. Confrontations with a territorial intruder, with a rival in a group, or with a lactating female, are situations that have begun to be successfully studied under laboratory conditions.

The behavioral analysis of aggression has several important implications for the study of underlying neural mechanisms and, especially, the role of neurotransmitters. First, each of the experimental paradigms differs in terms of: (1) the variables that are necessary for a selected form of "aggression" to occur; (2) the type of aggressive or defensive reaction; and (3) the preferred animal species. It is unlikely to expect a single neural network to mediate the various aggressive and defensive behavior patterns. Second, the "model" approach to aggression needs to be critically examined and ultimately should be abandoned. It appears more fruitful to pursue a study of mechanisms mediating functionally well-defined and meaningful sequences of aggressive behavior. Given the problems of identifying the biological functions of earlier research paradigms it has been difficult to clarify exactly what the experimental conditions and resulting behavior patterns are modeling.

MULTITRANSMITTER CONTROL OF AGGRESSION

Recent literature reviews have followed a similar format in summarizing the roles of acetylcholine (ACh), serotonin (5-hydroxytryptamine, 5-HT), dopamine (DA), and norepinephrine (NE) as well as other neurohumors in the mechanisms of aggression. One of the first summaries was presented by Reis (1974), who proposed that the release of NE primarily induces or enhances affective defensive reactions; this type of behavior appears to be facilitated also by ACh.

In Table 8.2 the summaries of several recent reviews have been synthesized (Daruna, 1978; Karczmar et al., 1978; Krsiak et al., 1981; Pradhan, 1975; Reis, 1974). It is apparent that each reviewer's perspective is determined by his or her own expertise with a given research paradigm and species. The arrows in Table 8.2 denote increased or decreased transmitter activity. Two basic methods have been used to determine neurotransmitter activity; first, neurochemical measurements in animals showing attack or defensive behavior, and secondly, more or less specific pharmacological manipulations of a neurotransmitter system.

The information on attack behavior (Table 8.2, top) is entirely based on isolated mice. There is good agreement on a facilitatory role for brain acetylcholine in attack and threat behavior that is mainly concluded from the potent antiaggressive effects of anticholinergic drugs. The respective roles of the monoamines (5-HT, DA, NE) are considerably less clear. The few neurochemical studies indicate substantial but divergent changes in catecholamine activity during and after attack (Eleftheriou & Boehlke, 1967; Hendley, Moisset, & Welch, 1973; Modigh, 1973).

The pattern of neurotransmitter activity on defensive reactions reveals several consistencies (Table 8.2, bottom). These reactions have been investigated in pairs of rats that are exposed to electric shock to their feet, in cats that are stimulated via electrodes in the medial hypothalamus, and to a lesser extent in

TABLE 8.2
Neurotransmitter Profiles of Agonistic Behavior

			Neurotransmitter Activity			
Paradigm	*Behavior*	*Species*	*ACh*	*5-HT*	*DA*	*NE*
A. Attack or Offensive Behavior						
Isolation-induced aggression	Attack, threat, pursuit	Mouse	↑	↑ ↓ (2) ↑ (3) ↓ (5)	 ↑ ↓ (2)	 ↑ (3) ↑ ↓ (2)
B. Defensive Reactions						
Electric shock-elicited aggression	Defensive postures	Rat	↑	↓ (2) ↑ ↓ (3)	↑	↑
Electric brain-stimulation-elicited aggression	Affective defensive reactions	Cat	↑ (1)	↓ (1)	↑ (2)	↑ ↑
Isolation-induced timidity	Defensive postures and acts	Mouse		↑ (5)		

(1) Reis, 1974
(2) Pradhan, 1975
(3) Daruna, 1978
(4) Karczmar et al., 1978
(5) Krsiak et al., 1981

mice that are considered "timid" after isolated housing. In spite of the marked differences in experimental conditions and in species, a facilitatory role of ACh and NE in defensive reactions is consistently found, whereas 5-HT and DA activities appear to depend on the experimental preparation.

In contrast to attack and defense as they occur in agonistic interactions between species members, a remarkably consistent profile of neurotransmitter activity has been suggested for predatory aggression (Table 8.3). In spite of less than compelling evidence, it appears that killing of mice by rats is facilitated by pharmacological treatments that enhance the activity of brain ACh, decrease 5-HT synthesis and storage, and inhibit NE (Barr, Gibbons, & Bridger, 1976; Pradhan, 1975; Sheard, this volume). The transmitter profile for predatory attack in cats parallels that for rats (Reis, 1974).

The current views of the role of various neurotransmitters in the mechanisms mediating aggressive and defensive behaviors emphasize the principle of balance between these substances. Experimental manipulations of one neurotransmitter usually lead to a concurrent change in an interacting substance. For example, simply restricting the amino acid tryptophan in the diet with the objective of altering brain 5-HT also leads to profound changes in the uptake processes for phenylalanine and tyrosine (Fernstrom & Hirsch, 1975).

TABLE 8.3
Neurotransmitter Profile of Predatory Aggression

Paradigm	*Behavior*	*Species*	*Neurotransmitter Activity*			
			ACh	*5-HT*	*DA*	*NE*
Muricide	Attacking and killing of mouse	Rat	↑	↓		↓
Predatory attack due to electrical brain stimulation	Quiet biting attack of rat	Cat	↑ ↑	↓	↓ ?	↓

A critique of the current multitransmitter concept has to begin with the observation that the pattern of changes in neurotransmitters associated with aggressive behaviors is not unique to this class of behaviors. Recently, we described the intriguing parallel findings after manipulations of androgens, DA, opioids, and also 5-HT in male aggressive and copulatory behavior (Miczek & DeBold, 1983). Of course, similar neurotransmitter profiles for these two classes of behavior may not necessarily imply identical mechanisms. Yet, at this level of analysis both behavior patterns share commonalities. Furthermore, there appear to be closely similar patterns of monoamine activity in defensive reactions to attack (often referred to as "affective aggression") and in the reactivity to other noxious and painful stimuli.

A second major criticism is directed toward the basic premise of specifying a causal relationship between the activity of transmitter substances in the brain and the occurrence of an aggressive act. Contrary to earlier beliefs, which labeled neurotransmitters with a uniform behavioral function such as excitatory or inhibitory, a considerably more sophisticated and differentiating approach emerges. Anatomically and functionally separate neural systems for each of the transmitter substances have already been identified. For example, DA-containing neurons originating in separate cell fields in midbrain and terminating in striatal, limbic, and cortical areas appear to be associated with completely separate behavioral functions (Iversen, 1977; Kelly, Seviour, & Iversen, 1975). Even within the striatum, DA receptors have been described with opposite influences on sequences of motor routines (Cools, 1977). Similar complex, anatomically discrete systems of specific monoamine-containing neurons, often at the level of receptor subpopulations, have already been studied for their role in ingestive behavior, sleep, reinforcement processes, and psychopathologies (Iversen, 1977; Leibowitz, 1978; Radulovacki, Wojcik, Fornal, & Miletich, 1980; Seeman, Tedesco, Lee, Chau-Wong, Muller, Bowles, Whitaker, McManus, Tittler, Weinreich, Friend, & Brown, 1978).

Profiles such as those in Table 8.2 and Table 8.3 attempt to present the overall trends, ignoring conflicting data. Detailed examination of the available evidence actually indicates little agreement, particularly regarding the role of the monoamines (Miczek & Barry, 1976; Miczek & Krsiak, 1979, 1981). For example, there are many instances under which decreased 5-HT activity does not lead to predatory killing (McCarty, Whitesides, & Tomosky, 1976; Vergnes & Kempf, 1981) or under which enhanced catecholamine functioning fails to activate attack or defense (Crowley, Stynes, Hydinger, & Kaufman, 1974; Krsiak, 1979; Miczek, in press; Sheard, 1981).

Future studies of neurotransmitter involvement in the mechanisms mediating aggressive behaviors will have to be considerably more specific with regard to anatomical and neuropharmacological systems. Summaries such as those in Table 8.2 and Table 8.3 already appear outdated and may even be misleading.

A third criticism deals with the reluctance to adopt biologically relevant, accurate, and comprehensive behavioral measurements into studies whose primary objective is the elucidation of the underlying neural mechanism. Table 8.2 and Table 8.3 indicate how limited and coarse the measures of aggressive and defensive behavior are, often a single index, in experimental situations that are frequently chosen for psychopharmacological and neurochemical studies. The lack of direct comparisons across species further limits the generality of transmitter profiles. The glaring absence of any information on neural mechanisms of aggression in females will have to be corrected.

ETHOLOGICAL ANALYSIS OF AGONISTIC BEHAVIOR

The ethological approach to aggression originated with investigations under field conditions where elaborate sequences of species-specific interactions are readily seen. It is possible to arrange experimental conditions in the laboratory that engender biologically relevant agonistic behavior. When, for example, a resident animal or an established group of animals confronts an unfamiliar adult member of the species, the resident attacks, threatens, and pursues the intruder, who typically reacts with defensive responses and eventually escapes or, alternatively, submits. Agonistic interactions follow a predictable course, that can be revealed by a sequence analysis. Variations in sequence and intensity of agonistic behavior are brought about by the opponent's behavior, the history of success and failure in previous encounters, the physical prowess, time within circadian and annual rhythms, the presence of mates or a litter, and other variables.

Agonistic interactions resulting from resident–intruder confrontations offer important advantages. First, resident–intruder fighting has wide species generality, ranging from insects to primates. Second, offensive and defensive behavior patterns and their dependence on each other are apparent in these encounters; the complex structure and dynamics of agonistic interactions are readily analyzed. Third, resident–intruder fighting can easily be reproduced in the laboratory. Fourth, resident–intruder fighting occurs under laboratory conditions without any noxious or painful stimuli. Exposure to electric foot shock, prolonged isolated housing, or deprivation and conditioning regimens as prerequisites for aggressive or defensive behavior (as specified in Table 8.1) are significant confounds for the study of the underlying neural processes.

The major limitation of studying aggression in the context of resident– intruder encounters, appears to lie in its restricted application to humans. Most instances of human aggression involve individuals who are familiar with each other and are even related.

The study of agonistic interactions presents a number of formidable methodological challenges; the patterns of behavior are highly species specific; they are composed of a substantial number of postures, movements, displays, and communicative signals; they include slow and extremely rapid, spectacular epochs; and most importantly they are the product of two or occasionally several interacting combatants. Research methods have been developed that faithfully, reliably, and accurately measure complex sequences of attack, threat, pursuit, defense, flight, and submission. The methodology for recording agonistic behavior relies on a video record of the entire confrontation. This is a particularly useful step when experimenting with fast interacting rodents. Infrared-sensitive

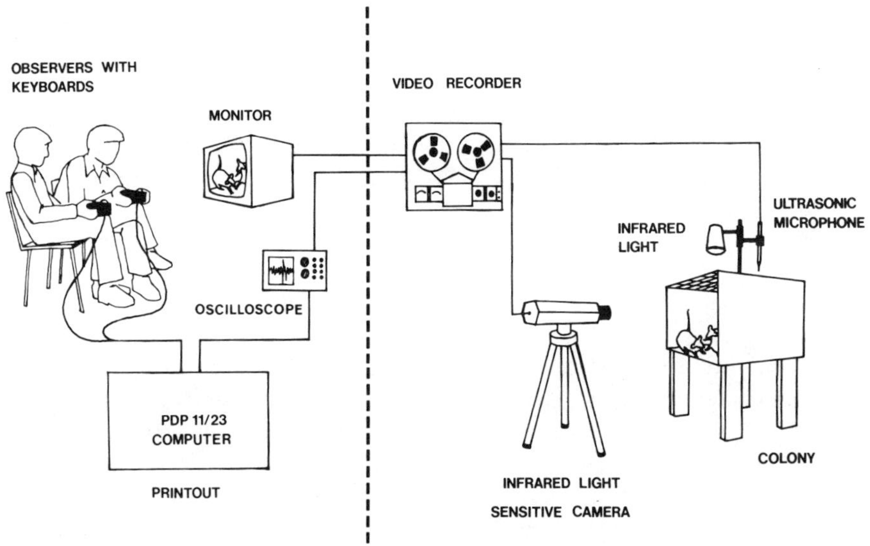

FIG. 8.1. Experimental setup for recording, measuring, and analyzing observational data. A microphone records vocalizations during aggressive encounters, such as audible sounds and ultrasounds in rodents. An infrared-light sensitive camera permits recording of aggressive behavior in nocturnal animals at a time of peak activity. Videotapes or cassettes may be reviewed at regular or slow-motion speeds. Onset and offset times of each defined behavior are encoded by activating keys on hand-held consoles. Programs for data tabulation and analysis allow rapid evaluation of the results (From Miczek, 1982).

cameras, ultrasound-sensitive microphones, and motor activity sensors can be used to supplement the observational records. Figure 8.1 depicts the experimental arrangement for recording, measuring, and analyzing observational data. Experienced observers record the behavioral events with the aid of keyboard consoles, which in turn transfer the records into computer files.

BRAIN CATECHOLAMINES AND AGGRESSION

A most critical problem in relating brain catecholamines and aggressive, defensive, and flight behavior derives from the way these behaviors are typically studied in the laboratory. As already discussed, the situational variables that are necessary to produce aggressive behaviors often involve a range of noxious stimuli; these aversive events such as electric shock, isolated housing, and extinction conditions result in themselves in substantial changes in catecholamines in the peripheral as well as central nervous system.

Environmental stress and pharmacological treatments that enhance CA functions tend to increase defensive reactions. These types of behavior involve pronounced activity of the autonomic nervous system and often are referred to as ''affective aggression.'' For example, ''affective aggression'' in cats, originally described by Hess (1948) as ''affektive Abwehr'' (affective defense), has been linked to increased NE metabolism and synthesis, particularly in the brainstem (Reis, 1974). There is also indication that the defensive posturing and biting in rats that are exposed in pairs to electric foot shock is associated with significant changes in NE as seen by heightened NE synthesis from ^{3}H-tyrosine (Stolk, Connor, Levine, & Barchas, 1974). Experiments with rubidium, lithium, clonidine, piperoxane suggest a facilitative role of NE receptor activation and heightened NE turnover on these defensive reactions, whereas evidence from 6-hydroxydopamine lesion experiments and intracranial infusion studies indicates an inhibitory role of NE in this type of behavior (see reviews by Eichelman, 1979; Sheard, 1981). Moreover, dopaminergic involvement is suggested by an increase in Vmax for DA uptake into rat striatal synaptosomes after 30 sec of shock-induced defensive posturing in rats (Hadfield & Rigby, 1976).

In contrast to ''affective'' defensive behavior, catecholaminergic activity in attack and threat behavior is even more complex. Drugs that block catecholamine synthesis or that block DA and NE receptors suppress all active motor functions, including aggressive and defensive behavior (reviews by Eichelman, 1979; Sheard, 1981). Preferential depletion of brain DA by intraventricularly administered 6-hydroxydopamine leaves attack and threat behavior by isolated aggressive mice unaltered, but increases the frequency of attacks in mice that are ''timid'' after isolation (Pöschlova, Masek, & Krsiak, 1976). Most of the pharmacological studies suggest that interference with the synthesis, storage, release, or receptor activation of catecholamines leads to a suppression of aggressive behavior (Miczek, 1981; Schiørring, 1981). However, under certain conditions, DA and NE receptor activation may enhance attack and, especially defensive and flight reactions.

The complex pattern of results is illustrated with a series of experiments using the catecholamine-releasing drug D-amphetamine and related agents in mice, rats, and squirrel monkeys (Miczek, 1974, 1977, 1979, in press; Miczek & Gold, in press; Miczek, Woolley, Schlisserman, & Yoshimura, 1981; Miczek & Yoshimura, 1982; Winslow & Miczek, in press). Drug action was assessed both on attack and threat behavior of dominant or alpha animals and on the opponent's defensive, submissive, and flight reactions.

In our initial studies of mice and rats we learned that attack and threat behavior were altered at lower doses of amphetamine than defensive and flight reactions, and that drug treatments did not alter both types of agonistic behavior in the same way. For example, D-amphetamine showed a biphasic dose-effect function on attack and threat by dominant rats (i.e., low doses enhancing and higher doses decreasing these behaviors) however, defensive reactions were facilitated only at higher doses (Miczek, 1974, 1977, 1979).

Amphetamine effects on attack behavior in mice and squirrel monkeys differ from those in rats; the drug effects on defensive and nonagonistic motor functions are closely similar in the three species (Miczek, in press; Miczek & O'Donnell, 1978; Miczek et al., 1981; Miczek & Yoshimura, 1982). D-Amphetamine, given to the resident mouse 30 min before confronting an intruder, decreases the rapid bursts of attack bites, sideways threats, and pursuits. When the drug is administered to the intruder mouse, its defensive postures and escapes become unrelated to the resident's attacks. Normally, the resident's attack behavior prompts nearly all the intruder's escapes and defensive postures, as indicated by high correlation coefficients (r = .6 to .9). Figure 8.2 represents a profile of amphetamine action on the repertoire of agonistic and nonagonistic behavior in mice. The motor-activating effects of amphetamine differ from those on agonistic behavior and appear similar in attacking and defending animals. Amphetamine increases the incidence and duration of walking in a monotonic fashion.

In recent experiments with squirrel monkeys, we confirmed that amphetamine increases the incidence of stereotyped head movements equally in dominant, subdominant, and submissive members of established social groups (Miczek & Gold, in press; Miczek et al., 1981). By contrast, the sensitivity to amphetamine's suppressive effects on agonistic behavior in squirrel monkeys was greatly determined by the social rank of the individual monkey.

It remains to be elucidated under which conditions catecholamine agonists such as amphetamine, apomorphine, or L-dopa enhance attack behavior. Species differences may provide significant clues for this puzzling pattern. Increased attacks and threats are readily seen in amphetamine-treated rats, but rarely in mice, and least likely in primates. In order to study this problem further in mice, we investigated drug effects following an experimental protocol that reliably

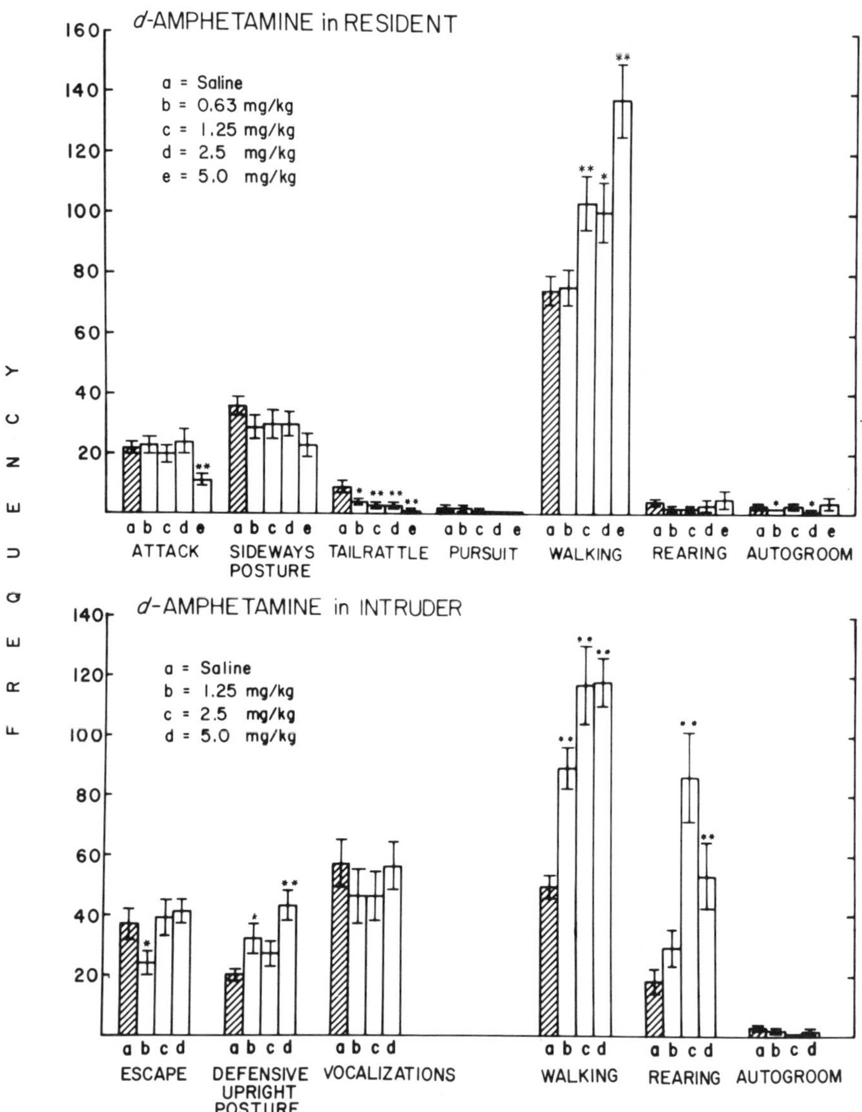

FIG. 8.2. *Top:* The effects of D-amphetamine doses on the frequency of seven behavioral elements measured in resident mice during 5-min resident–intruder tests. The resident mice were the drug recipients. The shaded columns indicate values from saline control tests. The vertical lines in each column mark 2 S.E.M. Statistically significant differences between amphetamine treatments and saline control are indicated by asterisks (* $p < .05$; ** $p < .01$). *Bottom:* The effects of D-amphetamine on six behavioral elements measured in intruder mice. Amphetamine was administered to the intruder only. The format is identical to that above. (From Miczek, in press.)

altered the level of fighting in a habituation paradigm (Winslow & Miczek, in press). In the course of ten 5-min confrontations that are distributed over 2 hours, the frequency of biting attacks and threats by resident mice directed toward conspecific intruders declines in a lawful fashion. Administration of D-amphetamine or apomorphine, 5 min before the first trial, counteracted the decrement of attacks and threats. The low rates of attacks in the late phase of the 10 encounters were increased by low and intermediate doses of both drugs; by contrast, changes in nonagonistic motor behavior followed a different dose-effect function, the highest does being the most effective.

Whenever systemic drug injections are given in order to alter brain catecholamine functions, it is possible that the resulting disruption of attacks, threats, and pursuits may stem from drug action on the autonomic nervous system or on the motor system. In an effort to block the potentially interfering drug effects on autonomic and motor responses, catecholaminergic receptor antagonists were used in conjunction with amphetamine (Miczek, in press). Pretreatment with the DA receptor blocker haloperidol, the alpha-adrenergic receptor blocker phenoxybenzamine, the beta-adrenergic receptor blocker propranolol or the 5-HT receptor blocker methysergide was ineffective in antagonizing the antiaggressive effects of D-amphetamine (Fig. 8.3, left). The motor-stimulating effects of D-amphetamine were completely blocked by haloperidol, in part antagonized by phenoxybenzamine and propranolol, and left unaffected by methysergide (Fig. 8.3, right).

In a similar series of experiments in squirrel monkeys (Miczek et al., 1981; Miczek & Yoshimura, 1982), amphetamine and cocaine severely reduced intense attack and threat behavior toward an unfamiliar intruder, nearly abolished rank-related agonistic interactions and affiliative behavior within the group, and, of course, produced clear signs of motor activation. After pretreatment with receptor antagonists, the observations paralleled those obtained in our studies with mice. Haloperidol and chlorpromazine failed to antagonize the pronounced reduction in social behavior—whether agonistic or affiliative in nature. Again, similarly to the findings in mice, amphetamine- and cocaine-induced stereotyped movements of head, torso, and limbs were effectively blocked by haloperidol and chlorpromazine.

The failure of catecholamine receptor blockers to antagonize the disruptive effects of amphetamine on aggressive behavior in mice and in squirrel monkeys contrasts sharply with the effective antagonism of motor activation. This pattern of results confirms that DA release or receptor activation is critical for heightened motor activity, but this mechanism cannot be extrapolated to aggressive behavior.

One of the key problems in predicting the effects of catecholaminergic drugs on aggression derives from the fact that aggressive behaviors in themselves cause changes in the dynamics of the various peripheral and central catecholamine systems. The initiation, execution, and consequences of aggressive and defen-

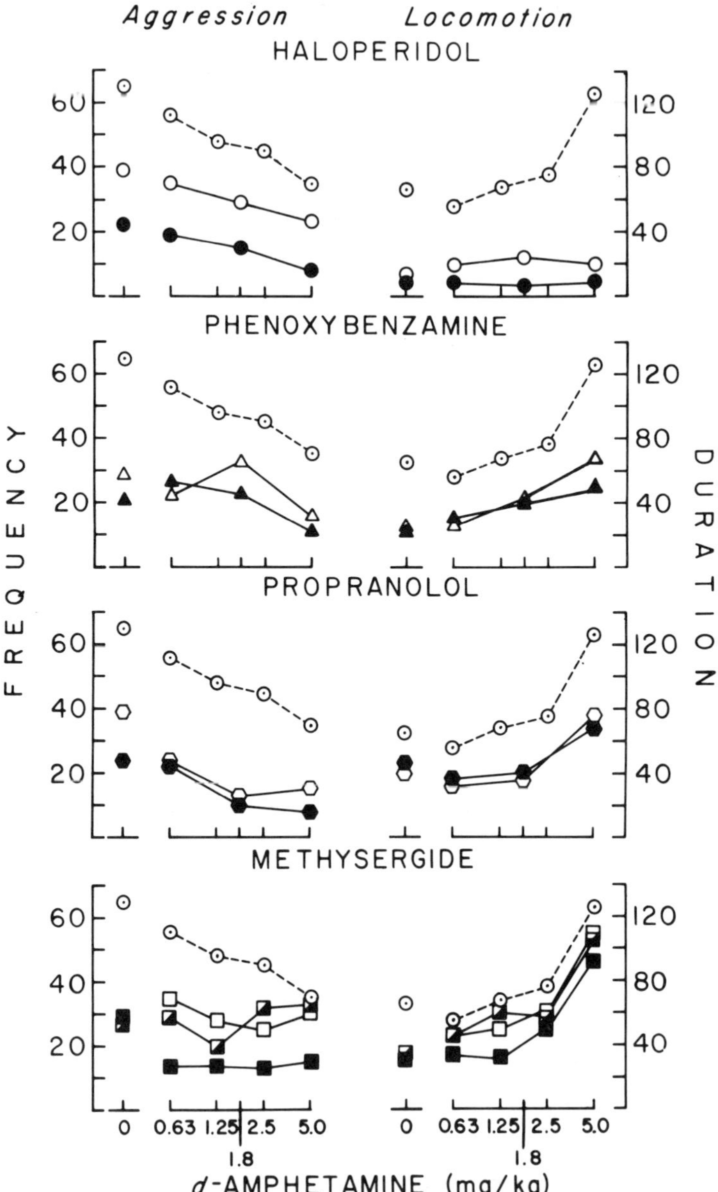

FIG. 8.3. The frequency of aggressive behaviors (*left*) and the duration of locomotor activity (*right*) in resident mice as a function of D-amphetamine dose. The results of D-amphetamine administration without any pretreatment are indicated in each of the four graphs as reference (⊙—⊙). Dose-response determinations of D-amphetamine are depicted after pretreatment with haloperidol (.25 mg/kg ○——○; 1.0 mg/kg ●——●), phenoxybenzamine (5.0 mg/kg △——△; 10 mg/kg ▲——▲), propranolol (10 mg/kg ⬡——⬡; 20 mg/kg ⬢——⬢), or methysergide (.3 mg/kg □——□; 1.0 mg/kg ◪——◪; 3.0 mg/kg ■——■). (From Miczek, in press).

sive behavior are linked in a correlative and possibly causative manner to large changes in catecholamines, which in turn are the substrate for drug action.

ENDOGENOUS OPIOIDS AND DEFEAT

In the context of agonistic interactions, marked changes in the functioning of endogenous opioids become apparent. We recently observed the physiological and behavioral sequelae of exposure to repetitive attacks in intruder mice (Miczek, Thompson, & Shuster, 1982). Defeat in a social confrontation with a resident mouse produces a large, lasting pain suppression that appears to be medicated by endogenous opioids, and that is associated with a specific behavior pattern. As described previously, in the initial phase of a confrontation intruder mice retaliate, then react with defensive postures, and eventually flee. If escape is barred, the intruder engages in specific defeat or submissive behaviors, portrayed in Fig. 8.4. The body is in upright position, the head is in an upright angle, the forepaws have low muscle tone, the ears are retracted. The defeated mouse squeals before being bitten and fails to orient toward the approaching opponent.

The analgesia in defeated mice is antagonized by low doses of naloxone and naltrexone (Fig. 8.5). Because the quaternary form of naltrexone does not enter

FIG. 8.4. Defeated mouse in characteristic posture. Resident mouse in the rear (Adapted from Miczek et al., 1982).

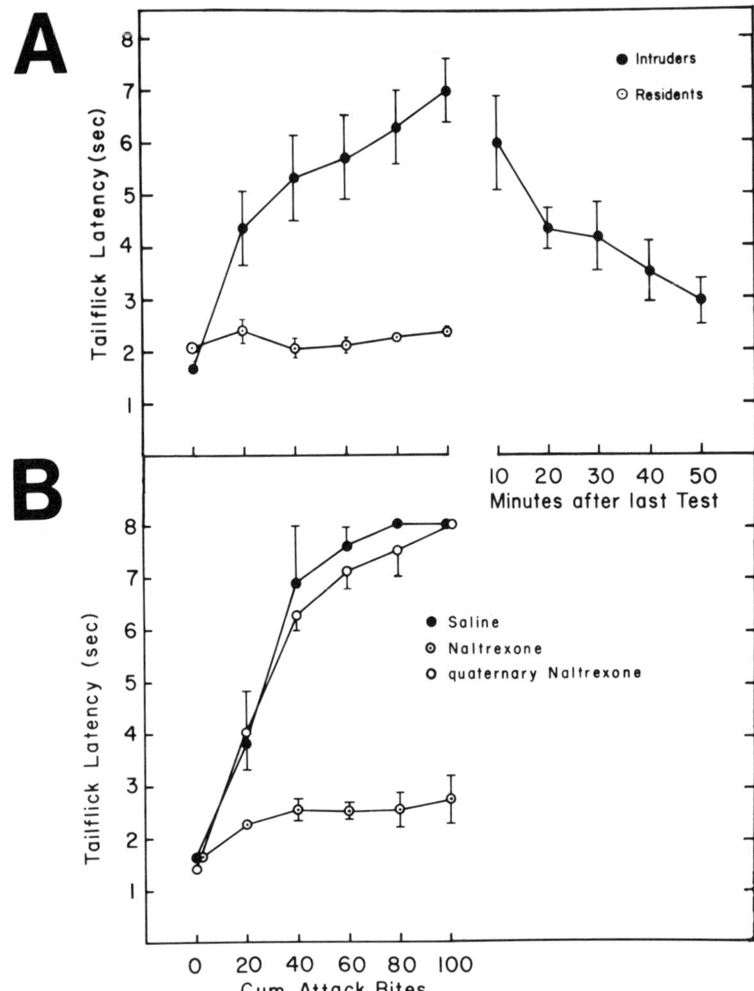

FIG. 8.5. (A) Tail-flick latencies in intruder mice (N = 9) as a function of being bitten, and in resident mice (N = 5) as a function of attacking an intruder. Values are means ± standard errors. Latencies were determined before any fighting experience and after 20 bites. The heat stimulus turned off automatically after 8 sec. (B) Tail-flick latencies in intruder mice that were injected with saline (N = 5), naltrexone (N = 7), or quaternary naltrexone (N = 6) 20 min before the first test, expressed as a function of exposure to bites by nontreated resident mice (From Miczek et al., 1982).

the central nervous system, its failure to block the defeat-induced analgesia points to a mechanism in the central nervous system rather than at peripheral sites.

Adrenalectomy or treatment with the synthetic glucocorticoid dexamethasone, or exposure to hypertonic saline as drinking fluid failed to alter the analgesia in defeated mice (Thompson, Miczek, & Shuster, 1981), again implicating central mechanisms.

In two separate experiments we further demonstrated that analgesia in defeated mice is mediated by endogenous opioids, as they developed tolerance to the analgesia-producing endogenous substances and became cross-tolerant to morphine. Conversely, morphine-tolerant mice failed to show defeat-induced anal-

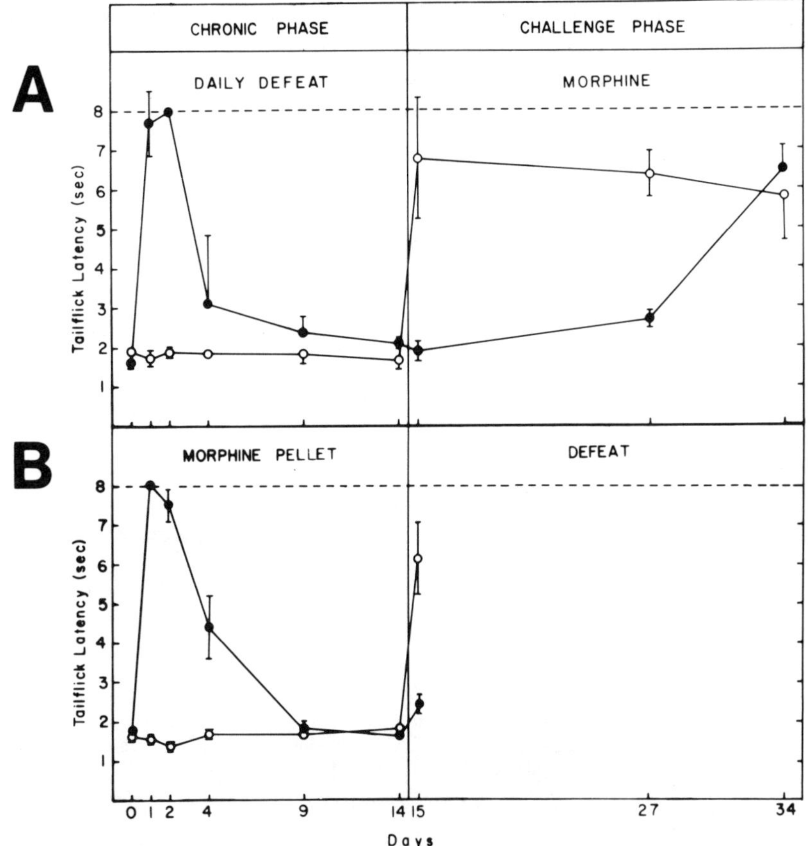

FIG. 8.6. (A) Tail-flick latencies in intruder mice ($N = 6$) subjected to 100 bites by resident mice every day for 14 days (●), and in control mice ($N = 6$) not subjected to attack (○). Tail-flick latencies were measured before the first attack (Day 0) and periodically thereafter (Days 1, 2, 4, 9, and 14). On Days 15, 27, and 34 the defeated mice and the controls were administered morphine sulfate and given tail-flick tests 30 min later. (B) Tail-flick latencies in mice implanted with a morphine pellet ($N = 10$, ●) or with a placebo pellet ($N = 5$, ○). Tail-flick tests were performed before pellet implantation (Day 0) and periodically thereafter (Days 1, 2, 4, 9, and 14). On Day 15, mice with morphine and placebo pellets were exposed to 100 bites and tested for tail-flick latency (From Miczek et al., 1982).

gesia (Fig. 8.6). Specifically, mice that were subjected to attack bites daily for 14 days showed maximal analgesia on Days 1 and 2, but eventually returned with their pain reaction to the range of control animals. Mice that were implanted with a 75-mg morphine pellet showed a parallel tolerance development to the chronically defeated mice. On Day 15, in tests for cross-tolerance, morphine-tolerant mice and chronically defeated mice did not show analgesia when challenged with the opposite treatment (Fig. 8.6A and Fig. 8.6B).

The role of endogenous opioids in stress-induced analgesia has been difficult to demonstrate, and non-opioid mechanisms have been suggested. Yet, the dramatic functional change in endogenous opioids in defeated mice may indicate that defeat is a biologically relevant stressor that readily activates these peptides.

ACKNOWLEDGMENTS

This work has been supported by United States Public Health Service Grants DA–02632 and AA–05122.

REFERENCES

Barr, G. A., Gibbons, J. L., & Bridger, W. H. Neuropharmacological regulation of mouse killing by rats. *Behavioral Biology,* 1976, *17,* 143–159.

Cools, A. R. Two functionally and pharmacologically distinct dopamine receptors in the rat brain. In E. Costa & G. L. Gessa (Eds.), *Advances in biochemical pharmacology* (Vol. 16). New York: Raven Press, 1977.

Crowley, T. J., Stynes, A. J., Hydinger, M., & Kaufman, I. C. Ethanol, methamphetamine, pentobarbital, morphine, and monkey social behavior. *Archives of General Psychiatry,* 1974, *31,* 829–838.

Daruna, J. H. Patterns of brain monoamine activity and aggressive behavior. *Neuroscience and Biobehavioral Reviews,* 1978, *2,* 101–113.

De Molina, A. F., & Hunsperger, R. W. Organization of the subcortical system governing defence and flight reactions in the cat. *The Journal of Physiology,* 1962, *160,* 200–213.

Eichelman, B. Role of biogenic amines in aggressive behavior. In M. Sandler (Ed.), *Psychopharmacology of aggression.* New York: Raven Press, 1979.

Eichelman, B., & Thoa, N. B. The aggressive monoamines. *Biological Psychiatry,* 1973, *6,* 143–164.

Eleftheriou, B. E., & Boehlke, K. W. Brain monoamine oxidase in mice after exposure to aggression and defeat. *Science,* 1967, *155,* 1693–1694.

Fernstrom, J. D., and Hirsch, M. J. Rapid repletion of brain serotonin in malnourished corn-fed rats following L-tryptophan injection. *Life Sciences,* 1975, *17,* 455–464.

Flynn, J. P., Smith, D., Coleman, K., & Opsahl, C. A. Anatomical pathways for attack behavior in cats. In M. von Cranach, K. Foppa, W. Lepenies, & D. Ploog (Eds.), *Human ethology: Claims and limits of a new discipline.* Cambridge: Cambridge University Press, 1979.

Grossman, S. P. Eating and drinking elicited by direct adrenergic or cholinergic stimulation of hypothalamus. *Science,* 1960, *132,* 301–302.

Hadfield, M. G., & Rigby, W. F. C. Dopamine-adaptive uptake changes in striatal synaptosomes after 30 seconds of shock-induced fighting. *Biochemical Pharmacology,* 1976, *25,* 2752–2759.

Hendley, E. D., Moisset, B., & Welch, B. L. Catecholamine uptake in cerebral cortex: Adaptive change induced by fighting. *Science,* 1973, *180,* 1050–1052.

Hess, W. R. *Das Zwischenhirn: Syndrome, Lokalisationen, Funktionen.* Basel: Benno Schwabe, 1948.

Iversen, S. D. Brain dopamine systems and behavior. In L. L. Iversen, S. D. Iversen, & S. H. Snyder (Eds.), *Handbook of psychopharmacology* (Vol. 8: *Drugs, neurotransmitters and behavior.* New York: Plenum Press, 1977.

Karczmar, A. G., Richardson, D. C., & Kindel, G. Neuropharmacological and related aspects of animal aggression. *Progress in Neuro-Psychopharmacology,* 1978, *2,* 611–631.

Kelly, P. H., Seviour, P. W., & Iversen, S. D. Amphetamine and apomorphine responses in the rat following 6-OHDA lesions of the nucleus accumbens septi and corpus striatum. *Brain Research,* 1975, *94,* 507–522.

Krsiak, M. Effects of drugs on behavior of aggressive mice. *British Journal of Pharmacology,* 1979, *65,* 525–533.

Krsiak, M., Sulcova, A., Tomaskikova, Z., Dlohozkova, N., Kosar, E., & Masek, K. Drug effects on attack, defense and escape in mice. *Pharmacology Biochemistry and Behavior,* 1981, *14,* Suppl. 1, 47–52.

Leibowitz, S. F. Identification of catecholamine receptor mechanisms in the perifornical lateral hypothalamus and their role in mediating amphetamine and L-dopa anorexia. In S. Garattini & R. Samanin (Eds.), *Central mechanisms of anorectic drugs.* New York: Raven Press, 1978.

McCarty, R. C., Whitesides, G. H., & Tomosky, T. K. Effects of *p*-chlorophenylalanine on the predatory behavior of *Onychomys torridus. Pharmacology Biochemistry and Behavior,* 1976, *4,* 217–220.

Miczek, K. A. Intraspecies aggression in rats: Effects of D-amphetamine and chlordiazepoxide. *Psychopharmacologia,* 1974, *39,* 275–301.

Miczek, K. A. Effects of L-dopa, D-amphetamine and cocaine on intruder evoked aggression in rats and mice. *Progress in Neuro-Psychopharmacology,* 1977, *1,* 271–277.

Miczek, K. A. A new test for aggression in rats without aversive stimulation: Differential effects of D-amphetamine and cocaine. *Psychopharmacology,* 1979, *60,* 253–259.

Miczek, K. A. Pharmacological evidence for catecholamine involvement in animal aggression. *Psychopharmacology Bulletin,* 1981, *17,* 60–62.

Miczek, K. A. Ethological analysis of drug action on aggression, defense and defeat. In M. Y. Spiegelstein & A. Levy (Eds.), *Behavioral models and the analysis of drug action.* Amsterdam: Elsevier, 1982.

Miczek, K. A. Ethopharmacological analysis of amphetamine action on agonistic behavior and motor functions in mice. *Psychopharmacology,* in press.

Miczek, K. A., & Barry, H. Pharmacology of sex and aggression. In S. D. Glick & J. Goldfarb (Eds.), *Behavioral Pharmacology.* St. Louis: C. V. Mosby Press, 1976.

Miczek, K. A., & DeBold, J. F. Hormone–drug interactions and their influence on aggressive behavior. In B. Svare (ed.), *Hormones and aggressive behavior.* New York: Plenum Press, 1983.

Miczek, K. A., & Gold, L. H. *d*-Amphetamine in squirrel monkeys of different social status: *Psychopharmacology,* in press.

Miczek, K. A., & Krsiak, M. Drug effects on agonistic behavior. In T. Thompson & P. B. Dews (Eds.), *Advances in behavioral pharmacology* (Vol. 2). New York: Academic Press, 1979.

Miczek, K. A., & Krsiak, M. Pharmacological analysis of attack and flight. In P. F. Brain & D. Benton (Eds.), *A multidisciplinary approach to aggression research.* Amsterdam: Elsevier, 1981.

Miczek, K. A., & O'Donnell, J. M. Intruder-evoked aggression in isolated and non-isolated mice: Effects of psychomotor stimulants and L-dopa. *Psychopharmacology,* 1978, *57,* 47–55.

Miczek, K. A., Thompson, M. L., & Shuster, L. Opioid-like analgesia in defeated mice. *Science,* 1982, *215,* 1520–1522.

Miczek, K. A., Woolley, F., Schlisserman, S., & Yoshimura, H. Analysis of amphetamine effects on agonistic and affiliative behavior in squirrel monkeys (*Saimiri sciureus*). *Pharmacology, Biochemistry and Behavior,* 1981, *14,* Suppl. 1, 103–107.

Miczek, K. A., & Yoshimura, H. Disruption of primate social behavior by D-amphetamine and cocaine: Differential antagonism by antipsychotics. *Psychopharmacology,* 1982, *76,* 163–171.

Miller, N. E. Chemical coding of behavior in the brain. Stimulating the same place in the brain with different chemicals can elicit different types of behavior. *Science,* 1965, *148,* 328–338.

Modigh, K. Effects of isolation and fighting in mice on the rate of synthesis of noradrenaline, dopamine and 5-hydroxytryptamine in the brain. *Psychopharmacologia,* 1973, *33,* 1–17.

Pöschlova, N., Masek, K., & Krsiak, M. Facilitated intermale aggression in the mouse after 6-hydroxydopamine administration. *Neuropharmacology,* 1976, *15,* 403–407.

Pradhan, S. N. Aggression and central neurotransmitters. *International Review of Neurobiology,* 1975, *18,* 213–263.

Radulovacki, M., Wojcik, W. J., Fornal, C., & Miletich, R. Elimination of REM sleep rebound in rats by α-adrenoreceptor blockers, phentolamine and phenoxybenzamine. *Pharmacology, Biochemistry and Behavior,* 1980, *13,* 51–55.

Reis, D. J. Central neurotransmitters in aggression. In S. H. Frazier (Ed.), *Aggression.* Baltimore, Williams and Wilkins, 1974.

Schiørring, E. Psychopathology induced by "speed-drugs." *Pharmacology, Biochemistry and Behavior,* 1981, *14,* Suppl. 1, 109–122.

Seeman, P., Tedesco, J. L., Lee, C. T., Chau-Wong, M., Muller, P., Bowles, J., Whitaker, P. M., McManus, C., Tittler, M., Weinreich, P., Friend, W. C., & Brown, G. M. Dopamine receptors in the central nervous system. *Federation Proceedings,* 1978, *37,* 130–136.

Sheard, M. H. The role of drugs affecting catecholamines on shock-induced fighting in rats. In E. Usdin (Ed.), *Catecholamines: Basic and clinical frontiers* (Vol. 2). New York: Pergamon Press, 1979.

Sheard, M. H. Shock-induced fighting (SIF): Psychopharmacological studies. *Aggressive Behavior,* 1981, *7,* 41–49.

Stolk, J. M., Conner, R. L., Levine, S., & Barchas, J. D. Brain norepinephrine metabolism and shock-induced fighting behavior in rats: Differential effects of shock and fighting on the neurochemical response to a common footshock stimulus. *The Journal of Pharmacology and Experimental Therapeutics,* 1974, *190,* 193–209.

Thompson, M. L., Miczek, K. A., & Shuster, L. Changes in brain β-endorphin and tolerance to morphine analgesia after a single defeat in mice. *Neuroscience Abstracts,* 1981, *7,* 881.

Vergnes, M., & Kempf, E. Tryptophan deprivation: Effects on mouse killing and reactivity in the rat. *Pharmacology, Biochemistry and Behavior,* 1981, *14,* Supp. 1, 19–23.

Wasman, M., & Flynn, J. P. Directed attack elicited from hypothalamus. *Archives of Neurology,* 1962, *6,* 220–227.

Winslow, J. T., & Miczek, K. A. Habituation of aggression in mice: Pharmacological evidence for catecholaminergic and serotonergic mediation. *Psychopharmacology,* in press.

9 Aggressive Behavior: Effects of Neural Modulation by Serotonin

Michael H. Sheard
Yale University

The assumption that aggressive behavior has been demonstrated to be under genetic control underlies several chapters in this volume. Thus it would be of considerable interest to identify specific neuronal mechanisms through which genetic control might be mediated. One such mechanism is differing thresholds in the basic neural substrates for aggression. Another is alteration in the activity of modulating monoaminergic systems, for example, the serotonergic system.

A review by Reis (1973) of the chemical coding of aggressive behavior provided scant evidence for a role of serotonin (5-hydroxytryptamine, 5-HT) in the display or modulation of aggressive behavior. In the last 10 to 12 years, however, considerable evidence has accumulated for such a role. The demonstration of 5-HT-containing neuronal systems in the brain by Dahlstrom and Fuxe (1965) and the development of relatively specific 5-HT synthesis inhibitors beginning with *p*-chlorophenylalanine (*p*-CPA) by Koe and Weissman (1966) made possible the investigation of central 5-HT's role in behavior. These investigations have depended on various methods of stimulating or inhibiting 5-HT with increasing specificity and observing behavioral changes, and/or manipulating behavioral changes and correlating these changes with changes in central 5-HT.

It is now evident that the central 5-HT neuronal systems are involved in the modulation of many behaviors. These include sensory and motor activity, sleep, eating, drinking, learning, sex, and aggression. Neuronal substrates for aggressive behavior have been worked out in considerable detail in the mammalian brain of the cat by Flynn and his colleagues (1976). The generality of these findings has extended to other mammals including the rat (Adams, 1979; Koolhaas, 1978; Panksepp, 1971). In summary these findings reveal a neural substrate for quiet biting attack (offensive or predatory) extending from the preoptic region through the lateral hypothalamus and midbrain to the region of the brachium conjunctivum in the pons. The substrate for affective or defensive aggressive behavior also runs through the hypothalamus, medial to the substrate for offensive aggression, and passes along the medial longitudinal fasciculus (Band of Shutz) into the central gray of the midbrain. Neural substrates that modulate these basic areas have been descirbed in the amygdala, hippocampus, thalamus, and septal region.

An examination of the distribution of the 5-HT system as described by Dahlstrom and Fuxe (1965), Moore, Halaris, and Jones (1978), and Parent, Descarries, and Beaudet (1980) reveals the anatomical basis for many possible sites of interaction between 5-HT and the neural substrates for aggression. This chapter provides a selective review of the data implicating both a direct and an indirect role for 5-HT in aggressive behavior. The review covers both offensive and defensive aggression in a variety of animal models including muricide (mouse killing), ranicide (frog killing), isolation-induced, pain-induced, brain stimulation-induced, and intermale aggression.

Depletion of Serotonin

p-CPA. The first clear demonstration of profound behavioral changes consequent to 5-HT depletion was provided by Dement (1968), who described unusual aggressive and sexual behavior in cats given *p*-CPA. This compound produces a depletion of 5-HT by inhibition of tryptophan hydroxylase (Koe & Weissman, 1966). A study with rats given *p*-CPA (Sheard, 1969) confirmed these findings and demonstrated a shifting pattern of behavioral changes over time that correlated with reduction in brain 5-HT and 5-hydroxyindoleacetic acid (5-HIAA), the main metabolite of 5-HT. The aggressive behavior was not only intraspecies (female–female, female–male, male–male) but also markedly interspecies in the form of muricide. The muricide appeared impulsive and unpredictable and did not occur in every rat treated with *p*-CPA. However, the percentage of rats killing mice was significantly higher than in controls. Later studies have also pointed out the fact that killing bites are often not well directed. It is interesting to note that pup killing in rats has also been found to increase following the administration of *p*-CPA (Copenhaver, Schalock, & Carver, 1978).

It appears then that lowering brain 5-HT can enhance some forms of aggressive behavior. *p*-CPA, however, is not completely a specific drug. It also depletes catecholamines to some extent (Peters, Filczewski, & Mazurkiewicz-Kwilecki, 1972) and equally important, has 5-HT agonist actions of its own (Sloviter, Drust, & Connor, 1978). Dominguez and Longo (1969) reported that *p*-CPA can decrease aggressiveness after septal lesions. In this case, the time of testing was relatively soon (2–3 hours) following the administration of *p*-CPA, and the decrease could be explained by the action of *p*-CPA itself or its metabolite chloro-B-phenylethylamine. This latter compound has been reported to have sympathomimetic efforts (Edwards & Blau, 1972). These findings make it important to test for behavioral changes after *p*-CPA itself has disappeared from brain, and catecholamine levels are restored to normal. For example, the increase in muricide can be seen after 48 hours and for up to 6 days. Another finding that implicates 5-HT more specifically in the increase in aggressive behavior following the administration of *p*-CPA is the reversible inhibition of the increase by 5-hydroxytryptophan (5-HTP), which restores levels of 5-HT by entering the synthetic pathway beyond the tryptophan hydroxylase block. Such a reversal is not produced by deoxyphenylalanine (DOPA), a precursor of catechomamines (Sheard, 1969). This latter finding also argues against the possibility that 5-HTP might be acting via catecholamine neurons.

In mice, predatory cricket killing is also enhanced by *p*-CPA (McCarty, Whitesides, & Tomosky, 1976). However isolation-induced aggression in mice appears to be blocked by *p*-CPA (Welch & Welch, 1969). Thus there appear to be important species differences. It is also known that 5-HT metabolism in mice is much more resistant to the action of *p*-CPA than in rats. Indeed in mice the action of *p*-CPA in enhancing cricket killing appears partly due to loss of weight, as food-deprived mice kill as many crickets as *p*-CPA-treated ones (Kantak, Hegstrand, & Eichelman, 1980). That a reduction of 5-HT in mice by *p*-CPA can in fact increase aggression can be seen from a report by Matte and Tornow, 1978, who gave *p*-CPA for 9 consecutive days and saw an enhancement of aggression in male wild mice isolated for 21 days.

In another model of aggressive behavior, electric-shock-induced fighting in rats, initial reports on the effect of *p*-CPA were controversial. On the one hand, Conner, Stolk, Barchas, Dement, and Levine (1970) reported that *p*-CPA did not influence fighting behavior in this paradigm, whereas Ellison and Bresler (1974) found fighting was increased. This discrepancy was resolved through an analysis of the shock parameters used in the two studies. It was shown (Sheard & Davis, 1976) that *p*-CPA enhanced fighting behavior in rats when a relatively long interstimulus interval was used, as in the Ellison and Bresler study, but not when a short interstimulus interval was used, as in the Conner et al. study. It would be surprising if *p*-CPA did not influence shock-induced fighting, as it has been shown to reduce pain thresholds (Tenen, 1967). However, an increase in pain sensitivity cannot account for the increase in fighting behavior because similar changes in pain sensitivity occur at both the long and short interstimulus intervals. These findings also provide evidence against a simple general role for serotonin in response suppression as postulated by Harvey, Schlosberg, and Yunger (1975).

There is current argument about the relevance of models of predatory aggression and shock-induced fighting, which is predominantly a form of defensive aggression, to offensive intraspecies aggression such as intermale fighting in rats. Close observation of pairs of rats in the shock-elicited fighting paradigm can clearly distinguish offensive from defensive patterns in this model of aggression, and frequently one rat will show the full submissive posture. However, it is correct to say that the stimulus for the aggression is highly artificial.

It was therefore of interest to examine the effect of *p*-CPA in a more naturalistic paradigm, that of territorial aggression. In this situation a home-cage rat fights intruding males placed in the cage. The home-cage rat is almost always dominant and successful in these encounters and the intruding male rapidly adopts submissive postures that usually terminate the fights and reduce their seriousness. This model was originally proposed for pharmacological studies by Chance and Silverman (1964, pp. 65–79). It was reported (Sheard, 1973a,b) that the administration of *p*-CPA to intruder rats 48 hours prior to the encounter greatly increased both the duration and intensity of fighting behavior. Possibly the stress of the novel situation normally enhances the release of 5-HT in the intruder rat and might thereby contribute to the inhibition of aggression. The administration of *p*-CPA blocks this inhibitory effect and induces enhanced aggressive behavior in the intruder rats, which secondarily stimulates increased aggression in the home-cage rat. A specific role for 5-HT is lent further support by the antagonizing effect on fighting in *p*-CPA encounters of administration of 5-HTP to the intruder 30 minutes before entering the cage. Although the behavioral effects of *p*-CPA are usually attributed to depletion of central 5-HT, it should not be forgotten that *p*-CPA as usually given depletes 5-HT in the periphery also, and this peripheral depletion can have significant behavioral effects. It has recently been possible for us to show both increased muricide and increased shock-elicited fighting in rats given *p*-CPA by the intraventricular route.

The conclusion may be drawn that several types of aggressive behavior are enhanced when brain 5-HT is lowered with *p*-CPA. This in turn suggests that central 5-HT is normally exerting a tonic inhibitory control over aggressive behavior. However before assuming a direct effect of this kind it is important to recognize that the mechanism underlying enhanced aggression might also be indirect, through changes in motor activity or sensory reactivity. *p*-CPA has been reported to impair habituation and increase the reactivity to novel stimuli in the auditory startle response in rats (Conner et al., 1970). The action of *p*-CPA on motor activity is complex and depends on the precise type of motor activity being studied. For example, *p*-CPA has been reported to reduce activity in running wheels but increase activity in novel field situations (Brody, 1968; Tenen, 1967). *p*-CPA does make animals hypersensitive (Tenen, 1967) and hyperreactive to foot shock (Fibiger, Mertz, & Campbell, 1972). Also, *p*-CPA can enhance certain types of learning such as brightness discrimination (Stevens, 1970). More evidence against an effect of general response suppression is provided by an experiment by Thornton and Goudie, 1978. They showed that extensive treatment with *p*-CPA, at doses that produce a prolonged depletion of 5-HT, fails to inhibit the adaptive witholding of responses produced by a positive reinforcement schedule. This is quite different from the disinhibition of behavioral suppression produced by aversive reinforcement contingencies. It is clear from these *p*-CPA results that reduction of 5-HT can differentially affect behavior and that aggressive behavior is directly and indirectly affected.

Lesions of Raphe Neurons

The main sites of central 5-HT neurons are the dorsal and medial raphe nuclei of the midbrain. Lesions of both these nuclei produce a very great depletion in central 5-HT and induce muricide in rats (Grant, Coscina, Grossman, & Freedman, 1973; Yamamoto & Ueki, 1977). On the other hand, small discrete lesions of either the dorsal or the median raphe nuclei fail to induce muricide (Vergnes, Mack, & Kempf, 1973; Vergnes, 1978). The production of muricide thus depends on the size of the lesion and the degree of depletion of 5-HT. In rats whose olfactory bulbs have been removed, which reduces 5-HT in the amygdala (Karli, Vergnes, & Didiergeorges, 1969), combined lesions of the median and dorsal raphe induce mouse killing in about 70% of the rats and this can be increased to 90% by the addition of *p*-CPA.

Discrete lesions of the median or dorsal nucleus also have a differential effect on foot shock-elicited aggression (Jacobs & Cohen, 1976). One week following a dorsal lesion, a great increase in fighting was observed in pairs of lesioned rats. However, no increase in fighting was observed in rats with lesions of the median nuclei alone.

In the interpretation of these results it is important to note that lesions of the dorsal raphe nucleus were not associated with changes in pain threshold despite an increase in aggression, whereas lesions of the median were associated with a marked increase in motor activity but with no increase in aggression. Thus depletion of 5-HT can specifically affect aggressiveness without necessarily altering pain threshold and specifically alter motor behavior without altering aggression. These discrete lesions are of course associated with specific regional depletions of 5-HT, as has been documented by Lorens and Guldberg (1974). They showed that lesions of the median are associated with depletion of 5-HT in the hippocampus, lesions of the dorsal with depletion of striatal 5-HT, and only dorsal lesions produced depletion in the brainstem.

It is not possible therefore to compare very exactly the behavioral consequences of depleting 5-HT by *p*-CPA with depletion by lesions, as the depletion with *p*-CPA is much more general, and widespread effects result.

Neurotoxins

Depletion of 5-HT can also be produced by the use of relatively specific neurotoxins such as 5,6 and 5,7-dihydroxytryptamine. The specificity of such agents is enhanced by the use of specific uptake blockers for other monoaminergic systems prior to use. Injections of 5,7-dihydroxytryptamine intraventricularly (Breese & Cooper, 1975, Penot, Vergnes, Mack, & Kempf, 1978), directly into the raphe nuclei themselves (Paxinos & Atrens, 1977; Vergnes, Penot, Kempf, & Mack, 1977), or into the ascending serotonergic pathways (Hole, Johnson, & Berge, 1977) induces muricide. These studies have reported widely differing rates of mouse killing by rats, ranging from 30–90%; part of this variability can be explained by the incidence of preoperative testing with mice, because Marks, O'Brien, and Paxinos (1977) have shown that such prior exposure has a marked inhibiting effect postoperatively. This evidence adds weight to the notion that 5-HT is involved in brain mechanisms mediating the control of aggressive behavior. These experiments, however, have not yielded further evidence as to whether the effect is a direct one or indirect via other behaviors such as irritability, motor activity, or general consummatory behavior. Some studies have suggested an independent effect (Breese, Cooper, Grant, & Smith, 1974; Hole et al., 1977) whereas others (Lippa, 1974; Paxinos & Atrens, 1977) report strong effects on other behaviors.

Recently Applegate (1980) has carefully studied the results of intraventricular 5,7-DHT on muricide irritability, food and water consumption, motor activity, and exploration. He found a significant effect on predatory behavior without any significant effect on the other behaviors. This strongly supports the notion of an independent effect of 5-HT on predatory aggressive behavior.

A further development has been the demonstration that a local injection of 5,7-DHT, which depletes 5-HT in the hippocampus, can induce an increase in shock-elicited fighting (Kantak, Hegstrand, & Eichelman, 1981). Thus very specific areas of 5-HT depletion can be associated with specific increases in aggressive behavior.

File, James, and MacLeod (1981) attempted to locate regional sites of action for 5-HT on aggressive behavior by administering 5,7-DHT bilaterally into the amygdaloid complex. They reported that dominant aggressive behavior was reduced in the intruder type of paradigm in lesioned animals. 5-HT was reduced 80% in the amygdala but norepinephrine was also reduced by 29%. Thus the lesions were not specific for 5-HT depletion. Moreover, in this study it was not possible to localize precisely the lesion within the amygdala, and it is known that different amygdaloid nuclei have different effects on aggression. File has demonstrated that 5,7-DHT lesions of specific raphe nuclei have different effects. For example, lesions of the median raphe nucleus produced an increase in dominance behaviors, whereas dorsal raphe lesions produced a decrease in both dominance and submissive behaviors (File, Hyde, & MacLeod, 1979). On the other hand, rats with lesions of both raphe nuclei showed no change in home-cage aggression (File & Deakin, 1980), suggesting that the effects of lesioning the dorsal and median raphe nuclei can sometimes cancel each other out. This latter finding was also reported in my study of raphe lesions (Sheard, 1969).

Tryptophan-Free Diet

The synthesis of 5-HT depends on tryptophan availability. Hence reduction in this availability can lower brain 5-HT (Fernstrom & Wurtman, 1978). If rats are maintained on a tryptophan-free diet for 4–6 days, nonkiller rats will turn into mouse killers and the muricide of killer rats will be enhanced (Gibbons, Barr, Bridger, & Leibowitz, 1979). Kantak, Hegstrand, Whitman, and Eichelman (1979) reported that shock-elicited fighting and pain sensitivity were increased in rats fed a tryptophan-free diet. However, they pointed out that although muricide was also enhanced, control rats fed some tryptophan and others pair-fed chow also showed muricide, and thus the increase in muricide was not specific to the lack of tryptophan.

In another study, Kantak et al. (1980) examined the effects of alterations of dietary tryptophan on isolation-induced and predatory cricket killing in male mice. They found that a tryptophan-free diet reduced brain 5-HT by about 28%, decreased isolation-induced fighting, and increased cricket killing. However, they also found that a food-deprived control group that lost the same amount of weight as the tryptophan-free diet group showed the same increase in cricket killing. This finding suggests that the increased predation was a response to dietary needs rather than related to 5-HT depletion. But these results have to be reevaluated in the light of data provided by Walters, Davis, and Sheard (1979). In this experiment the body weight of rats fed a powdered tryptophan-free diet declined in comparison with controls fed a diet supplemented with L-tryptophan. These two groups did not differ in acoustic startle amplitude despite a 28% decrease in whole brain 5-HT in the tryptophan-free diet group. However, when rats were tube-fed the diets to maintain equal body weights, the tryptophan-free diet group decreased whole brain 5-HT by 65% and showed increased startle amplitudes. These elevated amplitudes returned to normal when tryptophan was added to the diet and could be temporarily restored to normal by injections of L-tryptophan, supporting the notion that depletion of 5-HT was the cause of the elevated amplitude. These findings point up the great importance of preventing the weight loss induced by the tryptophan-deficient diet before behavioral consequences are evaluated.

Elevation of 5-HT by Tryptophan

In general it is much easier to demonstrate effects on behavior by depressing the 5-HT system than by enhancing it. Gibbons, Barr, and Bridger (1980) have shown that acute injections of L-tryptophan can inhibit mouse killing in rats in a dose-related manner. This effect was not completely specific for aggressive behavior, because at some doses food intake and motor behavior were also inhibited. These findings are not consistent with most reports on the effects on other behaviors, which by and large have been negative. Kantak et al. (1980), in their studies on the effects of the addition of tryptophan to the diet in rats and mice, did not find any effect in control rats. However, they did find that the addition of tryptophan to the diet could reverse the increase in aggression brought about by a tryptophan-deficient diet and also reverse the enhancement of shock-elicited fighting and mouse killing produced by septal lesions or 5,7-DHT lesions. In the unaltered animal the addition of tryptophan to the diet or administration by injection has little or no effect on behavior despite boosting 5-HT metabolism and brain levels. This appears to be because the functional 5-HT released at synapses is subject to rapid reuptake or destruction by monoamine oxidase (Grahame-Smith, 1971). Systemic administration of 5,hydroxytryptophan can also block muricide (Kulkarni, 1968).

In view of the aforementioned results, the author studied the effects of tryptophan on shock-elicited fighting in rats that had been pretreated with a monoamine oxidase inhibitor. Doses of L-tryptophan and pargyline (a monoamine oxidase inhibitor) were chosen that individually had no effect on fighting behavior. The combination, however, showed a powerful L-tryptophan dose-related inhibition of fighting (Sheard, 1981). This behavioral finding is supported by the work of Elks, Youngblood, and Kizer (1979), who concluded that only in tissue pretreated with pargyline do increasing concentrations of tryptophan increase the releasable pool of 5-HT. They were able to show that rates of 5-HT release and synthesis in brain slices may increase independently of tissue tryptophan concentration or tryptophan uptake.

Electrical Stimulation of Raphe Nuclei

Electrical stimulation of the raphe nuclei was shown to stimulate 5-HT metabolism as measured by an increase of 5-hydroxyindoleacetic acid in the forebrain of rats (Aghajanian, Foote, & Sheard, 1968; Aghajanian, Rosecrans, & Sheard, 1967; Sheard & Aghajanian, 1968). The effects of stimulating the raphe region of cats were also studied and it was shown that levels of 5-hydroxyindoleacetic acid, the main metabolite of 5-HT, rose in the cerebrospinal fluid and in many areas of the brain, which included the hippocampus, amygdala, cortex, thalamus, and hypothalamus (Sheard & Zolovick, 1971). Experiments were then performed on cats that had electrodes chronically implanted in both the raphe nuclei of the midbrain and in sites in the hypothalamus that could elicit quiet biting attack and affective defensive attack. The latency to attack an anesthetized rat by a cat that did not naturally attack rats was measured from the onset of hypothalamic stimulation. This latency to attack proves to be very stable for a given electrical intensity, provided that the distance from the cat's nose to the rat is kept constant. The electrical threshold for the attack can also be measured as the lowest intensity that produces an attack in under 20 seconds.

When stable attack latencies were obtained for sites that yielded both quiet biting and affective defensive attack, the effect of conjoint stimulation of the raphe electrode with the hypothalamic electrode was investigated. Actually the raphe stimulation was locked just prior to the hypothalamic stimulation. The results of these experiments showed a significant increase in the latency to attack with combined raphe stimulation, suggesting that serotonin release was exerting an inhibitory effect on the stimulated aggressive behavior. It should be noted that the stimulation to the raphe region alone was at an intensity that produced no observable behavior. Another variety of this experiment was performed with these cats by continuous stimulation of the raphe electrode for periods of 15–30 minutes and then following the change in latency to attack from repeated stimulation of a hypothalamic electrode over time. It was found that there was a significant lengthening of latency, which gradually returned to baseline (i.e., to the latency resulting from previous stimulation of the hypothalamic electrode alone).

Pretreatment of cats with *p*-CPA blocks this inhibitory effect of stimulation of the raphe electrodes, furthering the evidence that implicates 5-HT in the inhibitory action. *p*-CPA itself reduces the latency to attack from hypothalamic electrode stimulation (MacDonnell, Fessok, & Brown, 1971). Although it is correct to say in general that latency to attack is not a good measure of aggressive behavior, as many variables are at play, this is not true of the electrically elicited attack in the cat. Studies have revealed a very high correlation of the latency to attack with biting and a parametric relationship to the intensity of stimulation over a substantial range of intensities. Thus in this particular paradigm, latency to attack is a convenient and very reliable measure. There are other criticisms that can be leveled against interpretations that derive from the electrical stimulation of brain (Valenstein, 1973), which include stimulation of neuronal or axonal systems besides the targeted one, the effects of retrograde stimulation, nonspecific effects of stimulation, and others. However, these stimulation experiments are supportive of the evidence that 5-HT plays an important inhibitory role in aggressive behavior. Another set of experiments involving electrical stimulation of brain was performed on the model of ranicide. The reason to use this model resulted from the reliable and reproducible biting attack on a frog introduced into the home cage of a hooded rat. Chronic electrodes were implanted into the dorsal raphe region and comparisons made on the latency to attack between stimulation and no-stimulation trials. Postsession histological examination revealed that stimulation of the dorsal raphe region produced a significant inhibition of attack with longer latencies and decreased number of attacks. This finding was not true when electrode placement was outside the dorsal raphe nucleus, unless the stimulation excited mesencephalic motor pathways, which produced circling movements interfering with attacks. The only observable behavior on stimulation of the dorsal raphe region was some arousal at the onset of stimulation.

Alteration of 5-HT with Drugs

Hallucinogens. D-lysergic acid diethylamide (LSD) has been shown to inhibit the firing rate of 5-HT neurons when given intravenously (Aghajanian et al., 1968) or iontophoretically (Aghajanian, Haigler, & Bloom, 1972). This is associated with a fall in brain 5-HIAA and a rise in 5-HT in the brain.

Paired rats were tested in a shock-elicited fighting model with various doses of LSD against saline controls. It was found that small doses of LSD, which stimulate presynaptic 5-HT receptors preferentially, caused an increase in fighting, whereas with increasing doses there was first no change from controls and then a decrease in fighting (Sheard, Astrachan, & Davis, 1977). The latter changes were interpreted as resulting from the action of large doses of LSD on postsynaptic 5-HT receptors and thus acting like a 5-HT agonist. LSD then has a biphasic effect, with results that fit the notion of inhibition of 5-HT causing an increase in aggressive behavior and stimulation of 5-HT causing a decrease in aggression. Additional experiments were performed using *N,N*-dihydroxytryptamine and 5-methoxy *N,N*-dimethyltryptamine in the shock-elicited fighting model with rats (Walters et al., 1979). Both these hallucinogens differed from LSD in not showing any significant increase in aggression with low doses; rather, after moderate doses they both produced a dose-dependent decrease in fighting. Single-cell studies show that both these compounds act as potent postsynaptic 5-HT agonists. 5-Methoxy-*N,N*-dimethyltryptamine is unique in its powerful stimulation of spinal 5-HT receptors, resulting in a marked excitant effect on such behaviors as the auditory startle response. This might also interfere with the fighting behavior.

5-HT Agonists

If indeed 5-HT has an inhibitory function, then 5-HT agonists can be expected to have a dose-dependent inhibitory action on aggressive behavior. We have used the combination of tryptophan with a monoamine oxidase inhibitor and quipazine (Sheard, 1981). Both these agonists produce a dose-dependent decrease in fighting in the shock-elicited fighting model with rats. Glusman (1979) has also reported that Judith Gibbons in his laboratory studied the effects of quipazine, fluoxetine, a serotonin uptake inhibitor, and fenfluramine, a serotonin releasor. All three agents inhibited mouse killing in killer rats in a dose-related manner. Marks, O'Brien, and Paxinos (1978) found that chlorimipramine, another 5-HT uptake blocker, requires an intact 5-HT system for its antimuricidal effect.

Finally there is a drug called *p*-chloroamphetamine, which first releases 5-HT and then depletes it by a long-range inhibition of tryptophan hydroxylase and sometimes even 5-HT neuronal damage (Harvey, McMaster, & Yunger, 1975; Sanders-Bush, Gallager, & Sulser, 1974; Trulson & Jacobs, 1975). This drug could be expected first to inhibit aggressive behavior and then to enhance it, and these actions would be correlated with phases of 5-HT release and depletion. Experiments performed with rats on shock-elicited fighting revealed that following administration of *p*-chloroamphetamine, there was a profound inhibition of fighting for 15–30 minutes and then this inhibition wore off with the gradual onset of increased fighting. With large doses the increased fighting lasted at least 4 weeks. The prior administration to rats of *p*-CPA but not α-methylparatryosine blocked the early inhibition of fighting and provided further evidence for the specific role of 5-HT in the inhibition.

Behavioral Alterations of 5-HT

Eleftheriou and Church (1968) studied brain levels of 5-HT and norepinephrine (NE) in mice after exposure to aggression and defeat. They found an initial decline in brain 5-HT followed by a significant rise in the hypothalamus and amygdala during 16 days of exposure to aggression and defeat. However, the cortical levels of 5-HT showed a continuous decline over the same period. NE behaved in a reciprocal fashion in these same brain areas. Valzelli (1974) has reviewed the correlation between 5-HT and aggressiveness in isolated mice and rats. He points out that although brain levels of 5-HT may not change, nevertheless there are important relationships between the turnover of 5-HT and the aggressive behavior of isolated mice and rats. In general, when isolated rodents become aggressive, the turnover rate of 5-HT decreases. Valzelli and Garattini (1971) studied the biochemical and behavioral changes induced by isolation in rats. They found that the turnover rate of 5-HT increased in rats described as "friendly" toward mice after 6 weeks of isolation, but decreased in "muricidal" and "indifferent" rats. This study points up the importance of changes in relationship to actual behavior. These studies also support the notion that 5-HT is inhibitory to aggressive behavior.

Summary

Evidence has been collected from depletion, stimulation, drug, and behavioral studies to demonstrate that specific 5-HT systems are involved in both direct and indirect inhibitory control of aggressive behavior. Future studies need to concentrate on the delineation of specific 5-HT systems that are directly inhibitory to aggression.

REFERENCES

Adams, D. B. Brain mechanisms for offense, defense, and submission. *The Behavioral and Brain Sciences,* 1979, *2,* 201–241.

Aghajanian, G. K., Foote, W. E., & Sheard, M. H. Lysergic acid diethylamide: Sensitive neuronal units in the midbrain raphe. *Science,* 1968, *161,* 706–708.

Aghajanian, G. K., Haigler, H., & Bloom, F. Lysergic acid diethylamide and serotonin: Direct actions on serotonin-containing neurons. *Life Sciences,* 1972, *11,* 615–622.

Aghajanian, G. K., Rosecrans, J. A., & Sheard, M. H. Serotonin: Release in forebrain by stimulation of midbrain raphe. *Science,* 1967, 156, 402–403.

Applegate, C. D. 5,7-Dihydroxytryptamine-induced mouse killing and behavioral reversal with ventricular administration of serotonin in rats. *Behavioral and Neural Biology,* 1980, *30,* 178–190.

Breese, G. R., & Cooper, B. R. Behavioral and biochemical interactions of 5,7-dihydroxytryptamine with various drugs when administered intracisternally to adult and developing rats. *Brain Research,* 1975, *98,* 517–527.

Breese, G. R., Cooper, B. R., Grant, L. D., & Smith, R. D. Biochemical and behavioral alterations following 5,6-dihydroxytryptamine and 5,7-dihydroxytryptamine administration into brain. *Neuropharmacology,* 1974, *13,* 177–187.

Brody, J. F. *Effects of p-chlorophenylalanine (a serotonin-depleting agent) on behavior. Doctoral thesis,* University of Pittsburgh, 1968.

Chance, M. R. A., & Silverman, A. P. The structure of social behavior and drug action. In H. Steinberg, A. U. S. de Reuck, & J. Knight, (Eds.), *Animal behavior and drug action.* Boston: Little Brown, 1964.

Conner, R. L., Stolk, J. M., Barchas, J. D., Dement, W. C., & Levine, S. The effect of parachlorophenylalanine (*p*-CPA) on shock-induced fighting behavior in rats. *Physiology and Behavior,* 1970, *5,* 1221–1226.

Copenhaver, J. H., Schalock, R. L., & Carver, M. J. Para-chloro-D,L-phenylalanine-induced filicidal behavior in the female rat. *Pharmacology, Biochemistry, and Behavior,* 1978, *8,* 263–270.

Dahlstrom, A., & Fuxe, K. Evidence for the existence of monoamine-containing neurons in the central nervous system: Demonstration of monoamines in the cell bodies of brainstem neurons. *Acta Physiologica Scandinavica,* 1965, *62,* (Supplement 2).

Dement, W. C. *The true function of REM sleep together with some observations clarifying the role of serotonin in brain.* Paper presented at Psychiatric Research Society meeting, New Haven, Conn., 1968.

Dominguez, M., & Longo, V. G. Taming effect of *p*-chlorophenylalanine on septal rats. *Physiology and Behavior,* 1969, *4,* 1031–1033.

Edwards, D. J., & Blau, K. The in vivo formation of *p*-chloro-β-phenylethylamine in young rats injected with *p*-chlorophenylalanine. *Journal of Neurochemistry,* 1972, *19,* 1829–1832.

Eleftheriou, B. E., & Church, R. L. Brain levels of serotonin and norepinephrine in mice after exposure to aggression and defeat. *Physiology and Behavior,* 1968, *3,* 977–980.

Elks, M. L., Youngblood, W. W., & Kizer, J. S. Serotonin synthesis and release in brain slices: Independence of tryptophan, *Brain Research,* 1979, *172,* 471–486.

Ellison, G. D., & Bresler, D. E. Tests of emotional behavior in rats following depletion of norepinephrine, or serotonin, or of both. *Psychopharmacologia,* 1974, *34,* 275–288.

Fernstrom, J. D., & Wurtman, R. J. Brain serotonin content: Physiological regulation by plasma neutral amino acids. *Science,* 1978, 414–416.

Fibiger, H. C., Mertz, P. H., & Campbell, B. A. The effect of *p*-chlorophenylalanine on aversion thresholds and reactivity to foot shock. *Physiology and Behavior,* 1972, *8,* 259–263.

File, S. E., & Deakin, J. F. W. Chemical lesions of both dorsal and median raphe nuclei and changes in social and aggressive behavior in rats. *Pharmacology, Biochemistry, and Behavior,* 1980, *12,* 855–859.

File, S. E., Hyde, J. R. G., & MacLeod, N. K. 5,7-Dihydroxytryptamine lesions of dorsal and median raphe nuclei and performance in the social interaction test of anxiety and in a home-cage aggression test. *Journal of Affective Disease,* 1979, *1,* 115–122.

File, S. E., James, T. A., & MacLeod, N. K. Depletion in amygdaloid 5-hydroxytryptamine concentration and changes in social and aggressive behavior. *Journal of Neural Transmission,* 1981, *50,* 1–12.

Flynn, J. P. Neural Basis of Threat and Attack. In R. G. Grenell & S. Gabay (Eds.), *Biological foundations of psychiatry.* New York: Raven Press, 1976.

Gibbons, J. L., Barr, G. A., & Bridger, W. H. L-tryptophan's effects on mouse killing, feeding, drinking, locomotion and brain serotonin. *Pharmacology, Biochemistry, and Behavior,* 1980, *4,* 419–422.

Gibbons, J. L., Barr, G. A., Bridger, W. H., & Leibowitz, S. F. Manipulations of dietary tryptophan: Effects on mouse killing and brain serotonin in the rat. Brain Research, 1979, *169,* 139–153.

Glusman, M. *Brain mechanisms in aggression.* Paper presented at Seventh International Seminar in Comparative Clinical Criminology. Montreal, Canada. June 4–7, 1979.

Grahame-Smith, D. G. Studies in vivo on the relationship between brain tryptophan, brain 5-HT synthesis and hyperactivity in rats treated with a monoamine oxidase inhibitor and L-tryptophan. *Journal of Neurochemistry,* 1971, *18,* 1053–1066.

Grant, L. D., Coscina, D. V., Grossman, S. P., & Freedman, D. X. Muricide after serotonin-depleting lesions of midbrain raphe nuclei. *Pharmacology, Biochemistry, and Behavior,* 1973, *1,* 77–80.

Harvey, J. A., McMaster, S. E., & Yunger, L. M. *p*-Chloroamphetamine: Selective neurotoxic action in brain. *Science,* 1975, *187,* 841–842.

Harvey, J. A., Schlosberg, A. J., & Yunger, L. M. Behavioral correlates of serotonin depletion. *Federation Proceedings,* 1975, *34,* 1796–1801.

Hole, K., Johnson, G. E., & Berge, O. G. 5,7-Dihydroxytryptamine lesions of the ascending 5-hydroxytryptamine pathways: Habituation, motor activity and agonistic behavior. *Pharmacology, Biochemistry, and Behavior,* 1977, *7,* 205–210.

Jacobs, B. L., & Cohen, A. Differential behavioral effects of lesions of the median or dorsal raphe nuclei in rats open field and pain-elicited aggression. *Journal of comparative physiology and psychology,* 1976, *90,* 102–108.

Kantak, K. M., Hegstrand, L. R., & Eichelman, B. Dietary tryptophan modulation and aggressive behavior in mice. *Pharmacology, Biochemistry, and Behavior,* 1980, *12,* 173–179.

Kantak, K. M., Hegstrand, L. R., & Eichelman, B. Dietary tryptophan reversal of septal lesion and 5,7-DHT lesion-elicited shock-induced fighting. *Pharmacology, Biochemistry, and Behavior,* 1981, *15,* 343–350.

Kantak, K. M., Hegstrand, L. R., Whitman, J., & Eichelman, B. Effects of dietary supplements and a tryptophan-free diet on aggressive behavior in rats. *Pharmacology, Biochemistry and Behavior,* 1979, *12,* 173–179.

Karli, P., Vergnes, M., & Didiergeorges, F. Rat–mouse interspecific aggressive behavior and its manipulation by brain ablation and by brain stimulation. In S. Garattini & E. B. Sigg (Eds.), *Aggressive Behavior.* Amsterdam: Excerpta Medica, 1969.

Koe, B. K., & Weissman, A. *p*-Chlorophenylalanine: A specific depletor of brain serotonin. *Journal of Pharmacology and Experimental Therapeutics,* 1966, *154,* 499–516.

Koolhaas, J. M. Hypothalamically induced intraspecific aggressive behavior in the rat. *Experimental Brain Research,* 1978, *32,* 365–375.

Kulkarni, A. S. Muricidal block by 5-HTP and various drugs. *Life Sciences,* 1968, *7,* 125–128.

Lippa, A. An investigation of the role of brain monoamines in conditional and unconditional behaviors. *Dissertation Abstracts International,* 1974, *183,* 14–24.

Lorens, S. A., & Guldberg, H. A. Regional 5-,hydroxytryptamine following selective midbrain raphe lesions in the rat. *Brain Research,* 1974, *78,* 45–56.

MacDonnell, M. F., Fessok, L., & Brown, S. H. Aggression and associated neural events in cats: Effects of *p*-CPA compared with alcohol. *Quarterly Journal of Studies with Alcohol,* 1971, *32,* 748–752.

Marks, P. C., O'Brien, M., & Paxinos, G. 5,7-DHT-induced muricide: Inhibition as a result of preoperative exposure of rats to mice. *Brain Research,* 1977, *135,* 383–388.

Marks, P. C., O'Brien, M., & Paxinos, G. Chlorimipramine inhibition of muricide: The role of the ascending 5-HT projection. *Brain Research,* 1978, *149,* 270–273.

Matte, A. C., & Tornow, H. Parachlorophenylalanine produces dissociated effects on aggression, emotionality, and motor activity. *Neuropharmacology,* 1978, *17,* 555–558.

McCarty, R. C., Whitesides, G. H., & Tomosky, T. K. Effects of *p*-chlorophenylalanine on the predatory behavior of *Onychomys torridus. Pharmacology, Biochemistry, and Behavior,* 1976, *4,* 217–220.

Moore, R. Y., Halaris, A. E., & Jones, B. E.: Serotonin neurons of the midbrain raphe: Ascending projections. *The Journal of Comparative Neurology,* 1978, *180,* 417–438.

Panksepp, J. Aggression elicited by electrical stimulation of the hypothalamus in albino rats. *Physiology and Behavior,* 1971, *6,* 321–329.

Parent, A., Descarries, L., & Beaudet, A. Organization of ascending serotonin systems in the adult rat brain. A radioautographic study after intraventricular administration of {^{3}H}5-hydroxytryptamine. *Neuroscience,* 1980, *6,* 115–138.

Paxinos, G., & Atrens, D. M. 5,7-Dihydroxytryptamine lesions effects on body weight, irritability, and muricide. *Aggressive Behavior,* 1977, *3,* 107–118.

Penot, C., Vergnes, M., Mack, G., & Kempf, E. Comportement d'aggression interspecifique et reactivite chez le rat: Etude comparative des effects de lesions electro lytiques du raphe et d'injections intraventriculaires de 5,7-DHT. *Biology and Behavior,* 1978, *3,* 71–85.

Peters, D. A. V., Filczewski, M., & Mazurkiewicz-Kwilecki, I. M. Effect of *p*-chlorophenylalanine on catecholamine synthesis in rat brain, heart, and adrenals. *Biochemical Pharmacology,* 1972, *21,* 2282–2284.

Reis, D. J. The chemical coding of aggression in brain. *Advances in Behavioral Biology,* 1973, *10,* 125–150.

Sanders-Bush, E., Gallager, D. W., & Sulser, F. On the mechanism of brain 5-hydroxytryptamine depletion by *p*-chloroamphetamine and related drugs and the specificity of their actions. In E. Costa, G. L. Gessa, & M. Sandler, (Eds.), *Advances in biochemical psychopharmacology,* Vol. 10. New York: Raven Press, 1974.

Sheard, M. H. The effect of *p*-chlorophenylalanine on behavior in rats: Relation to brain serotonin and 5-hydroxyindoleacetic acid. *Brain Research,* 1969, *15,* 524–528.

Sheard, M. H. Aggressive behavior: Modification by amphetamine *p*-chlorophenylalanine and lithium in rats. *Agressologie,* 1973, *14,* 323–326 (a)

Sheard, M. H. Brain serotonin depletion by *p*-chlorophenylalanine or lesions of raphe neurons in rats. *Physiology and Behavior,* 1973, *10,* 809–811. (b)

Sheard, M. H. Shock-induced fighting (SIF): Psychopharmacological studies. *Aggressive Behavior,* 1981, *7,* 41–49.

Sheard, M. H., & Aghajanian, G. K. Stimulation of midbrain raphe effect on serotonin metabolism. *Journal of Pharmacology and Experimental Therapeutics,* 1968, *163,* 425–430.

Sheard, M. H., Astrachan, D. I., & Davis, M. The action of D-lysergic acid diethylamide (LSD) on shock-elicited fighting in rats. *Life Sciences,* 1977, *20,* 427–430.

Sheard, M. H., & Davis, M. Shock-elicited fighting in rats: Importance of intershock interval upon the effect of *p*-chlorophenylalanine (*p*-CPA). *Brain Research,* 1976, *111,* 433–437.

Sheard, M. H., & Zolovick, A. J. Serotonin: Release in cat brain and cerebrospinal fluid on stimulation of midbrain raphe. *Brain Research,* 1971, *26,* 455–458.

Sloviter, R. S., Drust, E. G., & Connor, J. D. Serotonin agonist actions of *p*-chlorophenylalanine. *Neuropharmacology,* 1978, *17,* 1029–1033.

Stevens, D. A. The effects of *p*-chlorophenylalanine on behavior: Facilitation of brightness discrimination in satiated rats. *Life Sciences* (Part 1), 1970, *9,* 1127–1134.

Tenen, S. S. The effects of *p*-chlorophenylalanine, a serotonin depletor, on avoidance acquisition, pain sensitivity, and related behavior. *Psychopharmacologia,* 1967, *10,* 204–219.

Thornton, E. W., & Goudie, A. J. The effects of *p*-chlorophenylalanine on behavior differentially reinforced for low rates of responding (DRL schedule). I.R.C.S. Medical Science Nervous System. *Pharmacology, Psychology, and Psychiatry,* 1978, *6,* 264.

Trulson, M. E., & Jacobs, B. L. Behavioral evidence for the rapid release of CNS serotonin by PCA and fenfluramine. *European Journal of Pharmacology,* 1975, *36,* 149–153.

Valenstein, E. S. *Brain Control.* New York: John Wiley and Sons, 1973.

Valzelli, L. 5-Hydroxytryptamine in aggressiveness. In E. Costa, G. L. Gessa, & M. Sandler (Eds.), *Advances in biochemical psychopharmacology* (Vol. II). New York: Raven Press, 1974.

Valzelli, L., & Garattini, S. Biochemical and behavioral changes induced by isolation in rats. *Neuropharmacology,* 1971, *11,* 17–22.

Vergnes, M. Interspecific aggression and reactivity in rats: Effects of selective raphe lesions and additional olfactory bulb ablation. *Aggressive Behavior,* 1978, *4,* 207–218.

Vergnes, M., Mack, G., & Kempf, E. Behavioral and biochemical effects of lesions of the raphe on rat–mouse interspecific aggressive behavior. *Brain Research,* 1973, *57,* 67–74.

Vergnes, M., Penot, C., Kempf, E., & Mack, G. Lesion selective des neurones serotoninergiques du raphe par la 5,7-dihydroxytryptamine effects sur le comportement d'aggression interspecifique du rat. *Brain Research,* 1977, *133,* 167–171.

Walters, J. K., Davis, M., & Sheard, M. H. Tryptophan-free diet: Effects on acoustic startle reflex in rats. *Psychopharmacology,* 1979, *62,* 103–109.

Welch, B. L., & Welch, A. S. Aggression and the biogenic amine neurohumors. In S. Garratini & E. B. Sigg (Eds.), *Aggressive behavior.* New York: John Wiley and Sons, Inc., 1969.

Yamamoto, T., & Ueki, S. Characteristics in aggressive behavior induced by midbrain raphe lesions in rats. *Physiology and Behavior,* 1977, *19,* 105–110.

IV SUMMARY

10 Synthesis and New Directions

Edward C. Simmel
Miami University

Martin E. Hahn
William Paterson College

James K. Walters*
White Haven Center

As we look back over the preceding nine chapters of this volume, and even further back over the several decades of research on aggression, we are struck by the lack of continuity between the theories, methods, and findings of the earlier investigations and those represented within these pages. The abruptness of this paradigm shift seems so unusual, even granting the recent "knowledge explosion" in the biological and behavioral sciences, that a comparison of some of the major determinants might help to provide a historical perspective to this topic.

One of the major dimensions on which many of the earlier approaches differ from those represented in this volume is the "universality" of the earlier approaches. Aggression was seen as a unitary concept, either a particular response or a drive or instinct, depending on the theory. Aggressive-like behaviors such as predation or self-defense that did not fit into the theoretical framework were often excluded by definition, or, on occasion, just ignored. Implicit in many of these definitions of a universal concept of aggression was a value statement: Aggression is harmful; it is antisocial; it is bad. Many of these earlier theories and definitions originated during times of great social violence when world wars and urban and racial violence threatened even the walls of the academic world. It

*Dr. Walters was formerly affiliated with William Paterson College, Wayne, NJ.

seemed natural and appropriate that theories of aggression developed within this historical context would attempt to explain such dire events.

A difficulty arose, however, when theories based on a universal concept of aggression were subjected to laboratory investigation. Although many of the experiments were technically sound, a troublesome gap developed between the operational definitions of aggression (and the settings in which the studies were performed), and the social violence that the theories had originally sought to explain: hitting Bobo dolls, attributing negative statements to cartoon figures, or administering electric shocks to "subjects" in ersatz experiments, or to induce fighting in laboratory animals seem quite remote from wars, riots, and felonious assault. Part of the problem has been not merely the artificiality of the laboratory setting, but the attempt in some cases to use individual psychological principles of motivation to explain social events that involve more than the sum of individual behaviors.

Another form of universality characteristic of the earlier conceptualizations of the determinants of aggressive behavior was individual similarity, as opposed to individual differences. Particular theories stressed either proximal environmental determinants (e.g., frustration or imitation), distal environmental determinants (e.g., reinforcement history), or innate factors (e.g., drives or action-specific-energy). Whatever determinant was assumed to play the major role, it was usually implicitly assumed that individuals would not differ in their aggressiveness if the appropriate internal or external conditions were the same. When such theories could be subjected to empirical verification, it is not surprising that the results were often disappointing. Furthermore, the division of the classical theories into "innate" or "learned" with respect to the key determinants of aggression encourages the once prevalent, but now obsolete nature *versus* nurture argument: a behavior was either inherent (and thus fixed and inevitable), *or* shaped through experience with the environment (and therefore infinitely plastic and malleable).

It is not surprising then, that there is little direct continuity between the views and findings of the authors in this volume and those of the earlier researchers and theorists. The authors represented within these pages have abandoned both the universal definition of aggression, and the search for any single major determinant. One result of this is the absence of any major unifying concept, such as could be found in any one of the earlier theories. There are, nevertheless, common threads among the varied presentations in the preceding nine chapters that typify the new directions in research on aggression. In order to facilitate the identification of these common threads, we will review the main points made by each contributor.

Chapter Summaries

In the first chapter, Scott outlined the principles of systems theory and discussed the utility of the systems approach to the study of aggression. For example, aggression between animals is always expressed within the social relationships of those organisms—a social system. Pressure on a social system, such as scarce food, might alter relationships among the organisms in the system and increase aggression. Also, according to systems theory, aggression can be studied while a social system changes from a developing system with poorly defined relationships to a mature system with clearly defined and stable relationships. Finally, Scott described a major cause of aggression, social disorganization. Viewed in terms of systems theory, the breakdown of relationships among members will typically result in increased aggression as that behavior is used to reestablish stable relationships among group members.

In the second chapter, Simon argued that there is a pressing need for integration within aggression research. He pointed out that poor communication among investigators in various disciplines and a lack of comparable methods has hampered progress in determining the mechanism that regulate aggression. As one example, he cited evidence from several laboratories using different experimental procedures which suggest at least three different unitary mechanisms through which testosterone might activate fighting in mice. Simon then presented the results of interdisciplinary studies (behavior genetics, molecular biology, and behavioral endocrinology) that strongly suggest that testosterone does not act in a unitary manner. Another example of poor communication that hindered progress in research is the use of many different composite or discrete measures of mouse aggressive behavior. Simon concluded by proposing that mouse aggression be measured with an index derived from multiple measures and factor analysis. The index can be used as a composite or the components can be analyzed individually if analysis of discrete behaviors is desired.

In the third chapter, Hewitt and Broadhurst applied the theoretical formulations of biometrical genetics to aggressive behavior. As they discussed in detail, biometrical genetic theory allows an investigator to make inferences about the fitness status of a behavior by examining the pattern of inheritance, the "genetic architecture," of that behavior. They then surveyed a number of studies in the mouse aggression literature and, by noting the patterns of inheritance in those studies, were able to assert that in situations involving two mice who had no prior relationship, moderate levels of aggression had been favored by natural selection. In more complex social situations involving several males, however, high levels of aggression have been favored.

In the fourth chapter, Hahn reported the details of studies using the methods of biometrical genetics to examine the fitness of aggression in three situations involving mice: In those situations (intermale aggression, food competition, and female nest defense) a common pattern of inheritance emerged. Of the total genetic variation for aggression, additive variation consistently made a larger contribution than did dominance variation. This pattern of results is consistent with an evolutionary history of stabilizing selection, indicating that moderate levels of aggression have been favored over extreme levels.

In Chapter 5, Lagerspetz and Lagerspetz pointed out many advantages of using animal behavior genetics for the general study of aggression. Among the advantages is that an investigator can selectively breed for different levels or types of aggressive behavior and thereby develop models of inheritance that are more precise than are possible using human subjects. They then reported on their long running genetics selection for high and low aggressiveness in male mice and their examination of correlated characteristics which have appeared during selection. Among their findings was that females of both the high and low aggressive lines were uniformly nonaggressive unless given injections of testosterone neonatally and as adults. This finding suggested that females of the high aggressive line carry genes for high aggression as do males in that line but that those genes are only expressed in the presence of androgens. They also reported that general activity, as measured in two separate situations, was positively correlated with aggressive behavior in male mice.

In the sixth chapter, Ebert described a genetic selection for aggressive behavior in mice that was similar to that of Lagerspetz and Lagerspetz, with two notable exceptions. First, Ebert selected for interfemale aggression, and second, she used wild *Mus musculus* as her base population. This selection study provided an empirical basis for Ebert to ask whether aggression is a unitary trait or whether it consists of several behaviors which may be similar in appearance but which have separate genetic and neural control mechanisms. Her research and that of her colleagues demonstrated a rapid and perhaps asymmetrical response to selection for interfemale aggression with high and low lines clearly emerging. Next, Ebert reviewed the results of studies looking for correlates of interfemale aggression. She examined interfemale, maternal and predatory aggression, and found that while maternal aggression was positively correlated with interfemale aggression, intermale and predatory aggression were unrelated to interfemale aggression.

In the seventh chapter, Svare described maternal aggression toward intruding conspecifics by female mice, rats, and hamsters. In general, this aggression increases with advancing pregnancy and declines with continuing lactation. Svare pointed out that suckling stimulation from pups is essential for the initiation and maintenance of postpartum maternal aggression. Although the hormonal status of adult females may affect their aggression during pregnancy, suckling-induced changes in prolactin, ovarian, and adrenal hormones are not involved in aggression during lactation. Svare provided evidence to suggest that the mechanism through which suckling influences aggression may involve changes in the turnover of brain serotonin or catecholamines. He further suggested that neuroendocrine or neurotransmitter functional differences may be responsible for the strain and individual differences in postpartum maternal aggression that have been demonstrated.

Miczek, in chapter eight, outlined the major laboratory paradigms of animal aggression. He suggested that the approach of treating each variety of laboratory based aggressive behavior in a selected species as a distinct ''model'' of aggression should be abandoned even though it is likely that various aggressive and defensive behavior patterns are mediated by more than one neural network. Instead, he suggested an ethological approach that would employ biologically relevant resident-intruder confrontations, sequence analysis, and sophisticated audio and video recording to study the neural mechanisms of aggression. He criticized the current multitransmitter concept of neural mediation of aggression, and emphasized that profiles of neurotransmitter involvement in aggression that attempt to present overall trends often ignore conflicting data. He presented the results of experiments from his and other laboratories on the role of catecholamines in aggression and high-lighted the methodological differences and general lack of agreement in that area. Finally, Miczek briefly described a new set of experiments which point to the presence of endogeneous opiods as analgesics in defeated mice.

Sheard, in the ninth chapter, suggested that genetic control of aggressive behavior may be mediated through alteration in the activity of modulating monoaminergic brain systems. He provided a selective review of the literature implicating the serotonergic system as having a role in various types of offensive and defensive animal aggression. He discussed various means by which brain serotonin can be depleted including the drugs *p*-CPA, 5,6-/5, 7-DHT; raphe lesions; and tryptophan-free diets. Sheard's review showed that all of these serotonin-reducing treatments tend to increase or induce various types of aggression in rats such as intermale, shock-induced, muricide, and pup killing. On the other hand, elevation of brain serotonin by such treatments as tryptophan, 5-HTP, raphe stimulation, or various drugs generally inhibited muricide, shock-induced aggression, and other forms of aggression in rats. Overall, Sheard's review strongly suggested that brain serotonergic systems are involved in direct and indirect inhibitory control of most forms of aggression in rats.

Common Themes

Methodology. We believe that two important themes run through the preceding chapters. The more clearly delineated theme is the choice of methods used in studies of aggression. It may well be that differing conclusions from investigations of similar phenomena are a function of the diverse methods used in the experiments rather than on the basic actions of the variables examined. The reviews in the chapters by Hewitt and Broadhurst, Miczek, and Simon provide excellent examples of this. Of course, it is reasonable that experimenters employ a diversity of species, ages, drug dosages, and genotypes; and also that they measure a diverse set of behaviors in a variety of situations. However, we suggest that in two areas of methodology, changes could be made that would facilitate progress in our understanding of the basic phenomena and mechanisms of aggression.

1. In what situations should aggression be measured? According to the views expressed in this volume by Scott, Miczek, and Hewitt and Broadhurst, aggres-

sion should be measured in situations that are biologically relevant. Shock-elicited aggression or isolation-induced aggression are less "realistic" than territorial conflict between mice or defense of a nest area by a female mammal. The choice, however, of an appropriate situation need not be based on face validity. Guidance comes from those who work with animals in natural settings and from the growing literature in biometrical genetics that has pinpointed situations where behavior has been subjected to selective pressures. Furthermore, the best situations for study are probably those that exist in the context of a social system. The study of two strange males meeting for the first time may be experimentally "clean" but socially sterile. It might be better, for example, to study aggression in those two males as they interact over a period of time and develop roles in a group.

2. What behaviors should be measured in studies of aggression? Clearly, an investigator should measure those behaviors which best illuminate the question or hypothesis under test. Further, there has been some standardization in the choice of behaviors to be measured, at least in rodents, thanks to the classic paper by Grant and Mackintosh (1963). We concur with Simon's ideas (Chapter 2) and suggest that investigators should measure as many aspects of the behavior as possible. While counting the numbers of wounds on an animal's flank may yield a quick "dominance index"—such a procedure certainly does not allow analysis of the rich behavioral responses possible in most social situations. The use of multiple measures allows the investigator to employ such sophisticated techniques as factor analysis or multiple regression but will also permit sequence analysis or a focus on a single behavior of interest.

Single or Multiple Substrates of Aggression. The second general theme that ties the contributions in this volume together is the question of whether there are single or multiple neural and genetic systems underlying aggression. Moyer (1976) has suggested that there exist several distinct types of aggression, each with its own neural and genetic substrates. The chapters of Ebert, Lagerspetz and Lagerspetz, Hahn, Sheard, and Miczek provide evidence on this matter. Fuller and Thompson (1978) suggested a general schematic for relating genes, physiological systems, and behaviors that may aid us. A modified and simplified version of their schematic, which we have applied to aggression, is represented in Figure 10.1: Section (A) illustrates a model in which a single genetic system establishes a single neural network that controls several types of aggression (intermale and predatory, for example); (B) shows two genetic systems, one of which establishes a single neural network and controls two behaviors, while the other genetic system has a single associated neural system and controls a single pattern of aggression; and (C) depicts separate genetic systems, each establishing a neural network for a particular type of aggression. This last model is the one suggested by Moyer (1976). Of course, many more complex models are possible and the figure represents only several simple ones that contain no interactions at the genetic, neural, or behavioral level.

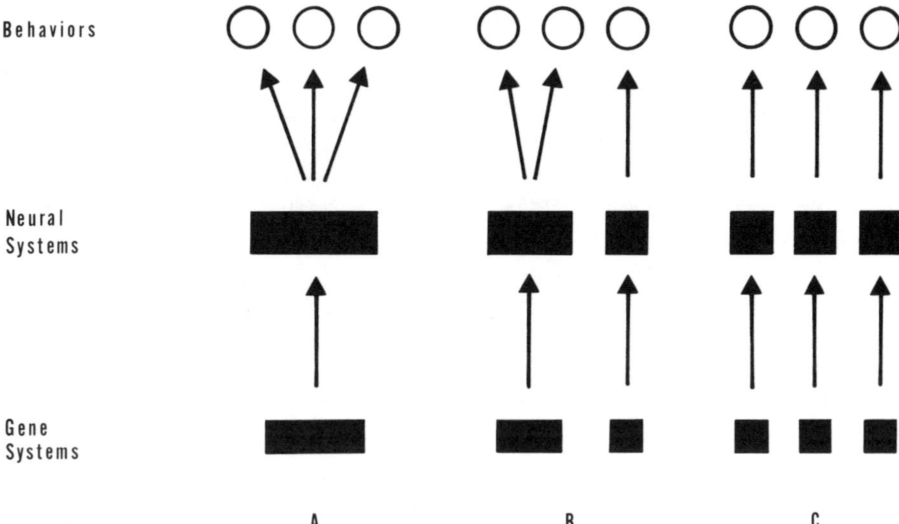

FIG. 10.1. Various models of the relationship between genetic systems, neural systems, and types of aggressive behavior.

Is there support for any of these models in the preceding chapters? Lagerspetz and Lagerspetz showed that female aggression in mice was a correlated character of intermale aggression, thus suggesting that a common genetic system could underlie both. Ebert also examined correlated characters and found that selection for interfemale aggression brought about a correlated response in maternal aggression, but not in intermale or predatory aggression. Hahn found that the same pattern of inheritance in an F_1 generation of mice characterized intermale aggression, food competition, and female nest defense. Comparison of inbred strains on several measures across those three situations revealed identical rankings for intermale and maternal nest defense but quite different rankings for food competition. The work of Ebert and that of Hahn suggests the presence of at least two genetic systems associated with the behaviors they observed.

The preceding chapters also contain information allowing for some evaluation of the number of neural substrates involved in aggression. Sheard presents evidence that across a variety of aggression provoking situations, serotonin has a uniform effect, at least in rats. His review of the mouse literature suggests that aggression other than predatory aggression is under unitary control. Miczek's views are in sharp contrast, however, as he summarized studies showing the nonunitary effects of norepinephrine and other neuromodulators on aggression. Definitive evidence on this point is scarce and precludes firm conclusions. The work of Flynn, Smith, Coleman, & Opsahl (1979) certainly supports the existence of two neural networks, one underlying a quiet biting attack (predatory) and one underlying an aroused, gesture-rich attack (conspecific).

On the basis of reports in this volume we cannot support a unitary model of the genetic and neural control of aggression as pictured in section (A) of Fig. 10.1. We also do not see support for a model in which there is a separate genetic and neural system for *each* of several types of aggression as is pictured in (C) of Fig. 10.1. Instead we do find support for a model with at least two genetic systems, one of which controls several types of aggression perhaps through a single neural system and at least one other genetic system that controls one type of aggression through a single neural system. Such a model appears in (B). We realize that this is still a very rudimentary scheme; one that will require a great deal of interdisciplinary research if it is to be redefined and extended. It does, however, provide one example of a direction for further research suggested by the contributions to this volume.

In a more general sense, both the common themes and the distinctive empirical contributions found in these chapters provide a promising step in the direction of integrated and interdisciplinary research on aggressive behavior.

REFERENCES

Flynn, J. P., Smith, D. Coleman, K., & Opsahl, C. A. Anatomical pathways for attack behavior in cats. In M. von Cranach, K. Foppa, W. Lepeines, & D. Ploog (Eds.) *Human ethology: Claims and limits of a new discipline*. Cambridge: Cambridge University Press, 1979.

Fuller, J. L., & Thompson, W. R. *Foundations of behavior genetics*. St. Louis, Mi.: The C. V. Mosby Company, 1978.

Grant, E. C., & Mackintosh, J. H. A comparison of the social postures of some common lab rodents. *Behaviour,* 1963, *21,* 246–259.

Moyer, K. E. *The psychobiology of aggression*. New York: Harper and Row, 1976.

Author Index

Numbers in *italics* denote pages with complete bibliographic information.

T

U

V

W

Y,Z

Subject Index

A

B

C

R

S

T

V